James Lee Wallar: A Life Well Lived

Nancy E. Wiseman

Carmel, Indiana   2025

ISBN: 979-8-218-64047-7

Dedicated to my mother,
Dorothy Elizabeth "Betty" (Bashears) Wiseman,
a great-great granddaughter of James Lee Wallar
I love you!

"We're all immortal, as long as our stories are told."
—Elizabeth Hunter, *The Scribe*

CONTENTS

PREFACE

Because of an untimely death and the resulting broken family, our Wallar ancestry remained a mystery to me for some time. When Mary Melissa "Mollie" (Bellew) Wallar died at age thirty-four in 1895, she left four small children, including my great-grandmother Florence Jeanette Wallar, age six. Mollie's husband, Harry Herbert Wallar, abandoned his little children, remarried, and started a new family. His granddaughter, Mary Kathryn "Katie" (Bashears) Parsons once told me that her grandfather was "a scoundrel." A scoundrel, indeed.

Once I learned about Harry Herbert Wallar and began tracing his ancestry, I was puzzled by my findings. His father James Lee Wallar was a well-respected Methodist minister and Freemason. Could he also be the Captain James L. Wallar who was dishonorably discharged from the Union Army during the Civil War? Did I have two men conflated into one? Thus began a five-year journey to discover more about my great-great-great-grandfather, James Lee Wallar.

Starting as something to do during the Covid-19 pandemic, I have spent countless hours researching James Wallar. I made several trips to West Virginia and Ohio and one trip to southern Illinois to learn more about this complicated man, to see where he lived and worked, and to experience the mountains where he fought in the American Civil War.

I hope all descendants of James Lee Wallar will find this book interesting. We are fortunate to have an ancestor who was intelligent, motivated, and charismatic, making it relatively easy to gather material for a book. I am honored to be one of James Lee Wallar's descendants.

NOTES

West Virginia did not become a state until June 20, 1863. When James Wallar joined the cavalry to fight in the Civil War, he joined a "Loyalist Virginia" (Union) cavalry unit. For clarity's sake, I have referred to western Virginia as West Virginia, and the loyalist Virginia troops as West Virginia troops, even before statehood.

Early in the war, the Union cavalry was often split to serve amongst infantry units. For this reason, it was occasionally difficult to determine where, exactly, James Wallar served at a given time. I have done my best to be accurate. In addition, war is a complicated, back-and-forth orchestration between rivals and I have simplified many campaigns to focus on the portions involving Captain Wallar. I've tried to portray him as a human facing difficult situations. Obviously, I have no idea how he felt at any time, so any feelings assigned to James Wallar are mere conjecture.

Harpers Ferry, West Virginia was spelled Harper's Ferry at the time of the Civil War, so I have used that spelling. The word "secesh" refers to a secessionist. This was a common nickname amongst the Union soldiers in West Virginia for those aligned with the views of the Confederate army. At the time of the Civil War, some county seats were called Raleigh Court House or Wyoming Court House instead of the current names Beckley and Pineville, for example.

I have often used newspaper articles, diary entries, and correspondence from the time. I very much enjoy the writing of the late nineteenth century and find it valuable to read the thoughts of the contemporary writers. I've retained spelling, grammar, and punctuation for authenticity.

It should be noted that most family members use the spelling "Wallar," while others use "Waller." I have tried to use the preferred spelling, and I have used the spelling of the name which appears on a document, preferred or not.

Lastly, I struggled with the formatting of this book. After writing, Microsoft Word and I were not getting along, so I switched to Atticus.io. This solved most of my formatting problems but isn't designed for nonfiction books, creating some limitations to the final layout of this book. I apologize for any perceived clunkiness. Done is better than perfect.

1

THE EARLY YEARS

Not much is known about James Lee Wallar's early years. There is even uncertainty about his birthplace and birthdate. In a list of deceased Methodist Episcopal ministers, James L. Wallar's birth year was given as 1819, and his birthplace was listed as Vermont.[1]

Son Charles M. Wallar, in a short biographical sketch, gives his father's birthdate as November 25, 1819, and birthplace as Rutland, Vermont. It mentions that he learned to cut stone there, then studied law and practiced for several years in Columbus and Marietta, Ohio. He later abandoned that and entered the ministry of the Methodist Episcopal church.[2]

To the contrary, on December 5, 1847, James L. Waller and Frances Gammon were married in Muskingum County, Ohio. James' father, Verden Wallar, gave permission for him to marry, and the words, "over the age of Twenty-one years" were crossed out, therefore suggesting a birthdate after December 5, 1826. Frances' father Robert Gammon also gave permission, indicating that she was not yet eighteen years old.[3]

This is a bit puzzling but after examining census records, it seems that this later birthdate might be more accurate. Most importantly, the 1830 census for the Virden Waller family shows four boys under the age of five years, and no boys over five.[4] Unfortunately, on the 1840 census page enumerating father Virden Wallar, there are no tick marks in the age categories for any males, so we cannot determine the age of Verden's sons in 1840.[5]

In 1850, James L. Waller, a stonecutter, was living in Circleville, Pickaway County, Ohio with wife Frances and son Lafayette. James was twenty-three years old and born in Ohio, suggesting he was born in 1826 or 1827.[6]

By the 1860 census the family had moved to Racine in Meigs County, Ohio and added four more children in addition to Lafayette, namely Laura, Charles, Harvey, and William. James S. [*sic*] Waller, a marble cutter, was thirty-two years old and born in Connecticut, suggesting he was born in 1827 or 1828.[7]

Supporting the later birthdate theory is a 1952 letter written by the grandson of one of James' brothers, James is listed as the third son of Verden and Edith (Layport) Wallar, suggesting a birthdate in the late 1820s.[8]

A newspaper article announcing his election as Captain of the Meigs County Rangers in May 1861 gave J.L. Wallar's age as forty-one and his nativity as, "amongst the rugged mountains of old Vermont."[9] This fits with a 1819 birthdate, such as that mentioned earlier in son Charles' biography. Additionally, in 1890, Wallar attended a dinner at which his seventy-first birthday was acknowledged, again pointing to the 1819 birthdate.[10]

In 1870, James L. Waller was employed as a Methodist Episcopal minister and living with his family in Robinson, Crawford County, Illinois. In this census, he was enumerated as having been born in Connecticut in 1828 or 1829 (age forty-one). Children Charlie, Harry H., William, and Lillie M. joined James and Frances.[11]

Up until this point, the census records are fairly consistent, at least as far as age is concerned. He was recorded as being twenty-three in 1850, thirty-two in 1860, and forty-one in 1870, with birth places of Ohio and Connecticut. In the ten years between the 1870 census and the 1880 census, however, James Wallar aged eighteen years, being enumerated as fifty-nine years old and born in New Jersey! It is unknown who answered the door when the census taker knocked, and this can certainly account for the variation in ages and birthplaces. A niece and a boarder lived with James and Frances in Enfield at the time of the 1880 census enumeration, so perhaps one of them gave the information to the census taker.[12] The last census James appears in was the 1900 census. James L. Waller and second wife Jeannette were living in Centralia, Illinois with a housekeeper. It is likely that the housekeeper spoke with the census taker, because of the three people in the household, only housekeeper Maria L. Dink has a birth month, birth year, and birthplace listed. No month or year of birth is given for James L. Waller, a Minister of the Gospel, and a birthplace of Vermont was reported. His wife Jeannette was reportedly born in July (no year given) in New York.[13]

It also seems likely, given an 1826-1829 birth year range, that James Wallar's mother was Edith Layport who Verden Waller married in 1825 in Harrison County, Ohio. Lending credence to this statement is the fact that the author shares identical DNA segments with several descendants of Edith Layport's father Isaac Layport, through siblings of Edith, meaning we share Isaac Layport as a common ancestor.

But how can we account for only one instance of an Ohio birthplace, the rest being East Coast locations? We know Verden Waller was in Harrison County, Ohio in 1825 (marriage) and 1830 (census). It would make sense, then, that James was born in Ohio, and quite possibly in Harrison County. In 1840, Verden was in Tuscarawas County, Ohio (census). James married Frances in 1847 in Muskingum County, Ohio before age twenty-one. James, Frances, and their young son Lafayette were in Pickaway County, Ohio in 1850 where he was working as a stone cutter. When did he go to Vermont to learn the art of stone cutting, if we are to believe the biographical sketch of son Charles?

In summary, I would like to suggest that James Lee Wallar was born to Verden and Edith (Layport) Wallar in 1829 in Harrison County, Ohio. I'm basing this on the 1830, 1850, 1860, and 1870 censuses, Verden and Edith's marriage in 1825 in Harrison County and residence there in 1830, the letter written in 1952, and my DNA matches with descendants of Isaac Layport.

Within a year of their 1847 marriage, James and Frances welcomed their first son, Lafayette Kent Wallar to the family. He was born on October 2, 1848 in Zanesville, Muskingum County, Ohio.[14] The little family was living in Circleville, Pickaway County in 1850, where James was working as a stonecutter.[15] Daughter Lauretta May "Etta" Wallar was born in Ohio in June 1852.[16]

Soon, however, James spread his wings to make a better life for his family. By the summer of 1853 he was in Davenport, Iowa working with his brother Elijah Davies Wallar. The two men were operating a branch of the Vermont Marble Works, selling "monuments, tomb-tables, or head and foot-stones" from a shop at the corner of Rock Island and Second streets.[17] Davenport, chartered in 1839, was growing rapidly in the 1850s. The population was slightly less than 2000 in the year 1850 and grew to over 11,000 by 1860.[18]

It is not known how much time James spent in Davenport, but based on the birthplaces of James' children, it's possible that Frances and the children stayed in Ohio. Son Charles M. "Charlie" Wallar was born in Washington County, Ohio on September 9, 1854.[19] The birthplace of the next child, Harry Herbert Wallar, was given as Ohio in every census where Harry appeared (1860-1910). His death certificate states he was born in Marietta in 1860, although this information was given by a friend rather than a family member.[20] It seems likely that he was born about 1856, since he was reported as being three years old in the 1860 census,[21] fourteen years old at the time of the 1870 census,[22] and twenty-three years old in the 1880 census.[23]

By April 1856, J.L. Wallar had returned to Ohio and was making himself known in Meigs County. He contributed to an exhibition "consisting of original orations, essays, comedies, tragedies, with a large variety of pieces selected for the occasion." Wallar contributed to a "burlesque county court" skit and presented an original tragedy which was well received by the captivated audience. He likely sang earlier in the evening. The newspaper named a "J.L. Wallace" as the vocalist.[24]

Contributing additionally to the interests of the community, J.L. Waller also served on a committee in 1858, organizing a "camp meeting," or religious revival, inviting traveling and local ministers from the area to participate.[25]

In Meigs County, the Wallar family lived in Racine, Ohio, a village of approximately 600 inhabitants on the Ohio River.[26] Racine was first called Graham Station, and the post office was established in 1818. The town grid was laid out in 1837 and Graham Station was incorporated in 1841. The town was renamed Racine in 1852—not long before the Wallars arrived. Area farmers and townspeople did their buying, selling, and trading in Racine. Tons of coal and salt were exported out of Meigs County. Packet boats frequently stopped at the landing, bringing mail, visitors, and items for sale from towns such as Pittsburgh, Wheeling, or Marietta.[27]

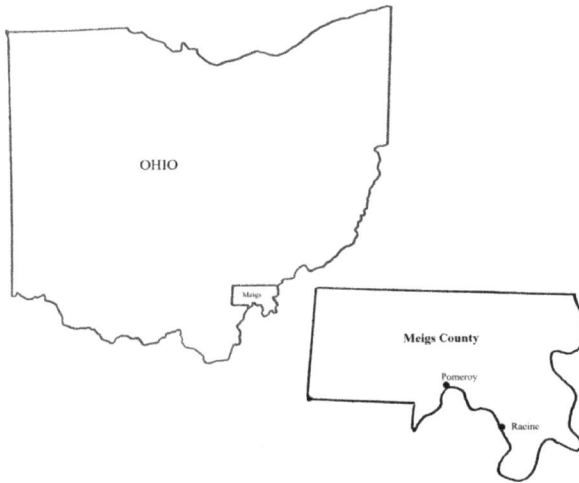

At this time, a new academy was ready to tend to the education of the children of Racine, presumably including the children of James and Frances. A factory manufacturing woolen goods had been recently outfitted with steam engines, and two flour mills were also steam-powered. Shops including a drug store, a furniture store, and machine shops lined the neat streets of Racine.[28]

In March 1858, James was carving stone for one of two Racine marble cutting firms, Skirvin & Smith. A Meigs County newspaper complimented James on his fine work:

While we give to the proprietors due credit for their enterprise, we cannot withhold from the public the real object that makes their works so attractive. It is the work of J.L. Waller. We rarely meet with one who is so perfect in the art. The design of a monument being executed for the Burnaps, is one of the most imposing we ever saw, and the design is wholly original. It is of a solid block of marble, probably two feet square, and about four and a half high, well polished, upon which is opened a large book, designed for a family record. It is well worth the time spent to stop and see this master-piece of workmanship.[29]

Silas Burnap grave marker

This monument was still standing in Mound Cemetery, ten miles northeast of Pomeroy, in September 2019.[30]

Perhaps in part because of the glowing review of his work earlier in the year, by July 1858 J.L. Wallar had opened his own marble shop with a partner in Racine.[31] The following year he showed off his handicraft at the Ninth Annual Fair of the Meigs County Agricultural Association:

Two lots of marble—one from Skirvin & Smith, of Racine, and the other from J.L. Waller, of the same place—were universally admired, and it would be difficult to procure more perfect specimens of workmanship anywhere than these.[32]

Business must have been good for James, because he purchased Lots #4 and #5 of Hopkins Addition in Racine on August 24, 1859 for $250.00.[33]

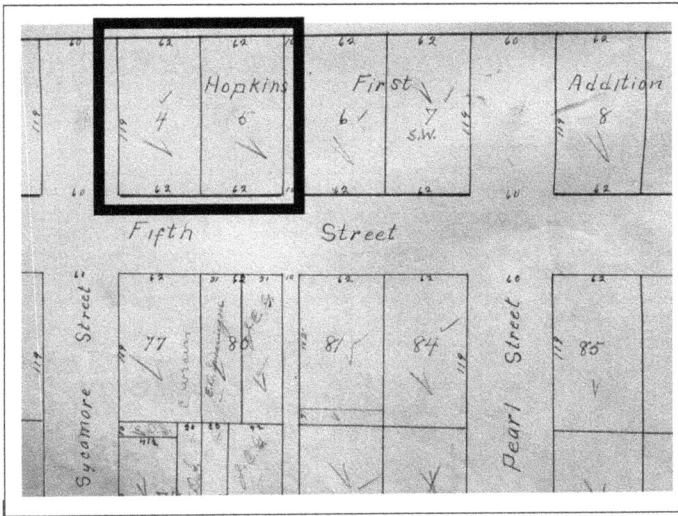

Map showing locations of Lots #4 and #5[34]

The Wallar family certainly needed more room for the growing family. Son William, known affectionately as "Willie," was born two days after the purchase of the lots, on August 26th.[35] In 2023, Lot #4 has the address of 201 Fifth Street. An old house sits on this lot. It is a simple, well-kept, two-story frame house to which additions have been added over time. Neither the county recorder's office nor the assessor's office could provide the age of the original structure, so I don't know if the Wallar family lived in a portion of this house. Lot #5 is currently an empty lot, and a smaller, 20th century home sits on Lot #6.

The family was enumerated in the 1860 census in Racine. James L. Waller was listed as a thirty-two-year-old marble cutter born in Connecticut. Thirty-year-old Frances was born in Ohio. Children Lafayette (age ten), Laura (age eight), Charles (age six), Harvey (Harry-age three), and William (age ten months) were all born in Ohio.[36]

House located at 201 Fifth Street, Racine[37]

By late 1859, J.L. Wallar was the mayor of Racine,[38] and was working as an attorney in mid-1860.[39] On July 12th of that year, a large crowd gathered at the courthouse in nearby Pomeroy. A band played patriotic music and the Stars and Stripes waved proudly. At this gathering, a prominent citizen of Meigs County announced he was leaving the pro-slavery Democratic Party for the Republican Party. James Wallar, "one of the most prominent and intelligent Democrats of [Meigs] County" was called upon to defend the principles of the Democratic Party:

Mr. Wallar is a gentleman of pleasing address, and one of the best speakers it has been our pleasure to hear. He proceeded in a clear, kind, logical argument to show why he was a Democrat. He passed, in review, the professed doctrines of the party in Ohio on the subject of slavery since 1840. He read from the platforms, and the inaugural address of Gov. Wood, and said he was a Democrat because he loved those principles, &c.—

...But here, the speaker showed that "he had come to a point where he must do one of two things—either, give up his long cherished sentiments, and go with the remnant of the party in their present pro-slavery position, or cast in his lot with the Republicans. After mature consideration, he

was constrained, in fidelity to his principles, the clearest conclusions of his judgement, the dictates of his conscience, and in view of the best and highest interests of his country, to unite with the great Republican party and give it his influence, his voice and his vote."

...every one in that large audience will agree with us that for courteousness of treatment to former political associates—clearness of argument—beauty of language—and effective deliverage, the speech was rarely surpassed in that house. We do not know that Mr. Wallar has been much in the habit of public speaking, but hope he will find time to let his fellow-citizens hear from him on the stump, during this campaign.[40]

The surprised crowd applauded and roared with cheers! What an unexpected turn of events! Now the darling of the Meigs County Republican party, James was named a member of the Meigs County Republican convention on July 31, 1860, representing Sutton Township,[41] and addressed the Republican Club of Pomeroy on August 22nd.[42]

Meigs County Courthouse in Pomeroy, Ohio, July 2022[43]

By late 1860, J.L. Wallar had turned his "Premium Marble Works" business over to a new proprietor, J.V. Smith, who was mentored by Wallar as he learned the business.[44] In an 1861 business directory, J.L. Wallar was listed as an attorney in Racine, as well as still being in the marble business.[45]

On April 22, 1861, just ten days after Confederate troops fired on Fort Sumter in South Carolina, James L. Wallar sold Lots #4 and #5 in the Hopkins Addition to the Town of Racine for $500.00. At this time, wives were interviewed separately from their husbands at the time of a sale to ensure that she agreed to the sale of the land and understood that she had no further interest in the property. Interestingly, there is no indication that this interview occurred in this real estate transaction.[46] The following year, on September 1, 1862, Frances E. Wallar purchased Lot #6 for $125.00.[47]

This is notable because the Ohio legislature, in 1861, passed a law allowing a married woman whose husband deserted her or became unable to provide for the family to purchase and own land. Before this law, Frances, as a married woman, would not have been able to buy real estate in her name. Were the couple separated or divorced? Was Frances considered deserted because James had joined the Union Army? Was James, using his knowledge as an attorney, using a loophole for a personal gain of some sort? Adding intrigue to the situation is the fact that James L. Wallar purchased Lots #4 and #5 again for $400.00 two weeks later, on September 16, 1862. Now James and Frances owned Lots #4, #5, and #6 between them. The deeds for these purchases appear consecutively in the deed book and were both recorded on October 6, 1862.[48]

2

GUARDING THE RAILROAD

I n late 1860 and early 1861, several southern states seceded from the Union, and on February 8, 1861, formed the Confederate States of America. Shortly thereafter, Confederate forces began to seize forts located in the southern states. On April 12, 1861, Confederate soldiers fired on Fort Sumter, a Union fort off the coast of Charleston, South Carolina. The United States troops surrendered the next day. This battle is generally considered the beginning of the Civil War.[49]

In Meigs County, Ohio, a county across the Ohio River from the Confederate-leaning state of Virginia, the citizens were concerned about the war. A meeting was held for:

...the citizens of Meigs County, without distinction of party or class, for the purpose of tendering to the Executive our heart-felt co-operation and influence in any measures he may adopt, having for their object the preservation of the Government, the enforcement of the laws, and the punishment of treason.[50]

At this meeting, held on Saturday April 27th, more than two hundred supporters from Mason County, Virginia joined the citizens of Meigs County in their support of the Union. Captain Wallar of the Meigs County Rangers gave a patriotic speech.[51] In a separate article on the same page of the newspaper a complimentary description of Captain J. L. Wallar appeared. He was described as six feet, one inch tall, "of pleasing address, easy manners, and commanding appearance—genial as a ray of sunshine in his disposition—is well adapted to inspire respect and good will among subordinates..."[52]

With the United States of America having existed for a mere seventy-five years, many men were anxious to preserve and protect the Union, including James Wallar. Wallar had, earlier in the week, enlisted in the Eighteenth Regiment, Ohio Volunteer Infantry.[53] Over two hundred local men volunteered to serve, either in the Meigs County Rangers—a group of men ready to serve if called upon by the governor—or the Pomeroy Guard—organized to protect the home front.[54]

Approximately two hundred men left Pomeroy for Athens, Ohio on Saturday May 25, 1861. A large number of these men were from the Meigs County Rangers, and some of the Pomeroy Guard chose to enlist, as well.[55] Their destination was Camp Jewett, located along the Hocking River, near the current West Elementary School in Athens.[56] The men bade a tearful farewell to their wives and children and prepared for their journey.

As the men marched west and north out of Pomeroy, they were escorted part of the way by the Middleport Brass Band and the Home Guard. Proud residents lined the roads and cheered as the men paraded past.[57] Captain Wallar's company stopped at Pageville, twenty miles from Pomeroy, for a much-appreciated dinner provided by townspeople. The company continued their march toward Athens, going another six miles to Albany, Ohio. Approaching Albany, the soldiers were met by the local Citizen's Guard who marched with them to the middle of town. From there, the unit was split into small groups and sent home with residents for the night. After what was hopefully a good night's rest, the companies reconvened Sunday morning for the final twelve miles of their journey to Athens.

On Sunday afternoon, the soldiers arrived in Athens and were treated to dinner on the Ohio University College Yard. Bellies full, they marched the last mile to Camp Jewett, also known as Camp Wool. The men pitched their tents and awaited further orders, not yet knowing that earlier that day, Major General George B. McClellan of the Department of the Ohio had already ordered Union troops, including the Eighteenth

Ohio, into West Virginia. In a letter of May 26th written to Colonel James B. Steedman in Marietta, McClellan requested that:

Monument to Meigs County Civil War Soldiers[58]

You will on receipt of this cross the river and occupy Parkersburg. The Eighteenth Regiment at Athens is ordered to report to you. You will at once move forward by rail towards Grafton, as far as can be done with prudence, leaving sufficient guards at Parkersburg and the bridges as you advance. Avail yourself of the assistance of the armed Union men. Preserve the strictest discipline, and do all in your power to conciliate. If you have to fight, remember that the honor of Ohio is in your hands. Communicate fully. See that the rebels receive no information by telegraph. Take one week's rations. See that the rights and property of the people are respected, and repress all attempts at negro insurrection.[59]

In an open letter published in West Virginia newspapers, McClellan assured the troubled citizens that the Ohio troops:

...come as your friends and brothers, as enemies only to the armed rebels who are preying upon you...Notwithstanding all that has been said by the traitors to induce you to believe that our advent among you will be signalized by interference with your slaves, understand one thing clearly—not only will we abstain from all interference, but we will, with an iron hand, crush any attempt at insurrection on their part.[60]

Early on Monday morning the troops quickly realized they were no longer merely citizens, but soldiers. Breakfast was a disappointing meal of salt pork, bread, and coffee—nothing like the delicious, home-cooked meals they'd eaten over the past two days! The troops were expecting to stay at camp for a while but were quickly organized into the Eighteenth Ohio Volunteer Infantry (O.V.I.) Regiment, serving with James L. Wallar as captain of Company H.[61]

The first Federal troops arrived in Parkersburg, West Virginia on Monday, May 27th.[62] The Eighteenth Ohio was not far behind. By late afternoon on that same day, the eager men were ordered from Athens, Ohio to Camp Putnam in Marietta, forty-five miles to the east.[63]

Like Camp Jewett, Camp Putnam was a training and staging camp for Ohio troops. It was located at the current site of the Washington County Fairgrounds along the Muskingum River and less than two miles from the Ohio River. On Wednesday, May 29th the men of the Eighteenth Ohio marched to the Ohio River, were armed with muskets, and boarded steamboats to take them fifteen miles south to Parkersburg, West Virginia where they arrived at Camp Union.[64]

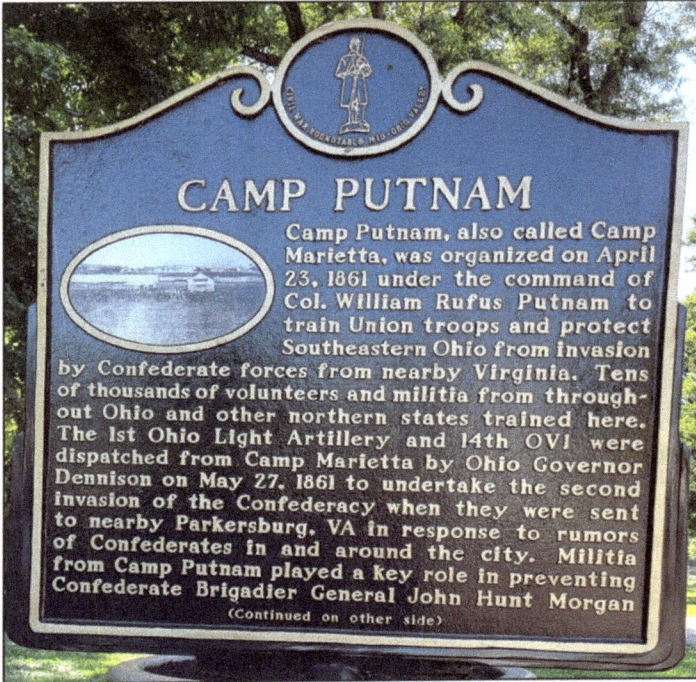

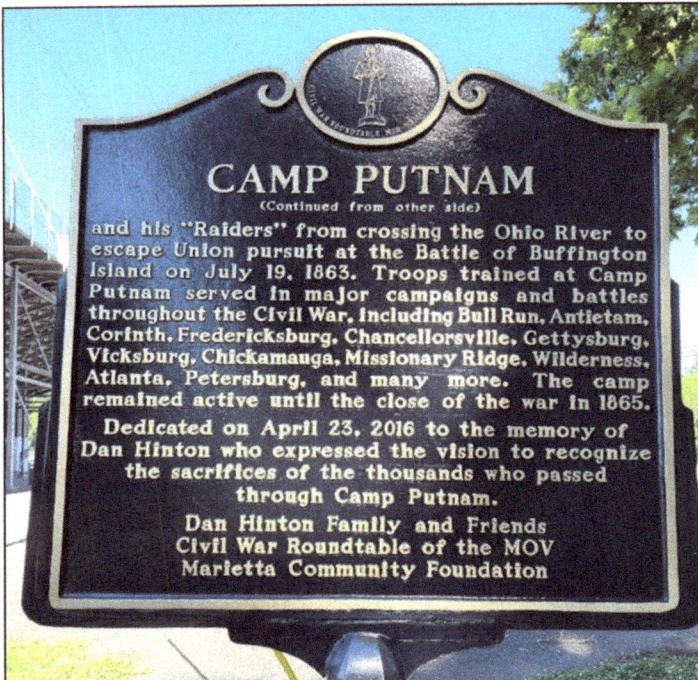

Camp Putnam Historical Marker, Marietta, Ohio[65]

Landing of Union Troops at Parkersburg [66]

Residents of the portion of Virginia comprising today's West Virginia, lying just across the Ohio River from Meigs County, were somewhat sympathetic to the Union. Virginia west of the Allegheny mountains was quite different from the remainder of the state, socially and economically. The western Virginians had long felt neglected. The influential legislators in Richmond were prosperous plantation owners and farmers from the Coastal Plain and Piedmont areas. Infrastructure improvements such as roads and railroads happened much more quickly in the eastern portion of the state.[67] While over 37% of the population of eastern Virginia were enslaved in 1860, only 2.5% of the inhabitants of Kanawha (as western Virginia was called during the early days of the Civil War) were enslaved.[68] Later in his 1863 inaugural speech the first governor of West Virginia, Arthur Boreman, spoke the following:

The mountains intervene between us, the rivers rise in the mountains and run towards the Northwest; and, as if to make the separation more complete, Eastern Virginia adopted the fatal doctrine of secession, while the West spurned and rejected it as false and dangerous in the extreme. Thus nature, our commerce, travel, habits, associations, and interests, all - all say that West Virginia should be severed from the East.[69]

Parkersburg in 1861 was a small river town of approximately 2500 and was of growing importance to the region. The North Western/Baltimore and Ohio Railroad reached Parkersburg in 1857, bringing with it the hope of new opportunity and industry. Repair shops, depots, and loading docks quickly sprung up. A railroad bridge was yet to cross the Ohio River so train cars were ferried across. Hope and optimism were quashed when the news arrived from Richmond on April 18th that Virginia would secede from the Union. The citizens of Parkersburg were fearful and concerned. Legally, they were now a part of the Confederacy, but for many, their hearts were with the Union. Chaos ensued, with fights breaking out in the crowd assembled to hear the proclamation from Richmond.[70]

The Wheeling, West Virginia newspaper reported:

A Row in Parkersburg—We learn from passengers on the steamer Liberty, which arrived last night, there was a serious disturbance in Parkersburg on Thursday, during which a large number of persons were badly injured, the Mayor of the town and Col. Jackson being of the number. It appears that certain secessionists attempted to seize some arms that were stationed in the jail, when the act was forcibly resisted by the Union men. A grand Union meeting was to have been held yesterday, in Parkersburg, when it was expected that there would be another outbreak.[71]

The Ohioans on the opposite shore of the Ohio River were understandably worried about the unrest in Parkersburg. City officials in Marietta, fifteen miles upstream from Parkersburg, sent a letter to Ohio Governor William Dennison expressing concerns that the secessionists would prevail in Parkersburg, leaving Ohio in a vulnerable position. Governor Dennison realized it was in Ohio's best interest to keep the Ohio River under control of the Federal troops so immediately requested Ohio militia groups from the Cleveland area to report to Marietta. Already the rebels occupied Grafton east of Parkersburg along the Baltimore and Ohio Railroad, and the fear of losing control of the railroad and ultimately Parkersburg was palpable. To that end, Governor Dennison proposed sending Ohio troops into West Virginia to secure the Ohio River from the opposite side of the river.[72]

With the influx of troops arriving in Parkersburg, also came vice. Seedy hotels, saloons, and brothels lined the streets near the Little Kanawha River, providing entertainment opportunities for the transient soldiers. Numerous camps popped up along the rivers, and, because of the absence of adequate warehouse space, supplies were stacked on the streets. Later in the war, there were several military hospitals and a large quartermaster's facility.

Camp Union was located a few blocks from the river at Stephenson's Grove near the home of James McNeil Stephenson, a former member of the Virginia House of Delegates. Stephenson was an enslaver and sympathized with the secessionists yet offered his grove to the Union army as a campground. His home, called "Oakland," was built in 1840 and was occupied and damaged by Union cavalry units during the war. It was added to the National Register of Historic Places in 1979.[73]

Stephenson House, Parkersburg, West Virginia[74]

The men of the Eighteenth Ohio Regiment had a miserable experience at Camp Union. A soldier from Company D reported that they'd received none of their provisions except their muskets and had to sleep on the bare ground.[75] A soldier from Company F mused later that,

We are informed that 'Bread is the Staff of life.' The staff we get is quite hard to break, being compelled, as we are sometimes, to use hammers in separating it into smaller particles. Our fare is Bread, Pork, Coffee and Beans; for a variety we change the order, having Beans, Pork or Coffee..."[76]

After a few days, the Eighteenth Ohio received orders to report to Grafton, West Virginia, and to move out as soon as they received uniforms and arms.[77] In a letter written to Confederate Colonel George A. Porterfield, Virginia Governor John Letcher instructed Porterfield and his subordinates in Grafton to:

...cut off telegraphic communication between Wheeling and Washington, so that the disaffected at the former place cannot communicate with their allies at headquarters, and, obstruct their passage by all means in your power, even to the destruction of the road and bridges.[78]

It was up to the men of the Eighteenth Ohio, among others, to prevent this from happening. With trepidation, the soldiers likely boarded boxcars fitted with backless wooden benches for their journey.[79] As the train carrying the men of the Eighteenth moved east along the B & O Railroad, corporals and privates from the Ohio regiment were let off along the way to guard bridges from Confederate sabotage.[80] Porterfield retreated only a few days later after learning the Federal troops would soon be closing in on Grafton. He then set up headquarters in Philippi, fifteen miles to the south.[81] General McClellan reported in a letter dated May 30, 1861 that Grafton had been successfully occupied by the Union troops with no loss of life.[82]

Colonel Timothy Robbins Stanley reported on June 10, 1861 that Companies F and H of the Eighteenth Regiment Ohio Volunteer

Militia were stationed along the along the North Western Virginia
Railroad between Parkersburg and Grafton. Clarksburg is approximately
seventy-five miles east of Parkersburg. Grafton lies 20 miles further
east. Colonel Stanley also reported that several men were ill with the
"measels."[83] Jewett Palmer, a soldier in Company B, stated that on June
13th, the regiment received their blouses and arrived in Clarksburg at
noon. A short time afterwards, they continued to Bridgeport, six miles to
the east. The camp there was, "the pleasantest camp of our three months'
experience." The day after their arrival in Bridgeport, a sympathetic
neighbor brought the soldiers a wagonload of food including bread and
milk.[84]

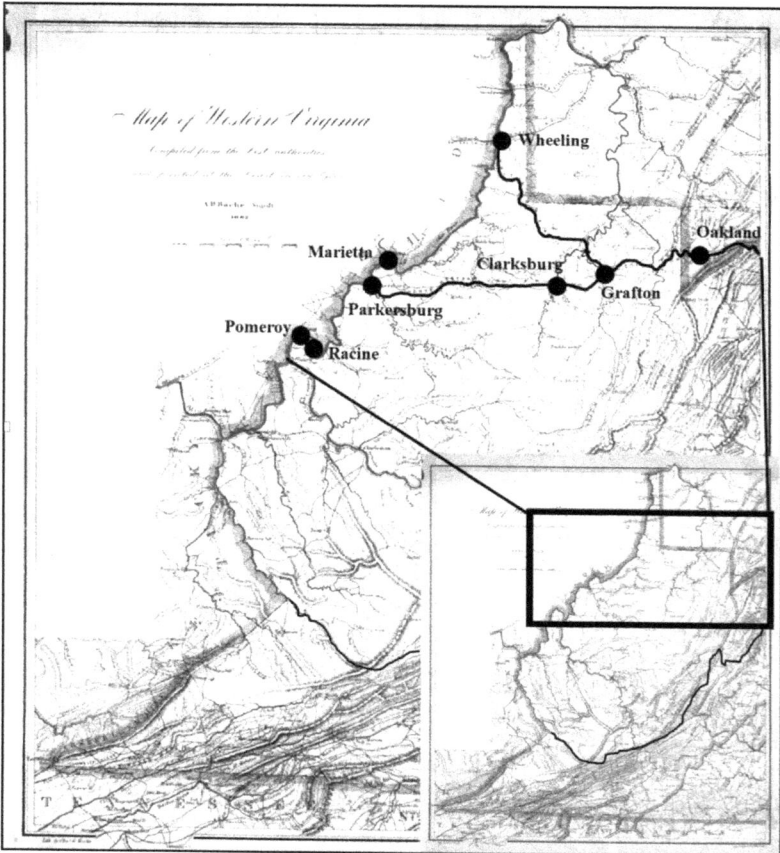

Map of Baltimore and Ohio Railroad, 1861[85]

In a June 20th letter home to Pomeroy, an Eighteenth Ohio Volunteer Militia soldier stationed at West Union (between Parkersburg and Clarksburg) reported that they'd encountered some Confederate scouts but had not seen much action other than that. He mentioned that most of the citizens of the area sided with the Union, and that trains transporting troops, horses, wagons, and provisions passed through nearly every day toward Grafton and the interior of Virginia.[86]

Railroad bridge at Grafton, West Virginia in 1859[87]

Clarksburg was a small village with fewer than one thousand inhabitants enumerated in the 1860 census.[88] For a short time, it was the headquarters of General George B. McClellan, commander of the Department of the Ohio. The soldiers stayed in camps in town, probably near the West Fork River. Although Confederate General Stonewall Jackson was born there, Clarksburg remained under Union control and was largely sympathetic to the Union throughout the war.[89]

In addition to guarding railroads, sometimes the soldiers ventured out on scouting expeditions, arrested successionists, and brought them back to camp, where the rebels would be released after they signed an oath pledging allegiance to the United States. This was against orders since the only arrests were to be those where secessionists were armed or in contact with the Confederate army.[90]

B&O RAILROAD

Chartered 1827 to connect Baltimore to the Ohio River, the railway was completed to Wheeling in 1852. Used to move Union troops and supplies during the Civil War. Its strategic importance made the B&O the target of destructive Confederate attacks. Postwar periods of prosperity were hampered by overexpansion. Rising debt led to a merger with the C&O Railroad in the late 20th century.

WEST VIRGINIA ARCHIVES & HISTORY, 2013

Historical Marker in Grafton, West Virginia[91]

Distribution of food, clothing, and supplies was often an problem. One soldier wrote home that, "Eating begins to look rather slim already, as we are allowanced to three crackers, a pint of coffee and fat pork in proportion."[92] Thankfully, though, sympathetic community members pitched in and the proud Union men at Camp Dunnington in Clarksburg were able to celebrate Independence Day on July 4th. After a foggy start to the day, the sun came out and shone brightly on the festivities.[93] Soldiers on bridge-guarding duty were brought to town for the day. Colonel Stanley of the Eighteenth O.V.M. addressed the soldiers from Ohio, Pennsylvania, and West Virginia gathered there. There was a band, choir, patriotic speeches, and a parade through the town. A fine dinner was served and no one went away hungry. Games were organized and violins played dancing tunes to the delight of both soldiers and young women from the community.[94] It's likely that Captain Wallar and most of Company H were present on this happy day.

On the evening of July 13th, nearly the entire regiment boarded train cars and traveled east to Oakland, Maryland, leaving only a few men to guard the camp. They arrived there on the morning of the 14th, and on the evening of the 15th, set out on foot for Greenland, West Virginia. They traveled along the Northwest Turnpike and crossed into West Virginia at the North Branch of the Potomac River at Gormania. The plan was to rendezvous with other units to present a large and imposing army of thousands of men to confront the enemy camped near Greenland.[95]

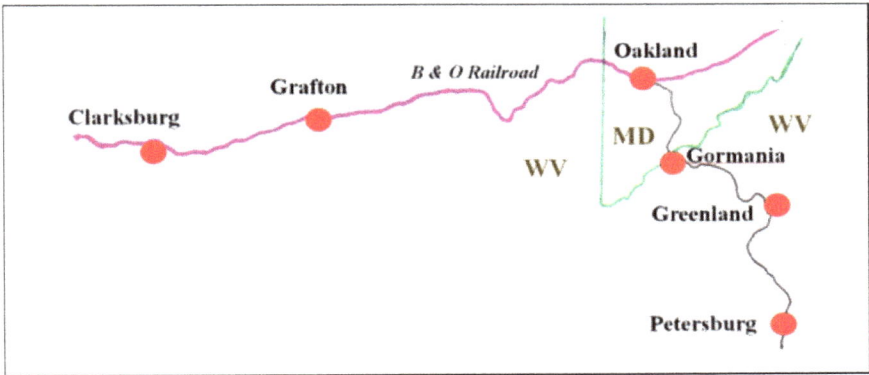

Map of route from Clarksburg to Greenland

After marching over thirty-five miles in twenty-four hours, the weary soldiers found themselves in the vicinity of Greenland only to learn that the Confederates had hastily retreated towards Petersburg when learning of the Union army's approach. Instead of pursuing the enemy, the Eighteenth O.V.M. were ordered back to Oakland.[96] They remained there until the morning of July 23rd, when the regiment packed their supplies and traveled west via the railroad, back to Clarksburg. On July 31st, they boarded the train again to go home to Ohio. From Parkersburg, they took the railroad ferry *Daniel Webster* to Marietta since there were no railroad tracks across the Ohio River at this location. Friends and family lined the banks of the Ohio and Muskingum Rivers to welcome the men home. After disembarking, the regiment marched to Camp Putnam. Townspeople lined the streets and cheered. Once assembled at Camp Putnam, Colonel Stanley bade the brave soldiers farewell, and the men were then free to return home.[97]

Since the Eighteenth Ohio Volunteer Militia was formed to serve only for three months, many of the men were willing to reenlist for a three-year period, and did so. Others were anxious to return home and resume life there. Before this could happen, however, the Eighteenth Ohio needed to be officially mustered out, and this order was given on August 1, 1861 by C. P. Buckingham, Adjutant General of Ohio.[98]

By August 9th, the soldiers of Company H were back in Meigs County. The newspaper reported, "The boys look sound and hearty. If they did have to live on "sheet iron crackers," they look none the worse for it..."[99] According to the records at the National Archives, the unit was mustered out on August 28th in Columbus.[100] The three-month volunteers who served in Company H met at the Meigs County courthouse in Pomeroy on August 31st to receive the remainder of their pay.[101]

There was some controversy regarding James Wallar. A mid-August newspaper article claimed that:

Captain Wallar will have a defense to make to the various unfounded rumors concerning his acts in Western Virginia, and asks the community to suspend judgement till he can properly make such defense.[102]

I was unable to find anything specific implicating Captain Wallar, but an article appearing in a Wheeling newspaper earlier in August reported that many Union horses died from lack of food and water in Clarksburg.[103] Perhaps this was the issue about which he wished to speak, or perhaps there was a darker side to Captain Wallar.

Wallar's Muster-out Record[104]

3

RAISING A COMPANY OF CAVALRY

Before this controversy could die down, Captain J.L. Wallar announced in the local newspaper that he would raise a company of cavalry for the Union army.[105] On August 28, 1861, James L. Wallar enrolled as a Captain in Company A, Second Regiment, Virginia Mounted Volunteers in Racine, Ohio for a period of three years.[106] This unit became known as Company A, Second Regiment, Loyal Virginia Cavalry, and subsequently the Second Regiment West Virginia Cavalry. Most of the members of the Second West Virginia were from southeastern Ohio. This regiment was formed under the assumption that it would be called the Fourth Ohio Cavalry, but the governor of Ohio refused to accept more cavalry units. The organizers then appealed to the provisional government of the western part of Virginia that had refused to secede from the United States—the future West Virginia.[107]

Men were eager to serve under Captain Wallar—the local newspaper claimed, "We know of no more popular Capt. in the service..."—and the enlistees left on the steamboat, *Hero*, for Parkersburg on Wednesday, September 11, 1861.[108]

Wallar, as an officer, was expected to supply his own horse and tack.[109] The enlisted men and noncommissioned officers were at the mercy of the U.S. government to supply horses. The horses offered to the men were often unfit for use. One officer mused... "I was obliged to receive everything in the shape of a horse which he [the quartermaster] sent in, whether he was good for anything or not." The noncommissioned officers had their choice of horse first, followed by the enlisted men.[110]

Monument to Civil War Horses, Middleburg, Virginia[111]

The use of cavalry in wooded and mountainous areas such as West Virigina was unprecedented, and commanders of Union cavalry were unsure how to train the troops or even what their role would be in the war. General George McClellan, who had studied European cavalry tactics during the Crimean War, and other Union leaders concluded that the best way to utilize the cavalry was to assign small detachments to infantry brigades to concentrate on duties such as scouting, escorting the infantry, and serving picket duty.[112]

Adding to the challenge was the fact that many of the Union's cavalry recruits had never ridden a horse. In northern states, horses were more commonly driven than ridden. After the war, a veteran exclaimed, "It seems as if each recruit for the cavalry thought the especial requirement for that branch of the service was that he could neither ride, saddle, nor groom a horse."[113]

The soldiers were often overburdened with gear. A cavalry soldier gave this account of packing:

Two woollen blankets and a coverlet brought from home were hurriedly rolled into a bundle two feet long and a foot thick, which was strapped on the saddle behind; the rubber dolman overcoat, carpet sack with several suits of underclothing, shaving-tools, shoe-brush and blacking, and perhaps a sheep-skin, had to be packed in front. The side-pockets, or saddle-bags, were filled with crackers and forty rounds of ammunition.[114]

The cavalryman then strapped on:

...a heavy cavalry sword; on one shoulder hung a monstrous shooting-iron (soon replaced by the carbine), and on the other a haversack holding three days' rations. Thus equipped, the horses were led into line, each with a nose-bag dangling on his neck containing a feed of oats, and a weight of one hundred and fifty pounds on his back...[115]

Typical uniforms of Civil War Cavalrymen[116]

While I don't have a color photograph of a Second West Virginia Cavalry uniform, the illustrations above show what the uniforms may have looked like. A Union cavalry jacket was made of dark blue wool with a high standing collar and twelve cavalry buttons down the front. The cavalry uniform trousers were reinforced to withstand wear and tear from the saddle and were of a sky-blue woven cloth with a gold stripe on the side. Calf-high boots completed the ensemble.[117]

The cavalrymen of the Second West Virginia regiment reported to Parkersburg, West Virginia for drills in mid-September but didn't receive their weapons until mid-December. Most of the soldiers were issued "horse pistols"— .58 caliber, one-shot guns with a 12" barrel. Others received single-shot Enfield rifles. They also received sabres, which would later prove to be "more ornamental than useful" for a cavalry soldier.[118]

The colonel oversaw drill instruction. The men learned and practiced facings, columns, lines, and how to march as a company, regiment, and battalion. Many men needed instruction on riding and maneuvering their horse. The frequency of drills was entirely dependent on the whim of the colonel. Wallar, as a captain, likely received additional tactical instruction. The men likely had instruction on using their sabres, but little target practice with their pistols or rifles.[119]

On November 8, 1861, James L. Wallar appeared on the company muster-in roll card in Camp Bolles,[120] a Union cavalry camp located on what was called Mount Logan on the south side of the Little Kanawha River south of downtown Parkersburg. The camp was later fortified and was renamed Fort Boreman. It is now the city's Fort Boreman Park.[121] Here, the eager men trained and drilled and waited to be called to action. Brigadier General J.D. Cox ordered that the Second West Virginia cavalry would "not be permanently attached to any Brigade, but it will make reports to the Brigade Commandant they may from time to time be serving with."[122]

Civil War soldiers were usually housed two to a tent and were responsible for keeping their mess kit, military equipment, and uniform in order. While in camp, the men were often bored or homesick. To pass the time, many played cards and games, like checkers or horseshoe pitching. Others wrote letters home or kept an account of their experience in a diary. Some men played music to entertain themselves and their fellow soldiers. Drinking and gambling weren't uncommon, and often led to life-altering disagreements. A bit of foreshadowing here, dear reader.

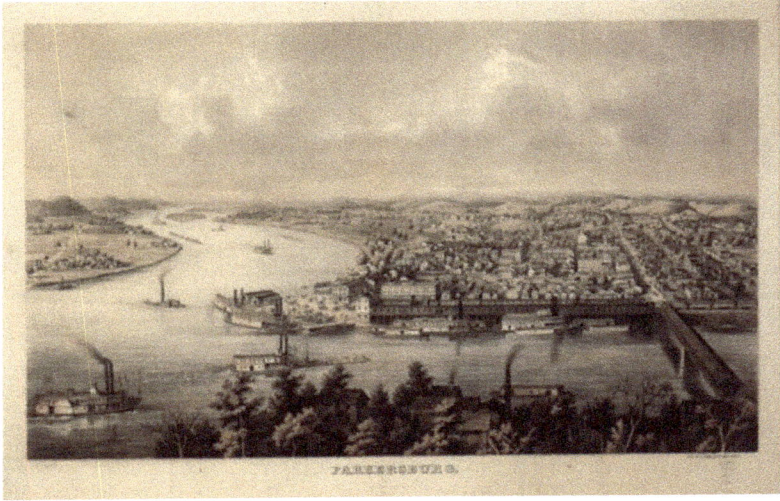

Parkersburg, 1861[123]

A typical day in a cavalry camp might begin with buglers calling "Reveille" before daybreak. The soldiers quickly dressed and lined up for roll call. Next, the "Stables" call was played, and the soldiers fed and cared for their horses, then ate breakfast. After breakfast, the horses were walked to the nearest stream for water. Sick call followed. "First Call for Guard Mount" sent the men who were to stand guard that day to leave for their assigned post. "Drill Call" was the signal for the sergeants to order the men into their companies. Once this was done, the sergeant would turn over his company to the captain by saying, "Sir, the company is formed." The captain would then command the men to form ranks and go to the parade ground for the day's drills. The buglers sounded the "Recall from Drill," and the men assembled for the main meal at lunchtime. More drilling often occurred after lunch. The men once again led their horses to the watering spot, and afterwards, retired the horses for the day. After supper, the men lined up for the evening roll call, and to end the day, "Taps" was played and the men retired to bed.[124]

Sundays were typically a day of rest from drills. The cavalrymen fed and tended to the horses, tidied their quarters, and cleaned their tack and equipment. Guards assumed their posts, and there was often an inspection and religious services later in the morning. If the camp was near the soldiers' hometowns, family and friends often visited camp on Sunday afternoons.[125]

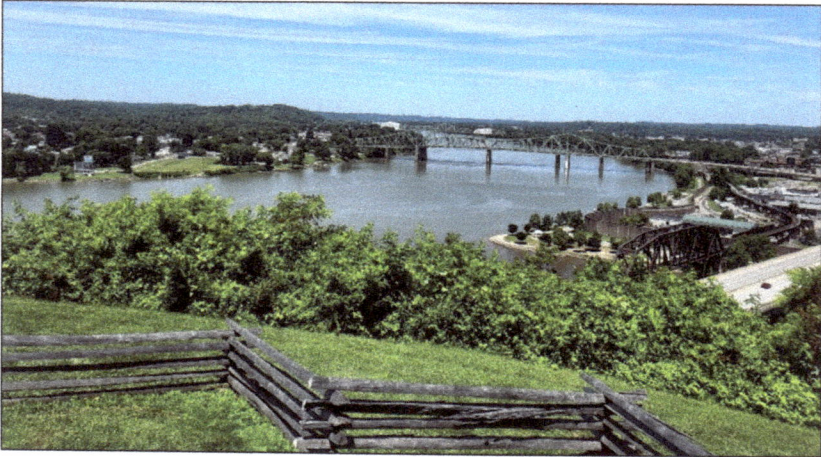

Looking north at the confluence of the Ohio River and Little Kanawha River at Parkersburg from Fort Boreman[126]

Today, Fort Boreman Park overlooks Parkersburg. To the west and north, one sees the Ohio River, and the Little Kanawha River flows in front of the park from the east. The well-maintained park has several overlooks, wooden walkways, and picnic shelters. At the uppermost overlook site, trenches and a small stone foundation are visible. Two cannons add to the historical aspect of the park.

On December 16, 1861, the regiment was ordered to their winter camp at Guyandotte on the south bank of the Ohio River in Cabell County, West Virginia.[127] Guyandotte is now a historic neighborhood of Huntington, West Virginia. There, the men received their horses and readied for battle. Only a month earlier, the town of Guyandotte was nearly destroyed. A small group of untrained, sickly Union soldiers who were stationed at Guyandotte were raided by a larger group of Confederate cavalrymen and secessionist townspeople. In retaliation, Union troops from the nearby town of Ceredo set fire to the business district and homes of Confederate sympathizers and drove the secessionists out of town.[128] The "better class of citizens" moved across the Ohio River, and the remaining townspeople were thankful to have the protection of Union troops.[129]

While the other companies of the Second West Virginia were stationed for the winter in Guyandotte, Wallar's Company A left Guyandotte for Ceredo, West Virginia in mid-December.[130] Ceredo was located ten miles west of Guyandotte on the southern shore of the Ohio River. It was a new town, founded in 1857 by New England abolitionists who thought the quickest way to end slavery would be to move to Virginia, establish themselves in leadership positions, and vote to abolish slavery. At the start of the Civil War, the men of Ceredo quickly organized into the Fifth Virginia Infantry.[131]

It was not long before Company A embarked on their first adventure. From December 17th through the 20th, the men of Company A made a scouting trip to the county seat, Wayne, twenty miles south of Ceredo through winding, mountainous terrain. Less than a week later, on Christmas Day, the company again embarked on a scouting trip, this time engaging with Confederate troops. One Union guard was injured in this skirmish.[132]

Historical marker in Ceredo, West Virginia[133]

4

❧·•———•••———•·❧

FINDING THEIR FOOTING

W inter in West Virginia can be cold, rainy, and snowy. Many of the mountain passes weren't navigable in the winter months, so there were extended periods of inactivity in camp waiting for nicer weather. In early January 1862, many of the Second's companies assisted General James A. Garfield's troops against Confederate General Humphrey Marshall in Eastern Kentucky. Company A, however, remained in Ceredo into February or March, drilling and going on occasional scouting expeditions.[134] As winter turned to spring, Company A, along with companies D, E, G, and H of the Second West Virginia Cavalry, were sent east and south to Raleigh Court House (now called Beckley), where they would form the Second Battalion, commanded by Lieutenant Colonel John C. Paxton. At Raleigh Court House, the men were quartered in deserted buildings, churches, and the courthouse. Their job was to patrol Raleigh, Fayette, and Wyoming counties, to keep the pro-secession residents under control, fight "bushwhackers," and to assist the infantry with the goal of securing the Virginia and Tennessee Railroad, which ran from Lynchburg to Bristol. Bushwhackers were southern sympathizers who were not soldiers in the Confederate army. A group of bushwhackers might position themselves on a hill and take shots at Union soldiers who were foraging or guarding a cache of supplies, for example. It was common for Union soldiers to burn the homes of suspected bushwhackers.[135]

A fellow cavalryman later wrote in his memoirs:

If there was one thing more than another that the Second Virginia Cavalry hated, it was the detestable bush-whackers. We did not object to being shot at on general principles, but to have some unprincipled scoundrel who was too cowardly to join the army and fight as a man, sneak around like a thief in the night and shoot from behind a tree or from some inaccessible position, was more than we could patiently stand.[136]

The Kanawha Valley was important to both the Union and Confederate armies because of the nearby salt deposits that could be used to preserve meat, and the fertile farmland in the northern and western parts of the valley could supply grains. In addition, the valley provided a route between eastern Virginia and Ohio, and a ready source of soldiers loyal to one side or the other. The populace was divided in its support, often neighbor against neighbor, and it was not difficult to find men willing to join. The Kanawha River was obviously a source of transportation and allowed access to eastern Virginia via the James River Turnpike on the eastern end of the valley and to the Ohio River on the west. The Federal army wished to maintain control of the Baltimore and Ohio Railroad on the north, and the Confederate army needed the Virginia and Tennessee Railroad in northern Virginia.[137]

Farther south, the Virginia and Tennessee Railroad was an important supply line for the Confederate army. It was used to transport troops, food, and raw materials such as copper and salt. The Union army hoped to secure the railroad line by gaining control of the depot at Dublin, Virginia, some eighty miles south of Raleigh Court House. Confederate Brigadier General Henry Heth was well aware of the importance of the railroad, and of the Union army's plans. Heth called for the men in the counties of southwestern Virginia to rendezvous at either Lewisburg or Peterstown with the militia or to join the regular army.

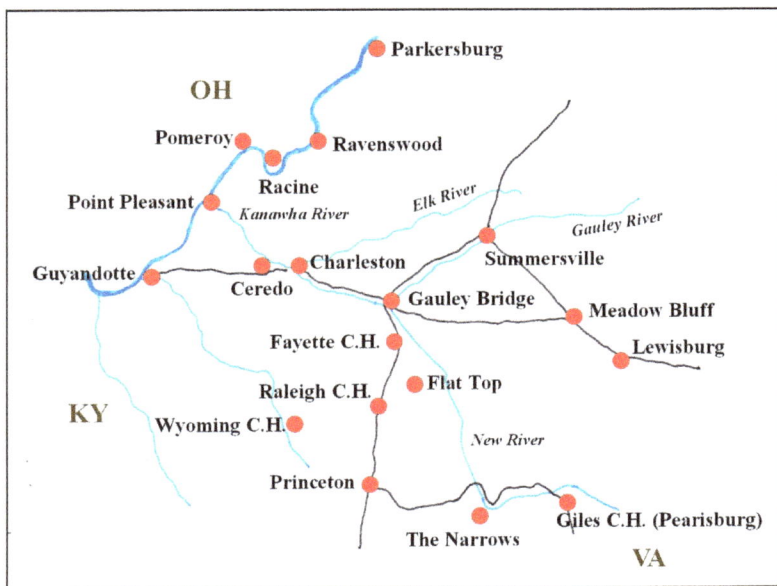

The Kanawha and New River Valleys

The Second West Virginia Cavalry's Second Battalion set off for Flat Top Mountain on April 8, 1862. The camp at Flat Top was officially known as Camp Jones and was in Mercer County about thirty-five miles south of Raleigh Court House and seven miles north of Princeton. Incessant spring rains made for poor roads, and the regiment moved slowly. Horses became ill from drinking sandy water, and troop morale was low. Many horses were lost, and the troops were forced to abandon much of their equipment along the way.[138] On the same day, a notice was printed in the *Pomeroy Weekly Telegraph*:

We are authorized to announce that Capt. J.L. Wallar will find place in his Cavalry Company for eight able-bodied men, if application be made immediately. Those who contemplate entering the service cannot secure a better place, as it is acknowledged on all hands that Capt. Wallar is as kind an officer as is in the service. Apply to the Captain, at Ceredo, Va., or at this office.[139]

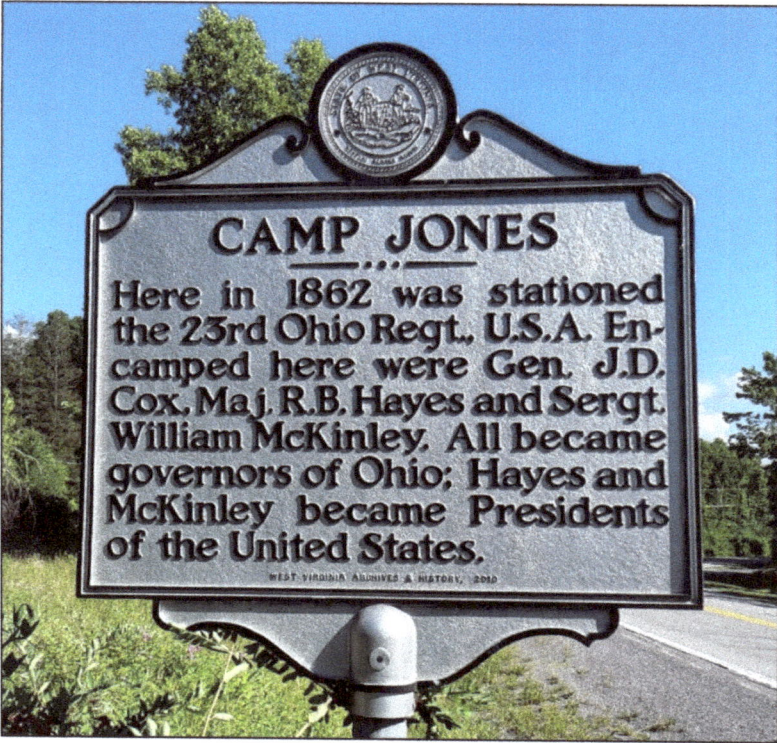

CAMP JONES

Here in 1862 was stationed the 23rd Ohio Regt., U.S.A. Encamped here were Gen. J.D. Cox, Maj. R.B. Hayes and Sergt. William McKinley. All became governors of Ohio; Hayes and McKinley became Presidents of the United States.

WEST VIRGINIA ARCHIVES & HISTORY, 2010

Historical marker at Flat Top, West Virginia[140]

James Wallar and his fellow Ohioans must have been awed by the beautiful landscape of this part of West Virginia. The Kanawha River runs from Gauley Bridge northwestward through Charleston and on to Point Pleasant, where it empties into the Ohio River. The mountains here are old—with rounded tops covered with trees. The forest is dense, dark, and rocky. Today's paved roads are narrow and winding; it's unimaginable how a cavalry unit would've navigated the muddy paths of the 1860s through such terrain.

Breastworks, or trenches, were dug along the road for a few miles from Camp Jones toward Princeton and an outpost was configured to watch for the approach of the Confederate army from the Princeton and Camp Creek area. Outpost duty could be a miserable affair. A member of the 5th New York Cavalry later penned:

Mounted upon their shivering horses, the poor fellows with nothing cheering, but their courage, go out to sit in the saddle for two hours, facing the biting wind, and peering through the storm of sleet, snow or rain which pelts them in the face mercilessly. Happy if the guerrilla does not creep through bushes impenetrable to the sight to inflict his cruel blows, the two hours expired, relief comes and the Vedette *[mounted guard] returns to spend his four, six or eight hours off duty as best he may.*[141]

Later Captain Wallar wrote a letter to the newspaper in Pomeroy, Ohio detailing the events of what would later be called the Battle of Clark's House or Clark's Hollow. This was a skirmish between Company C of the 23rd Ohio Infantry and the "Flat Top Copperheads"—a band of secessionists aligned with the Confederate army:

Dear Telegraph:--According to promise, I propose to give you an account of our doings since we have taken the field this spring. On the 26th of April we left Gauley Bridge; on the 27th we arrived at Raleigh Court House, where we remained until the 29th, when we started for Princeton, in Mercer County. The night of the 29th we encamped on Flat Top Mountain; next morning being May 1st, we moved forward. The night previous Company C, of the 23d O.V.I. had been sent forward about four miles as an outpost, where they occupied a large log house. About daylight in the morning they were attacked by about 400 rebels under command of Lieut. Col. Fitzhugh. After a severe fight the rebels fled, leaving seven killed, and about thirty wounded on the field; our loss was one killed, three dangerously wounded and sixteen slightly. Here our Cavalry took the advance; only the first Battalion of our Regiment was present. Our Battalion is composed of the following Companies: Capt. Wallar, Co. A.; Capt. Hamilton, Co. D.; Capt. McMahan, Co. G; Capt. Emmons, Co. K., commanded by Lieut. Col. J.C. Paxton and Maj. R.L. Curtis; Lieut. Cranson, Battalion Adjutant.[142]

Much of Wallar's account is corroborated in the diary of Lieutenant Colonel Rutherford B. Hayes, commander of the 23rd Ohio Infantry, and future 19th president of the United States:

Camp 5, Princeton, May 1, 1862. Thursday.—Marched at 6 A.M. Heard firing in advance. Turned out to be Company C on Camp Creek, attacked by Lieutenant-Colonel Fitzhugh with four companies, dismounted, Jenkins' Cavalry and Foley's bushwhackers. The company was in line ready to move off to return to camp when they saw a party of bushwhackers coming down the road who called out (Captain Foley called): "Don't fire; we are Richmond's men." Immediately after a volley was fired into our men from all sides. They were surrounded by three hundred Secesh. Finding the attack so heavy, Company C was ordered by Lieutenant Bottsford to take shelter in the log house where they had quartered. They kept up such a spirited fire that the enemy retreated, leaving four dead, four mortally, four more dangerously. All these we got...

I came up to the scene of the conflict soon after the enemy fled. They say our coming drove them away... We immediately pushed on in mud and rain after the retreating foe...I then sent the cavalry under Lieutenant-Colonel Paxton in advance.[143]

Again, from Wallar's letter:

After moving about five miles we were attacked by the rebels, who occupied a ridge right in front of us and partly concealed by a fence. We saw them just before they fired, and I recognized Col. Fitzhugh, and was in the act of taking a gun from one of the men to shoot him, when he gave the command, "fire!" and the firing commenced. The first shot struck my favorite horse, "Harry," about an inch below the eye, knocking him down. At the same time Col. Paxton gave the order to dismount and bushwhack them, which we did in less time than it takes to tell of it. We soon routed the rebels, killing one and wounding several. No loss on our side, thought I confess the enemy's balls whistled around our heads rather close for comfort.[144]

Hayes' diary continued:

They soon were fired on by a gang of bushwhackers from a hill and their horses badly stampeded. One horse threw his forelegs over Colonel Paxton's horse's neck. The cavalry dismounted, charged up the hill, and caught one dragoon.

Finding the cavalry would dismount and skirmish all the bad hillsides (and they were abundant—being twelve miles of defiles), I again put the Twenty-third in advance...

We pushed on rapidly, crossing Wolf Creek, and wading Bluestone waist-deep—rain falling, mud deep and slippery. We came in sight of the wagons of the retreating foe, but for want of cavalry familiarized to the business, we were unable to overtake them.

Reconnoitering[145]

It was commonly believed that it took upwards of two years to train a cavalry soldier and his mount. Clearly with only a few months' training under their belts, the Union cavalry companies such as Captain Wallar's Company A were somewhat ill-prepared for the war. Not surprisingly, Hayes was not impressed with the fighting skills of the Second West Virginia Cavalry. In a May 2nd letter home to wife Lucy, he wrote:

We would have caught Lieutenant-Colonel Fitzhugh and his men, if our cavalry had had experience. I don't report to their prejudice publicly, for they are fine fellows—gentlemen, splendidly mounted and equipped. In three months they will be capital, but their caution in the face of ambuscades is entirely too great. After trying to get them ahead, I put the Twenty-third in advance and cavalry in the rear, making certainly double the speed with our footmen trudging in the mud, as was made by the horsemen on their fine steeds.[146]

Wallar's letter continued:

We again mounted, and learning that the rebels were to be reinforced by the 45th Va. Regiment, we turned to the left on a road leading up Blue Stone river and coming into the road leading from Princeton to Giles Court-House, about four miles from Princeton. It was over this road that the 45th were moving, and they would have to retreat the same way; the 23d was moving on the direct road to Princeton. We pushed forward until within about two hundred yards of the Giles road, when we halted and my Company dismounted and went up the hill to reconnoiter. Just as we got to the top of the ridge a rebel in the road yelled halt, which was no sooner said than crack went the scoundrel's rifle, and he jumped behind a log leaving only a small portion of his head visible. Sergeant E.D. Robinson, from Chester, let him have the contents of his Enfield, which put daylight through his cap, blowing it off his head. By this time about twenty of my men, and about the same number of Capt. McMahan's men, were in the brush, near the road, when we discovered about 600 rebels coming up the road. We sent down the hill for more men, and then, without waiting for our men to get up, we dashed out of the woods toward the rebels, firing at them and yelling like demons. The rebels hesitated for a moment, then broke and run like dogs, throwing away knapsacks, clothing, guns and everything that incumbered them. By this time the balance of our force had got up and we followed them out into an open field, where they made a stand and fired at us several volleys, which we returned. Moving toward them on double-quick, away they went again, "helter skelter"—that is, every man for himself. We learned afterward that they numbered six hundred men, while our force in the field was at no time over two hundred, the rest being with the horses, and when they broke and run they had not seen over forty men, the others being concealed by a hill. I really never appreciated the term "skedaddle" until that day. In this affair the enemy lost three killed and about twenty wounded. It was now sundown, and we moved on toward Princeton, where we found the 23d. They in retreating, fired the town, and it was completely destroyed.[147]

Imagine the tragedy and chaos—the roads leading away from Princeton packed with women, children, and elderly men fleeing the inferno with whatever possessions they could quickly grab, the retreating rebels, and the Union soldiers trying to press onward to Princeton to extinguish the flames set by the Confederate troops.

Hayes' diary reported:

We were told of great reinforcements at Princeton or soon to be at Princeton. The Forty-fifth there or coming. We kept ahead. On approaching town we saw great clouds. Some thought it smoke, some supposed it was clouds. Within two miles we knew the Rebels were burning the town. We hurried forward; soon reached an elevated ground overlooking the place. All the brick buildings, court-house, churches, etc. were burning. I ordered up the howitzers to scatter out the few Rebel cavalry who were doing it...

And so ended the first of May—twenty-two miles in mud and rain. An exciting day. Five enemy killed, nine badly wounded that we got; three unwounded prisoners, and about a dozen Rebels wounded. Total five killed, three prisoners, twenty-one wounded. A good day's work.

In a May 2nd letter to Colonel Scammon from Princeton, Rutherford B. Hayes penned:

Lieutenant-Colonel Paxton with the cavalry reached here by the Giles Road about dark. He left the direct road to Princeton at Spanishburg and took the Bluff Road, which strikes the road from Giles to Princeton four miles from Princeton. We found it impossible to send the cavalry to the Tazewell or Wytheville Road, at least in time, and they went to the Giles Road hoping to catch the enemy retreating on that road. The enemy took the Wytheville Road to Rocky Gap and escaped. The cavalry on entering the Giles Road found a great number of fresh tracks leading to Princeton. Hastening on, they came suddenly on the Forty-fifth Virginia coming to the relief of Princeton. As soon as the cavalry came in sight there was a "skedaddling" of the cavalry for the hills and a scattering of knapsacks very creditable to their capacity to appreciate danger. There was a good deal of hurried firing at long range, but nobody hurt on our side and perhaps none on the other...[148]

James and his fellow cavalrymen probably found their ten day stay in Princeton a welcome respite from the hunt. The weather was finally decent, and Lieutenant Colonel Hayes called Princeton "...the best camping for an army I have seen in western Virginia." Although the town was nearly burned to the ground, the Union soldiers found ample provisions for stabling and feeding their horses, a few large homes to use as headquarters, and smaller houses for storage purposes. The men were fortunate to find cattle, sheep, chickens, and hogs, as well, left behind by the fleeing townspeople. It must have been unsettling, however, to have the remaining women of Princeton pleading for their lives and protection. [149]

James likely thought of his wife Frances holding down the fort back in Racine where the Ladies' Soldiers' Aid Society was collecting items such as sheets, pillows, towels, shirts, socks, dried fruit, bandages, pickles, jam, eggs, and butter for the ill and wounded Union soldiers at recently captured Fort Donelson in northwest Tennessee. With James away, Frances and older daughter Etta likely did their part to help the cause.[150]

Wallar's letter continued:

On the 4th, the 23d and two companies of our Cavalry moved to Giles Court-House, distant from Princeton 28 miles, where they remained until the morning of the 10th, when they were attacked by a superior force of the enemy and forced to retreat, which they did; fighting over every inch of the ground; but the enemy had 5 pieces of artillery, our force having none.[151]

Late in the evening on May 9th Hayes wrote to Colonel E.P. Scammon requesting reinforcements immediately. The enemy had artillery present, and the Union army had none. The following day, Hayes detailed in his diary their defeat and retreat to the Narrows:

We were attacked at 4 o'clock this morning. I got up at the first faint streak of light and walked out to see the pickets in the direction of the enemy. As I was walking alone I heard six shots. "No mistake this time," I thought...Led the whole to the front beyond the town; saw the enemy approaching—four regiments or battalions, several pieces of artillery in line of battle approaching. The artillery soon opened on us. The shell shrieked and burst over heads, the small arms rattled, and the battle was begun. It was soon obvious that we would be outflanked. We retreated to the next ridge and stood again. The men of the Twenty-third behaved gloriously, the men of Gilmore's Cavalry, ditto; the men of Colonel Paxton's cavalry, not so well...And so we fought our way through town, the people rejoicing at our defeat, and on for six hours until we reached the Narrows, five and one-half miles distant...In the Narrows we easily checked the pursuit of the enemy and held him back until he got artillery on to the opposite side of New River and shelled us out...The Second Virginia Cavalry left us! Bad state of things.[152]

Wallar's letter reported:

We received the news and started to reinforce them with the 30th O.V.I. and 4 howitzers of McMullen's Battery.

We met our retreating force about eight miles from Giles Court-House. The enemy right behind our force had contended manfully for the "Narrows," a place on New River, which is a natural fortification; but their shells drove us from the position. They now occupy the upper end of the "Narrows"—we the lower end. The pickets are cursing each other, and firing on each other continually.[153]

Dutifully, Hayes wrote to his wife Lucy about the day, concluding with the following:

It was a retreat (which is almost a synonym for defeat) and yet we all felt grand over it. But warn't the men mad at somebody for leaving us? We were joined by a battery and the Thirtieth [Ohio Infantry] Regiment at 4 P.M. under Colonel Scammon, starting at the seasonable hour of 7 A.M.! We are now strong again, but driven from a most valuable position with a loss of stores we had captured worth thousands.

I am reported dangerously wounded by some of the cowardly cavalry (not Gilmore's) who fled forty miles, reporting us "routed," "cut to pieces," and the like. Never was a man prouder of his regiment than I of the Twenty-third...

Since writing the foregoing, we have got information which leads me to think it was probably well we were not reinforced. There would not have been enough to hold the position we had against so great a force as the enemy brought against us. You see we were twenty miles from their railroad, and only six to twelve hours from their great armies.[154]

Wallar's Company A was not part of the "cowardly cavalry" which abandoned Hayes and the Twenty-third. They were a part of the reinforcements, arriving after the battle at Pearisburg.

By Monday, May 12th, Lieutenant Colonel Hayes and the entire First Brigade of the Army of the District of Kanawha were retreating toward Princeton and were at a camp north of the East River near the line between Giles and Mercer counties, eleven miles from Pearisburg, Virginia. This army, commanded by General Jacob Dolson Cox, consisted of five thousand men. Hayes wrote in his diary that the camp was on a hill overlooking both the New River and the East River, surrounded by high mountains, and was quite picturesque. The First Brigade was commanded by Colonel Eliakim Parker Scammon and consisted of the Twelfth, Twenty-third, and Thirtieth Ohio infantry regiments, McMullen's artillery battery (two brass six-pounders and four howitzers), and four companies of Paxton's or Bowles' Second Virginia Cavalry (including Company A) and Captain Gilmore's Cavalry.[155]

Lieutenant Colonel Hayes' frustration with the Second West Virginia Cavalry continued during the stay at the East River camp. His diary entry for Tuesday May 13th contained the following snippet:

The Second [West] *Virginia Cavalry, out foraging, came rushing in covered with foam; reported a great force of Rebel cavalry near by! Turned out to be our own—Gilmore's Cavalry! What a worthless set they are proving to be.* [156]

Wallar's letter of May 16th to the *Pomeroy Weekly Telegraph* concluded with the following:

A big fight will come off here soon; when it occurs I will let you know the result. Suffice it to say, we are confident of success. Let me here say, that Meigs County has no braver boys in the field than those in Company A. I always had confidence in them; but they did better than I could have asked. There was none of that unnecessary recklessness sometimes exhibited; but there was that coolness and strict obedience to orders, when the balls were hissing all around them, that made me feel proud of them, and it appears a miracle that none were killed. Only one was touched by a ball; that was S. Sprague, of Syracuse, who got a very slight wound on the hand. My men are well, and eager for another chance at the rebels. [157]

On May 16, 1862, Captain Wallar was stationed at a camp near the mouth of the East River in Giles County, Virginia. This area, just north of the community of Glen Lyn, was called Adair's.[158] On May 17th, Colonel Scammon's command, including Captain Wallar's Company A, joined Lieutenant Colonel Hayes in the camp near the Bluestone River. The enemy had cut the Union army's telegraph lines and their supply routes had been disrupted. The Union army had issued the last of the rations and the horses were suffering. Scammon brought news that the enemy was being reinforced by troops from Eastern Virginia and were now 15,000 strong. Brigadier General J.D. Cox ordered the troops to fall back to Flat Top.[159]

The Union troops at Princeton camped near a ridge called Pigeon's Roost. Unbeknownst to the Union army, the Confederate troops were lying in ambush. Scammon's brigade, and presumably Wallar, arrived at Princeton on the evening of the 17th. The Union army soon continued their retreat to Flat Top, and the campaign to destroy the train depot at Dublin was abandoned.[160]

Confederate Brigadier General Humphrey Marshall reported about the same encounter to General Robert E. Lee in Richmond:

My advance was unexpected by Brigadier-General Cox, who had his headquarters and body guard at Princeton at the time with a force variously estimated at from 500 to 1200 men, the former probably nearer to the truth than the latter. The pickets of the enemy were encountered by my advance guard about 4 miles from Princeton, and a skirmish continued from that place through the woodlands and brushwood to a point something over 1 mile from the Court-House.

...In this skirmish the enemy lost some 16 or 20, who were left on the field. ...After a while I was informed that the enemy had fled before us, leaving his tents, clothes, swords, officers' uniforms, and even the lights burning in his tents. It is probable, had we not halted before night-fall, we might have captured many prisoners, possibly the general himself, for I was informed he did not leave town until twilight; but none of us could foresee, and, so far as I know, every one acted for the best; the regiments went in with hearty good will and promptly.

So the town of Princeton fell into my hands about 10 p.m. on May 16; the line of the enemy's communication with Raleigh was cut, and the headquarters of the Kanawha division was abruptly stampeded. A mass of correspondence fell into my hands. Letters and orders, dated from May 10 down to May 16, fully disclosed the intentions of the enemy and his strength...

I found that the ruins of Princeton occupy a knoll in the center of some open, level meadows, entirely surrounded by woodlands, with thick undergrowth which fringe the open grounds, and that through the entire circuit about the town the central position at the Court-House can be commanded by the Enfield rifle. Roads lead in through these woods in several directions.

...After daylight I received a dispatch from Colonel Wharton, dated the 16th, at the Cross-Roads, 11 miles from Princeton, promising to come to town by 9 a.m. on the 17th. Before he arrived the enemy had reentered the town, a force I could not estimate, but which was provided with artillery, and displayed more than two full regiments...

The enemy was at the time throwing forward his skirmishers to dispute with mine the woods and points overhanging the road which led in from the Cross-Roads to Princeton, which road ran nearly parallel to the one by which I had advanced...My estimate is I now had some 2800 men, of whom one-half were raw recruits.

A regiment of the enemy, coming down from the direction of the Cross-Roads to Princeton about this time, appeared in the rear of Colonel Wharton's command, and were attacked by it furiously. The struggle lasted but a short time. The havoc in the enemy's ranks was terrible. Colonel Wharton reports to me 211 as the dead and wounded of the enemy. I understand that more than 80 bodies were buried on the field.

The enemy appeared with a flag of truce, asking to bury their dead and to remove their wounded. I refused; but hearing, after about an hour, that some officer had allowed it, and that the enemy were then engaged in burying, I directed Brigadier-General Williams to permit the ambulances of the enemy to pass along my right, for the purpose of carrying away their wounded also. There was no further battle.

I confidently expected at night-fall on the 17th that the enemy, in superior force would attack me in the morning, or that a junction with General Heth would enable me to attack his whole force, which was apparently concentrating around Princeton. He was in plain view under my glass; his wagons deliberately parked; his regiments exercising, and all the appearances given which indicate the purpose to give battle. My force was masked to him. He could have no idea of its amount. In this fact was my safety until Heth could come up. It seems Brigadier-General Heth did advance to the mouth of East River and found the enemy had abandoned tents and camp equipage both there and at French's, where he had been fortifying. The general passed on until he came within 4 or 5 miles of Princeton, on the evening of the 17th, when, hearing in the country from somebody that I had been repulsed and was retreating, he fell back in the night to the mouth of East River.

...The enemy had during the night vacated Princeton, taking the Raleigh road, his rear passing Blue Stone River about sunrise. I ordered my battalion of Mounted Rifles to follow him.

I ascertained that on the night of the 18th he encamped about 10 miles from Princeton, in a very strong position, having some seven regiments with him in retreat; in all from 5,000 to 7,000 men.

On the 19th I again sent forward on his line of retreat and ascertained that he had passed the Flat Top Mountains; had burned some of his caissons and gun-carriages, and had abandoned some of his wagons the preceding night. He was now 25 miles from Princeton.

...I left 71 of the enemy's wounded in the hospital at Princeton too badly shot to be moved at all. His surgeons were left in attendance and a chaplain was permitted to be with them. I return a list of 29 prisoners...

The enemy has lost largely, and, indeed, I should not be surprised if in killed and wounded his loss reached 400. One of his regiments scattered in the woods, threw away guns and uniforms, and its members are daily picked up by the country people.[161]

Battle of Pigeon's Roost marker[162]

5

CONFLICT NEAR AND FAR

A t some point, Captain Wallar left the company of Lieutenant Colonel Rutherford B. Hayes and traveled to Raleigh Court House (now Beckley, West Virginia). From there, on May 31, 1862, James L. Wallar sent a telegram to Assistant Adjutant General Henry Thrall in Wheeling asking if his leave of absence had been granted. It's unknown why Wallar was requesting this leave of absence, but it's possible that he wanted to travel home to see his new daughter. Based on her age in the 1870 census, James' and Frances' youngest child Lillie May Waller was possibly born in 1862.[163]

Contents of telegram sent by Wallar, May 31, 1862[164]

Regardless, James Wallar was forced to resign from the Union army in early June 1862. The following was reported in a diary entry of Rutherford B. Hayes:

Lieutenant-Colonel Paxton of the cavalry called to see me about Lieutenant Fordyce. Would he do for captain? Is he not too fond of liquor? My reply was favorable. He says he has three vacancies in the regiment. Captain Waller seduced Colonel Burgess' daughter; had to resign in consequence. I recommended both Avery and Bottsford for captains of cavalry; both would make good captains...[165]

Was Captain Wallar "too fond of liquor"? Hayes seemed to imply so. Who was Colonel Burgess? Hayes, in a March 13, 1862 diary entry, wrote:

Colonel Burgess was a venomous Secesh but is now mollified and so strong a Union man that with a body of our troops he attacked a gang of his old Secesh friends at Jumping Branch and killed one of them![166]

I have been unable to learn the identity of this Colonel Burgess.

James dutifully penned his resignation and was granted an honorable discharge. Note the approval by Lieutenant Colonel J.C. Paxton, Colonel E.P. Scammon, Brigadier General J.D. Cox, and Assistant Adjutant General H. Thrall. After a few weeks at home, James found himself in charge of Company A again. For the second time, he was mustered in as a Captain in the Second Regiment, Virginia Volunteer Cavalry in Wheeling, West Virginia on July 22, 1862,[167] and quickly rejoined the Second Battalion with their scouting and skirmishing activities.[168]

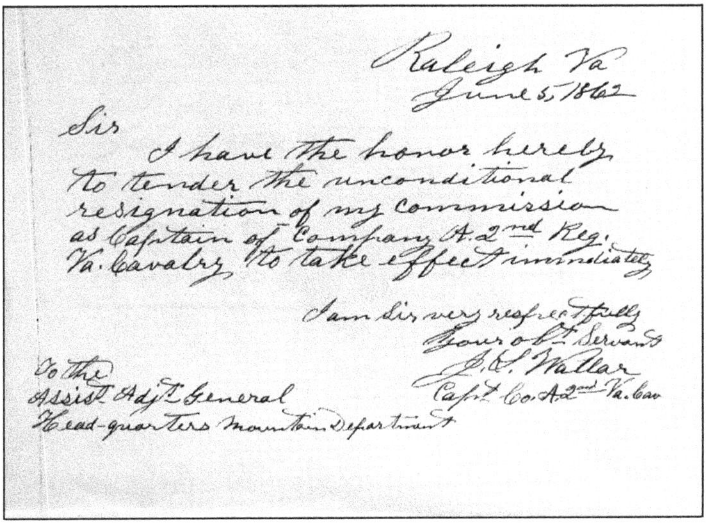

Front and back of Wallar's resignation[169]

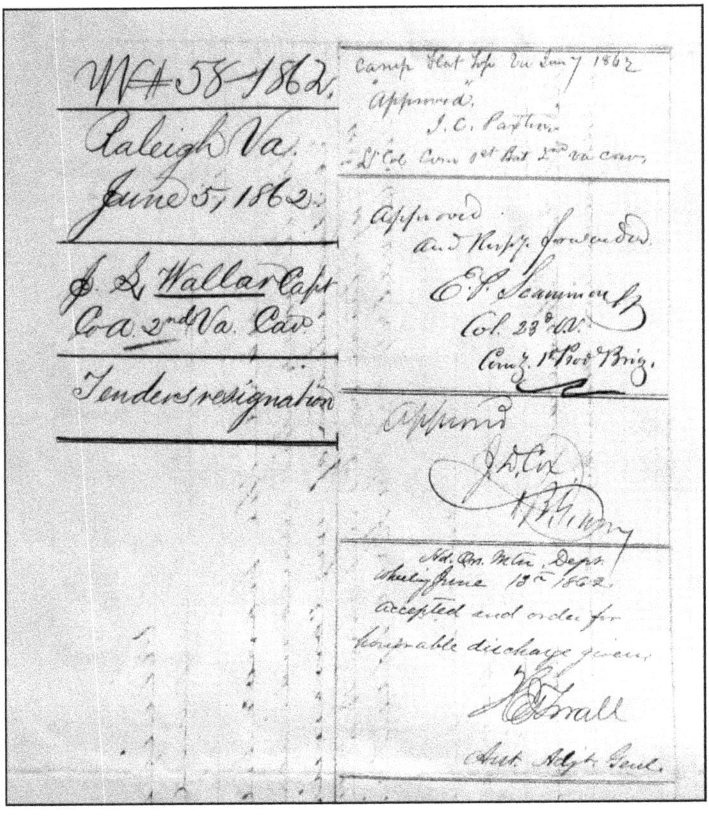

An August 1862 report written by Colonel Edward Siber of the 37th Ohio Volunteer Infantry recounts what I imagine was a typical campaign for a Union cavalry unit serving in West Virginia. On August 2nd, three companies of the 37th left Raleigh Court House and traveled toward Wyoming Court House (now called Oceana), a distance of about forty miles. The soldiers cleared a pass over and around Guyandotte Mountain. One company stayed at a farm near present-day Glen Daniel, West Virginia, owned by a man named Trump, while the other two companies, led by a Captain Messner, continued to Wyoming Court House. Upon arriving, citizens told Messner that Confederate scouts were confiscating cattle and grain from Union sympathizers about fifteen miles south on the Tazewell Road. Messner sent a scouting party to the Confederate-leaning farm where the goods were being held with the intention of burning the wheat. A skirmish took place when the Union troops were surprised by 140 Confederate cavalry. Captain Messner ordered his troops to retreat to Wyoming Court House and later, back to Trump's farm at Coal River. [170]

Word of the skirmish got back to headquarters at Raleigh Court House around noon on August 6th. Later that day, Captain Wallar and twenty-five of his cavalry accompanied Colonel Siber and some of the 37th Ohio Volunteer Infantry from Raleigh Court House toward Wyoming Court House. The first day's journey was about fourteen miles to Trump's farm. After a brief rest, the soldiers left the farm at 3:00 a.m. and arrived in Wyoming Court House late in the evening of August 7th.[171]

Early in the morning of August 8th, Siber sent James Wallar and his cavalry forward on the Tazewell road as far as the Guyandotte River, near Pineville, West Virginia. There Wallar was told that the enemy had already passed the river. Captain Wallar and his men pursued the fleeing Confederate soldiers but were unable to catch them.

Back at Wyoming Court House, many rebel sympathizers fled the town, and a Union militia was formed to maintain order. Several skirmishes took place in this area during this week with several fatalities on both sides, none of whom served in Captain Wallar's cavalry.[172]

Crossing to Fayetteville[173]

On the 9th, Colonel Siber wrote that he was "sending the horses back to Raleigh," which I presume means James Wallar's cavalry. Siber was confident that:

There is no danger that the enemy would march from Wyoming to Raleigh. Guyandotte Mountain and Clear Fork cannot be passed by wagons in the present state of the road. This circumstance caused me to march back to Raleigh, being already two days without rations, notwithstanding the pressing demands of inhabitants [of Wyoming Court House] to stay...[174]

Around the 14th of August 1862, Captain James L. Wallar and Company A moved to Gauley Bridge by way of Fayetteville.[175] On the 17th of the month, General J.D. Cox turned over the command of the District of the Kanawha to Colonel Joseph Andrew Jackson Lightburn and was instructed to lead brigades of Union troops from the Kanawha

Valley to the Washington DC area. Lightburn was left in command of the 37th, 44th, and 47th Ohio Volunteer Infantry, the 4th, 8th, and 9th West Virginia Volunteer Infantry, the 2nd West Virginia Cavalry, eight mountain howitzers and three rifled and three smooth-bore field-pieces of artillery. The massive shift in troops to the eastern theater left a mere five thousand or so Union soldiers in West Virginia.[176]

Filed May 6th 1862

CAMP, GAULEY BRIDGE.

Camp at Gauley Bridge from across the Gauley River[177]

On the 24th of August, Colonel Lightburn ordered "Captain Wallar's Co. A. 2 Va Cavalry to report without delay, at the Head Quarters of the regiment"—meaning Gauley Bridge, West Virginia.[178] The secluded community of Gauley Bridge lies at the eastern end of the Kanawha Valley. The Kanawha River is formed here from the confluence of the New River and the Gauley River, and meanders north and west approximately 100 miles until it empties into the Ohio River at

Point Pleasant. The Federal forces had been in control of the Kanawha Falls/Gauley Bridge area since September 1861.[179]

General J.D. Cox, in his *Military Reminiscences of the Civil War* penned:

Southwestward the country was extremely wild and broken, with few and small settlements and no roads worthy the name. The crossing of the Gauley was therefore the gate through which all important movements from eastern into southwestern Virginia must necessarily come, and it formed an important link in any chain of posts designed to cover the Ohio valley from invasion. It was also the most advanced single post which could protect the Kanawha valley. Further to the southeast, on Flat-top Mountain, was another very strong position, where the principal road on the left bank of New river crosses a high and broad ridge, but a post could not be safely maintained there without still holding Gauley Bridge in considerable force, or establishing another post on the right bank of New River twenty miles further up. All these streams flow in rocky beds seamed and fissured to so great a degree that they had no practicable fords. You might go forty miles up New River and at least twenty up the Gauley before you could find a place where either could be passed by infantry or wagons. The little ferries which had been made in a few eddies of the rivers were destroyed in the first campaign, and the post at the Gauley became nearly impregnable in front, and could only be turned by long and difficult detours...

Nothing could be more romantically beautiful than the situation of the post at Gauley Bridge. The hamlet had, before our arrival there, consisted of a cluster of two or three dwellings, a country store, a little tavern, and a church, irregularly scattered along the base of the mountain and facing the road which runs from the Gauley valley into that of the Kanawha. The lower slope of the hillside behind the houses was cultivated, and a hedgerow separated the lower fields from the upper pasturage. Above this gentler slope the wooded steeps rose more precipitately, the sandstone rock jutting out into crags and walls, the sharp ridge above having scarcely soil enough to nourish the chestnut-trees...In the angle between the Gauley and New rivers rose Gauley Mount, the base a perpendicular wall of rocks of varying height, with high wooded slopes above. There was barely room for the road between the wall of rocks and the water on the New River side, but after going some distance up the valley, the highway gradually ascended the hillside, reaching some rolling uplands at a distance of a couple of miles. Here was Gauley Mount... Across New River the heavy masses of Cotton Mountain rose rough and almost inaccessible from the very water's edge. The western side of Cotton Mountain was less steep, and buttresses formed a bench about its base, so that in looking across the Kanawha a mile below the junction of the rivers, one saw some rounded foothills which had been cleared on the top and tilled, and a gap in the mountainous wall made room on that side for a small creek which descended to the Kanawha, and whose bed served for a rude country road *leading to Fayette C.H. At the base of Cotton Mountain the Kanawha equals the united width of the two tributaries, and flows foaming over broken rocks with treacherous channels between, till it dashes over the horseshoe ledge below, knows far and wide as the Kanawha Falls. On either bank near the falls a small mill had been built, that on the right bank a saw-mill and the one on the left for grinding grain.*

Our encampment necessarily included the saw-mill below the falls, where the First Kentucky Regiment was placed to guard to road coming from Fayette C.H. Two regiments were encamped at the bridge upon the hillside above the hedgerow, having an advanced ost of half a regiment on the Lewisburg road beyond the Tompkins farm, and scouting the country to Sewell Mountain. Smaller outposts were stationed some distance up the valley of the Gauley. My headquarters tents were pitched in the door-yard of a dwelling-house facing the Gauley River, and I occupied an unfurnished room in the house for office purposes. A week was spent, without molestation, exploring the country in all directions and studying its topography. A ferry guided by a cable stretching along the piers of the burnt bridge communicated with the outposts up the New River, and a smaller ferry below the Kanawha Falls connected with the Fayette road. Systematic discipline and instruction in outpost duty were enforced, and the regiments rapidly became expert mountaineers and scouts. The population was nearly all loyal below Gauley Bridge, but above they were mostly Secessionists, a small minority of the wealthier slaveholders being the nucleus of all aggressive secession movements.[180]

Tompkins' Farm (Camp Gauley Mount)[181]

Two and a half miles above the bridge was a farm with a large barn, an overseer's home, slave quarters, and several outbuildings. This was Gauley Mount, the summer estate of Colonel Christopher Q. Tompkins, who resigned from the U.S. Army in spring 1861 and retired to Richmond. The Union army commandeered the farm in October 1861, and Mrs. Tompkins and her children uneasily occupied the home until December of that year. Upon leaving, Mrs. Tompkins wrote to a friend:

I expect to leave very soon and hardly hope ever to see this house again as even the majors say it ought be used as a hospital, then burned. It makes one very suspicious to have a person very friendly in the house, talking, and then before they reach the gate to hear such remarks. I shall go to Richmond and no matter what happens stand my ground. I have been very busy packing, arranging things, and am filled with disgust to see this beautiful place torn to pieces by the soldiers, when I remember the cost of money and trouble to build all the houses, etc. It is a perfect desolation now. Fences are all gone. The fields set in clover hard as roads from the encampments. What a pity

we ever saw the place. I cannot remain here this winter to save it, as in
the Spring the fighting will begin again. I have had as many cannon balls
roaring around me as I wish to hear. There is no hope of peace for years. The
South will not accept the terms offered by the North. The wind is roaring,
rain, hail, and snow falling. I dread this journey.[182]

Unfortunately, Mrs. Tompkins would never see Gauley Mount again. The home was burned later in the war.

Shortly after taking command, Lightburn became aware of Confederate troops amassing at the Narrows of the New River for an attack on the Kanawha Valley. Confederate General William W. Loring had been ordered to "Clear the valley of the Kanawha and operate northwardly to a junction with our army in the [Shenandoah] valley," and to destroy the B&O railroad. Not having enough men to face such an attack, Lightburn ordered Colonel Siber at Raleigh Court House to fall back to Fayette Court House, and Colonel Gilbert to retreat to Gauley Mount. The majority of the Second West Virginia Cavalry, including, I believe, Wallar and Company A, was sent to "keep after" Confederate Brigadier General Albert G. Jenkins. Jenkins and 500 cavalrymen left the area of Salt Sulphur Springs, West Virginia on August 22nd with the intention of preventing a Union retreat to the Ohio River and reclaiming the Kanawha Valley and the saltworks upriver from Charleston.[183]

Jenkins and his cavalry had an easy trip through Greenbrier and Pocahontas counties. In Randolph County, he learned of 1500 Union troops near Beverly, blocking his route to the railroad. Nearing Buckhannon in Upshur County, Jenkins encountered pesky, scattered fire from the Home Guard (or Lincolnite bushwhackers, as Jenkins referred to them). The Confederate cavalry made quick work of the Union troops and sympathizers located at Buckhannon, and Jenkins was able to rearm his poorly armed men with Enfield and Harper's Ferry rifles from the Federal stash before destroying "everything of value." The marauders continued their northwestward trip toward the Ohio River through Weston, Glenville, and Spencer, where Jenkins captured Colonel John C. Rathbone and five companies of infantry without firing a shot.[184]

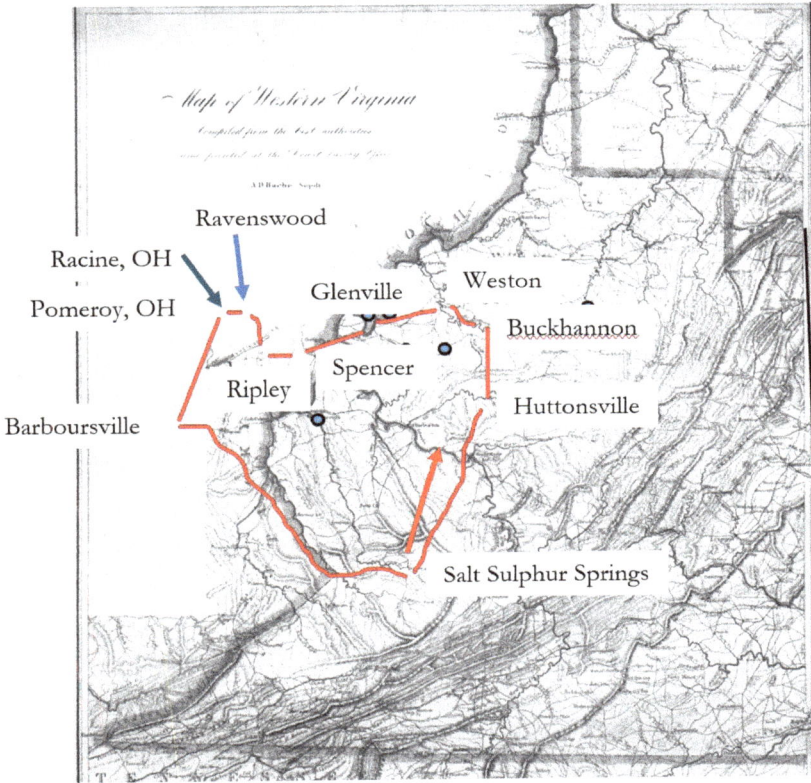

Jenkins' Raid 1862[185]

The following day, September 3rd, Jenkins and his cavalrymen arrived in Ripley, Virginia, a mere twelve miles from the Ohio River. Here they captured a Union paymaster and stole $5525—over $138,000 in 2019 dollars.[186]

The next morning, Jenkins arrived at Ravenswood, a small village of a few hundred people, located on the Ohio River:

The enemy, comprising near 200, fled across the Ohio on our approach. We rested most of the day at Ravenswood, and about an hour before sunset I crossed the Ohio with the larger portion into the State of Ohio, losing one man by being drowned. The ford was deep and the bar upon which we were compelled to cross narrow, and a number of the horses got into swimming water, but no other loss occurred...In a short time all were over, and in a few minutes the command was formed on the crest of a gentle eminence and the banners of the Southern Confederacy floated proudly over the soil of our invaders. As our flag was unfurled in the splendors of an evening sun cheers upon cheers arose from the men and their enthusiasm was excited to the highest pitch. [187]

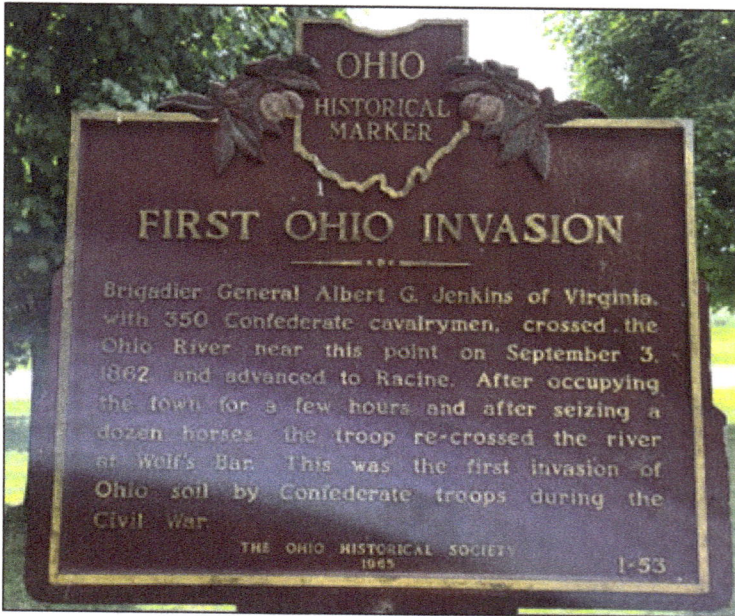

Jenkins' Raid historical marker[188]

The newspaper in Pomeroy recounted the events in the following week's issue:

...Coming nearer home, we have had our share of excitement. On Tuesday of last week, a company of rebel Guerrillas, under the notorious Jenkins, captured Spencer, in Roan County, Va. We had about four hundred troops there with considerable stores. The troops surrendered without a fight and were paroled. Of course the arms, ammunition and stores fell into the hands of the marauders. The next day they came to Ravenswood, where we had but about one hundred and fifty soldiers.—That place was also surrendered without a contest. This was in the morning.—The news came to Pomeroy, and our Home Guards turned

out in fine style, and the people of the country came into town with their rifles and shot guns as fast as the news reached them. By night there were some three hundred armed men in our streets, expecting an attack, as we had information of the crossing of the river at Buffington Island, by a portion of the rebel band.—Three hundred and fifty of the Rangers crossed to this side and came down to Racine, which place they captured about 9 o'clock in the evening. They shot a deaf and dumb man who could not hear the order to halt, and it is said wounded one or two others. They told the citizens that they were after horses and arms; that if they were not resisted they would not injure any one personally, but if fired upon they would burn up the town. They then gathered up all the good horses they could find in town, getting twelve, we believe, and after some hours, crossed over to Va. again at Wolf's Bar, below Racine.—From what we can learn, they took about 25 horses from this side of the river. Thursday and Friday they camped a few miles back from the river, and on Saturday, being reinforced to about 1200, struck the Kanawha at Buffalo, from which time and place we have no certain information of their movements.

While in Racine, the Rangers swore the most terrible vengeance on Pt. Pleasant and Gallipolis, declaring that they would not leave a stone or brick of either standing. But the prompt turn-out of the people of Mason and Gallia Counties made the raid too dangerous, and the band passed on for the present. It is reported that several large forces under Floyd and others are making for the border. Without a large army sent into Western Virginia immediately, the rebels will have complete possession, and all the border will be at their mercy.[189]

In a report from the headquarters of the cavalry brigade, Brigadier General Jenkins remarked:

It was a subject of the very greatest interest with me to observe the state of feeling in Ohio and the impression our presence would produce. I may say in brief that the latter was characterized by the wildest terror—so much so that but for the pity for the subjects of it one could only view it as an absurdity. Women inquired for officers wherever our troops appeared, and, having found them, begged them not to permit them to murder them. Others came

out of their dwellings and urged as a reason for our not burning them
that they contained invalids too much afflicted to be removed. To these
requests we replied that, though that mode of warfare had been practiced
on ourselves, though many of the soldiers of our command were homeless
and their families exiles on account of the ruthless warfare that had been
waged against us, we were not barbarians, but a civilized people struggling
for their liberties, and that we would afford them that exemption from
the horrors of a savage warfare which had not been extended to us. It was
manifest that they had not expected such immunity, and could scarcely
credit their senses when they saw that we did not light our pathway with
the torch.[190]

Marker commemorating Jenkins' Raid in Racine[191]

Think of the fear and trepidation that Frances Wallar and the
children must have felt when the rebels entered Racine. Frances surely
tried to protect the children the best she could. Did she beg for her life?
Did the Wallar family lose a horse to the raiders? Perhaps Frances and the
children hid in the root cellar or basement or sought refuge in the nearby
church. Maybe they fled to Pomeroy, in hopes of being protected by the
home guard.

After reentering Virginia after midnight on the 5th, Jenkins and his
men rested before reuniting with some troops he'd previously ordered to
the Point Pleasant area. Jenkins then proceeded through the community
of Buffalo and set up camp at Barboursville with plans to move toward
Charleston and cut off the Union's retreat from Charleston to the Ohio

River. Lightburn didn't treat this situation seriously and Colonel J. C. Paxton requested permission to challenge Jenkins with eight companies of cavalry, including, I believe, Wallar and Company A.[192] On September 8th, the 300 or so cavalry troops with Paxton arrived in Barboursville, and after a skirmish, Jenkins and his 1200 or more cavalrymen retreated to Wyoming Court House by way of Logan Court House, and then north to the Kanawha River at the mouth of the Coal River.[193]

Colonel Lightburn, in a September 24th letter to Major General Horatio G. Wright, Commander of the Department of the Ohio, praised the cavalry:

The Second Virginia Cavalry, under Colonel Paxton, did good service in keeping Jenkins' force at bay, thereby preventing an attack in our rear. I wish, also, to state that Colonel Paxton, with 300 men, attacked Jenkins' whole force (from 1,200 to 1,500), and drove them from Barboursville, which, no doubt, kept them from an attempt to harass our retreat.[194]

In the wee hours of September 11th, Colonel Lightburn reported from Gauley Bridge:

Fayette attacked to-day at noon by a superior force of the enemy. Fighting continued all the afternoon, our troops holding the post at sundown. Jenkins, with heavy cavalry force, on my right flank, in the rear. I am compelled to fall back, probably to Point Pleasant, Ohio River.[195]

As Lightburn was writing his letter, the Federal troops began their retreat toward Charleston. On the 12th of September, those under the command of Lightburn and colonels Samuel A. Gilbert and Edward Siber united at Camp Piatt, a few miles upstream from Charleston. At about 2:00 a.m. on September 13th, the column moved to Charleston, and by evening, the Union army had been soundly defeated.[196] Reportedly upwards of $1,000,000 worth of clothing, horses, ammunition, food, and other supplies—approximately $25,000,000 in 2019 dollars[197]—was lost to the Confederate army.[198]

With Jenkins in the rear of Lightburn at Coalsmouth (now St. Albans, West Virginia), and the Kanawha Valley now in the hands of the Confederate army, Lightburn's defeated army continued to retreat, burning what they could. Along the way, terrified citizens and formerly enslaved people accompanied the troops on the march west and north. Wisely avoiding the Kanawha River, the Union wagon train headed north by road, passed through Ripley, and most of the troops crossed the Ohio River near Ravenswood on September 16th. They then moved through Racine and Pomeroy before travelling down the Ohio side of the river to a point opposite Point Pleasant. Others boarded steamers and headed downriver to Point Pleasant or Gallipolis, Ohio.[199] The Second West Virginia Cavalry under the command of Colonel Paxton stayed on the Virginia side of the Ohio River and scouted around the clock along the Ohio and Kanawha rivers in the vicinity of Point Pleasant. They were the only regiment under Lightburn that remained on "the sacred soil of Virginia."[200]

The *Pomeroy Weekly Telegraph* reported:

...Safely upon the Ohio side, the train commenced its movement toward Pt. Pleasant, which brought it through this place. We don't know the number of teams, but were told that the train occupied eight miles in length. It was such a show as was never before seen in Pomeroy. It occupied a good portion of Tuesday and Wednesday in passing through town. It was followed by a host of fugitives, both white and black. For two or three days they have been resting themselves in groups under every shade-tree along the road. Many of the soldiers had not an hour's rest for four days and nights, and the fugitives, had none for more than half that time. They might well be weary. Scores of old men and women, scarcely able to walk, and little barefooted children, from three years old and upward, walked all the weary march without stopping to sleep. We passed along the road from this place to Racine on Tuesday morning, and found it literally lined with these weary pilgrims, who had laid them down to sleep and rest on the free soil of Ohio, which, to them, was a land of Canaan, reached at last. We stopped and talked to many of them, and heard tales that the novelist could never coin from his fertile brain to grace his fiction...

The retreat was undoubtedly a masterly movement, and does great credit to Col. Lightburn. The rebels were undoubtedly apprised of the immense train of horses, mules and wagons left in the charge of Col. L., and of the inadequacy of his force to protect it.—The bait was a tempting one, and worth a great expedition if it could be captured. With this train, and the Kanawha salt works in their possession, they could return to "Dixie" with salt enough for a winter's supply. The masterly retreat of Col. L. disappointed them in their prey. A large amount of Government stores at Charleston, which could not be brought away, was destroyed, so that the rebels will have their raid pretty much for nothing. True, they will strip the Valley of what is left in it, and will leave it a desolation, but it will yield them neither friends, nor, in large amount, the material of war. Unless they make a raid into Ohio, we think they will not find supplies enough to last them long, at Charleston. Will they attempt to cross the Ohio? We cannot say. But it behooves the citizens to perfect their military organizations at once, and be prepared for the worst.

The newspaper report continued:

The Union slaveholders generally told their slaves to escape as best they could and take care of themselves, being all fugitives alike; while the slaves of the secesh, took advantage of the general confusion, and joined the swelling throng. We confess the sight was one we never hope to see again. And yet it had its bright spots. We saw men, and women, too, who, a week before, were wealthy and surrounded with all the elegances of life, and slaveholders at that, speak to the fugitive slaves as they chanced to meet, in tones of the most unaffected kindness and sympathy, as if a common calamity had brought into action the heaven-born sentiment of a common humanity. We passed along the road the wanderers traveled, and saw and conversed with very many, both white and black, and did not hear an unkind word, or tone of voice that betokened prejudice or hatred from any. And all seemed amazed at the reception they met with in Ohio. And we must say we feel proud of our citizens, and are sure these wanderers from their homes will not forget the reception they met on their march.

From the time it was known that this army of fugitives were with the train, as if by instinct, the women, all along the line as well as in town, began to prepare for them, by baking bread and pies, and cooking everything eatable to supply their wants. And angels, we doubt not, looked upon the scene with heavenly delight. We saw by the doorways of the humble homes of laboring men, who have no large stock of this world's goods, piles of bread and pies, and the busy hands of their wives and children dealing out, with full hearts, the willing offering to the hungry and weary way-farers. God bless them for it! And he will, too. We also saw many with buckets of water by the roadside, with cups to quench the thirst of all the crowd...[201]

I imagine James Wallar felt some disappointment remaining with a retreating, downtrodden army in West Virginia rather than fighting in the more important Eastern theater. Just 250 miles to the east, the Second Battle of Bull Run was fought in late August, Harper's Ferry fell to the Confederates, and the Battle at Antietam occurred in September 1862.

Wallar was certainly in Meigs County on September 16th, when he and Frances purchased the adjacent lots in Racine,[202] and the official records show Company A as posted at Point Pleasant, about thirty-five miles from Racine.[203] I'm sure James and his family appreciated the opportunity to spend some time together. Before long, though, it was time to return to war. Early on September 21st, the Second was ordered to move up the Kanawha. It was reported that,

...the rebels have now occupied Guyandotte and taken two government boats. They occupy the three counties around us, Jackson, Putnam & Cabell. We hold Mason and expect to retreat no further. Their scouts come within two miles of the Pt [Point Pleasant] on the south side of Ka [Kanawha] [204]

General J.D. Cox was called to serve over the Department of the Ohio and the Kanawha Division. On October 15th, the Second West Virginia Cavalry was at Point Pleasant, likely with a few days' worth of rations in their haversacks. The move back to the Kanawha Valley was imminent and the men needed to be ready to go on short notice. Cox received word that Loring had left Charleston for Gauley Bridge, and that Charleston was not well protected.

The *Richmond Dispatch* printed an excerpt from a letter received from Cincinnati:

From Western Virginia we have news that the rebels are preparing to evacuate the Kanawha valley, as they have supplied themselves with all the salt that they could readily transport away. They have succeeded in obtaining an immense supply of the much needed article, and as there is nothing to be gained by loitering in the valley longer, in any great force, they have very sensibly determined to get out of it, and leave only a few cavalry or guerrillas to attend to their affairs there. We [the Union Army] have a very large force in Western Virginia, which is likely to effect something very soon, although in which direction it is not proper to state.[205]

Loring had begun his retreat on October 9th, and on the 11th, arrived at Kanawha Falls. Only small pockets of Confederate soldiers remained in the Kanawha Valley. Within days, the Confederates were nearing the Narrows and Lewisburg. Again, the Kanawha Valley was nearly free for the taking.[206]

6

RETAKING THE KANAWHA VALLEY

On October 20, 1862, Lightburn moved up the Kanawha. Major General J.D. Cox ordered him to clear the river at Red House and to repair roads and bridges as he progressed. Lightburn received word that Confederate General Echols had returned to Charleston and was attempting to reoccupy the Kanawha Valley.

The Second West Virginia Cavalry was ahead of Lightburn and split in two to occupy both sides of the Kanawha River. As they advanced toward the mouth of the Pocatalico River seven miles upriver from Red House, they encountered the enemy's pickets on the 22nd and engaged in a skirmish. Cox ordered Lightburn to stop at Poca and wait for reinforcements, fearing upwards of ten thousand rebels at Charleston, another twenty miles upriver. Echols, in fact, had closer to three thousand men, and hearing that Cox had arrived to support Lightburn, prudently began to retreat. The Federal troops comprised three and a half brigades and several supporting regiments. The Union advance cavalrymen skirmished with the enemy until arriving at Gauley Bridge on the 27th, having been slowed by a miserably cold rain and sleet. On October 30, 1862, the Federal troops once again occupied Charleston and the Kanawha Valley.[207]

The cavalrymen stayed at Gauley Bridge until November 15th, when they arrived at Camp Piatt. Camp Piatt was located about twelve miles southeast of Charleston on the east bank of the Kanawha River. Barracks were laid out in a square encompassing about an acre, with a cold-water spring in the center of the square. A soldier from the Second West Virginia Cavalry wrote:

The camp life at this time was of the highest type of enjoyment. The quarters were in the shape of a square and consisted of good log houses, with kitchens for the different messes. The houses on the east side of the square were occupied by the company officers, the regimental headquarters being in a house near the Kanawha river on the west. The stables were a short distance north of the camp. To the rear of the officers quarters there was a mountain of considerable height, its sides steep and almost inaccessible. In front of the camp, flowed the Kanawha river, with Brownstown on its opposite bank. It was four miles down the river to Malden, and ten miles to Charleston. During the month of June the regimental surgeon recommended that the men be supplied with ale, as it would be conducive to their health. When this became known, the file of the regiment readily expressed their willingness to take the perscribed [sic] medicine, and were ready to bless the name of Dr. McKeown. Word was sent to some Jewish merchants in Charleston that they might sell a few dozen bottles of ale to the regiment daily. Two or three of those enterprising dealers soon appeared in camp, and disposed of their merchandise at a good profit. This was a bonanza for the vendors, for ordinarily they were not allowed to sell to soldiers. There was no indication that the men would abuse the privilege, and the merchants obtained leave to make another visit within a few days. On the next trip they brought a considerable quantity of the stimulant, and with the large demand and their former success, determined to make a larger profit. The soldier has his own ideas of right and wrong, and will quickly resent a wrong, especially when his finances are involved. No sooner had they learned that ale was suddenly advanced in price, than they reached the conclusion that ale was a contraband of war, and so confiscated the entire lot. This ended the administration of ale as medicine in the regiment; but by this time it was unnecessary, as the men were in splendid health, the result, no doubt, of the ale.[208]

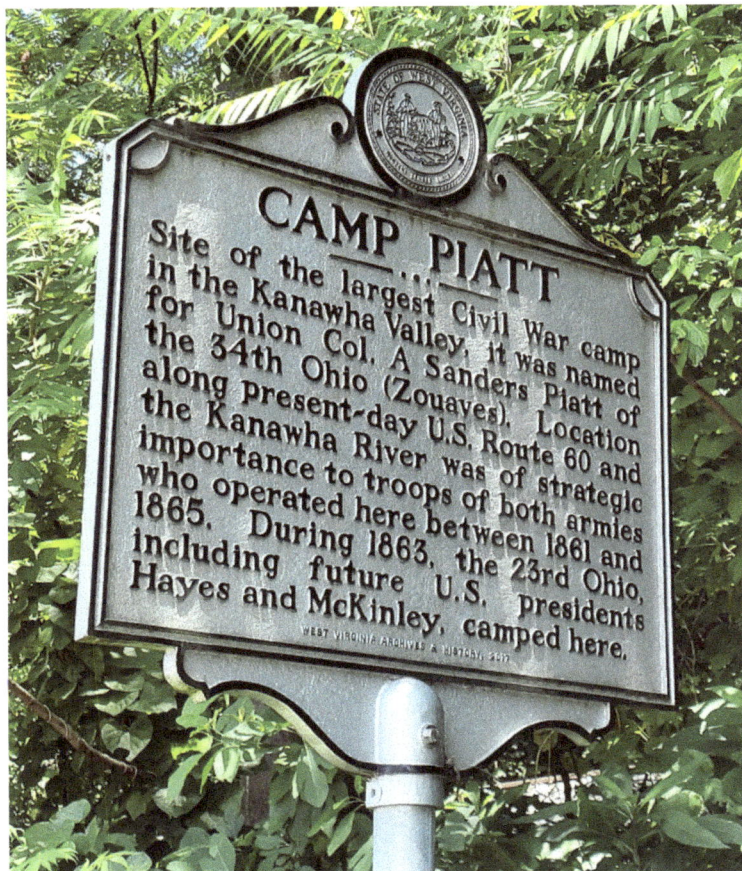

Camp Piatt marker[209]

From here, Captain Wallar wrote a letter on November 23rd to the editor of the *Pomeroy Weekly Telegraph*:

Mr. Editor:—Several members of my Company sent their over-coats home last Spring, to prevent losing them during the Summer. The weather is now so cold that an over-coat is quite comfortable. I take this method of informing the persons to whom the overcoats were sent, that the boys wish them sent to this place. I would suggest that the owner's name be marked on them, and that they be left at the "Remington House," in Pomeroy, in the care of Mr. Dunn, who will box them up and direct them to me. We start this evening on a raid into "Dixie," to be gone ten or twelve days; we expect to see the "gray-backs" on our return. I will give you the incidents of the trip.—J.L. Wallar, Capt. Co A, 2d Va. Cavalry[210]

And what a trip this would be! By this time in the war, Federal cavalry troops were more experienced, better equipped, and had begun to be used as a fighting force by commanders who appreciated their value as a unit rather than being divided among the infantry. The necessity to preserve the horses was apparent, and cavalry troops were just as likely to dismount and fight as to risk the health of their valuable steeds. Often the men remained mounted only to battle another cavalry unit. The opportunity to prove their value was overdue.[211]

On November 24th, Colonel J.C. Paxton received orders from Brigadier General George Crook to leave the relative comfort of Camp Piatt with several cavalry companies, including Wallar's Company A, on a daring mission to raid Confederate camps in Sinking Creek Valley. The men were undoubtedly excited to be back in the saddle! Colonel Paxton's official report follows:

Sir: In obedience to your order, I marched my command, consisting of Companies G, I, F, A, K, D, E, and H, Second West Virginia Volunteer Cavalry (in all, 475 men, rank and file, in good order), on the morning of November 24, for Summerville, arriving there at 10 p.m. the same day, a distance of 53 miles.

Left Summerville next morning at 7 o'clock, and arrived at the Hinkle farm at 4 p.m., 35 miles, and, being able to obtain some hay there, remained until 4 a.m. the 26th, when we took up the line of march, in a blinding snow-storm, for Greenbrier, via Cold Knob Mountain, where we arrived at 10 a.m. the same day; distance, 20 miles. Met Colonel Lane, Eleventh Ohio Volunteer Infantry, who was to assist me in breaking up a camp of the rebels at the foot of the mountain; but, on account of the severity of the weather and hard marching, he wished to return to his camp at Summerville. I asked him to take the advance, until we met the enemy's pickets, which he did, and, in about 1 mile, exchanged shots with 6 of the enemy, wounding 1. Colonel Lane at once opened his ranks, and gave us the road. We pushed rapidly into the enemy's camp, a distance of some 5 miles, effecting a complete surprise, at 12 m., the enemy scattering in all directions.

We killed 2, wounded 2, paroled 1, and captured 2 commissioned officers (1 captain and 1 second lieutenant), 111 non-commissioned officers and privates, 106 horses, and 5 mules; burned and destroyed about 200 Enfield and Mississippi rifles and 50 sabers, with other accouterments, stores, and supplies, and their camp tents, &c. I had 2 horses killed in the enemy's camp, and lost 10 on the march from fatigue and exhaustion.

The enemy was found 3 miles from the foot of Cold Knob Mountain, on Sinking Creek, Greenbrier County, West Virginia, at Lewis' Mill, and consisted of a part of five companies of cavalry, viz, Rockbridge Cavalry, Braxton Dragoons, Churchville Cavalry, Valley Cavalry, and Nighthawk Rangers. They were men who had been in the service fifteen months, and were located at this point to guard the mountain pass, and to organize a part of A. G. Jenkins' brigade. Our success was complete. We never lost a drop of blood.

After securing the prisoners and horses and destroying the camp, &c., we marched at 4 p.m. (26th) for Summerville, where we arrived on the 27th at noon, making 120 miles for men and horses, without food or rest, except one feed of hay for horses, over the most rugged, and mountainous part of Western Virginia. Remained in Summerville until the 29th. Left for Camp Piatt, and arrived in camp on the 30th at noon. My men suffered severely from frost. I left 2 men in the hospital at Summerville, whose boots we cut from their feet. Others were more or less frozen. My horses were very much cut down.

I cannot close this report without deservedly complimenting the officers and men; but, where all behaved so gallantly, it is impossible to particularize. But all honor is due Major Powell, who led the charge, and Company G, Captain McMahan, who led the column. I have the honor to be, your obedient servant, J.C. Paxton, Colonel, Comdg. Second West Virginia Volunteer Cavalry[212]

Joseph J. Sutton, in his regimental history, wrote the following:

From the nearly continuous march of seventy hours, the deep snow, insufficient rest and food and loss of sleep, officers, troops and horses were nearly exhausted. They fell asleep along the road, causing frequent gaps in the column, and necessitating the greatest vigilance on the part of the officers to keep it closed up in the rear of the prisoners guard.

At daybreak on the 27th the bugle sounded a halt, in response to which men cheered and horses neighed. Roll call showed all the prisoners present.

While horses are being fed, and breakfast made ready, let us attempt to draw a pen picture of our surroundings. Imagine a wild and sparsely settled region, where it was more than five miles between houses, and snow over a foot deep everywhere. All along the road the bushes added to our discomfort, by depositing great piles of snow in our faces, in our laps, and sometimes down our backs. At breakfast time with nearly frozen feet and limbs, we dismount in the snow to cook our humble meal. Are the men disheartened in the midst of all these gloomy surroundings? Not at all, but with cheerful hearts all hands join in, and soon hundreds of fires are burning; and within a few minutes the fragrant odor of coffee and bacon is borne upon the frosty air. Even the prisoners joined in to make the best of it, and were as cheerful as any.

The horses were fed by clearing away the snow and placing the grain on the ground; or it was put in canvass bags, these strapped to the animal's head, the bag coming up, just below the eyes. It was very amusing to watch the horses use this contrivance when it was first put on them, but they would soon grow accustomed to it and manage it very well.[213]

Paxton and the remainder of the regiment, including Company A, arrived after the surrender but assisted in destroying the camp and collecting horses, guns, and ammunition that might be of use to the Union army. From Lewisburg, Confederate colonel Jenkins pursued the regiment in hopes of freeing the rebel prisoners. While Paxton continued north with the spoils of the raid, Powell held off Jenkins' cavalrymen until they turned back toward Lewisburg, defeated.[214]

The rebel prisoners were taken by steamer to Wheeling and then to the prison camp for Confederate prisoners at Camp Chase on the west side of Columbus, Ohio.[215] For his leadership at Sinking Creek, Major William Henry Powell was awarded the Congressional Medal of Honor. The citation read, "Distinguished services in raid, where, with 20 men, he charged and captured the enemy's camp, 500 strong, without the loss of man or gun."[216] A newspaper article in the *Cincinnati Commercial Tribune* reported:

Major Powell is certainly one of the most industrious and indefatigable officers in the Union army. He is eager at all times to face any danger necessary. In the engagement he fired six shots from his navy revolver at a rebel; neither taking effect, he threw his revolver at him, which struck him on the head, inflicting a dangerous wound.[217]

Sinking Creek Raid Marker near Trout, West Virginia[218]

7

NO TIME TO REST

I n 1863, Charleston was a small town of about 1500 inhabitants located at the confluence of the Kanawha and Elk Rivers. Over 7000 Union soldiers were stationed at Charleston at the beginning of 1863, including Company A of the Second West Virginia Cavalry.[219] The exact location of their encampment is unknown. Union camps were set up at the mouth of the Ferry Branch on the south side of the Kanawha, near the Littlepage Stone Mansion (one of only six extant houses in Charleston that were built before the Civil War) at 1809 West Washington Street, and on Fort Hill. Fort Hill, later named Fort Scammon, rises above the south side of the Kanawha River and would have allowed a strategic view of the surrounding area.[220]

The weather was cold and wet, but on Thursday, January 8, 1863, the Second West Virginia Cavalry regiment left on a mission to destroy a bridge crossing the New River at Dublin, Virginia—a round trip of 250 miles. They overnighted at William Tompkins' Farm in the small community Cedar Grove, about seven miles upstream from Camp Piatt. The Tompkins' house, called Cedar Grove, was built in 1844, still stands today, and is on the National Register of Historic Places.[221] Up early the next morning, the regiment continued along the James River and Kanawha Turnpike (now U.S. Route 60) through Gauley Bridge, past Lookout Mountain and Big Sewell Mountain to within the sight of Meadow Bluff. Here, the regiment split in two, and three companies accompanied Colonel Paxton, including Company A.[222]

To pass through the area safely, Paxton informed his command that they would be impersonating the rebel cavalry, with Paxton assuming the persona of rebel Colonel John Clarkson. The astonished Union men took off and stored their blue overcoats, replacing them with blankets over their shoulders. The detachment crossed the Greenbrier River at Alderson's Ferry and moved past Wolf Creek. Eventually they arrived at Centerville (now Greenville, West Virginia).[223] J. J. Sutton recalled:

The little column encountered the rebel pickets near Centerville, and were allowed to pass without question. The pickets informed our men that there was a force of infantry in the town, but nothing daunted; they marched boldly into Centerville, and halted. To throw the enemy entirely off their guard, the colonel ordered the men to remain in column in the street and feed their horses; this was done, the men bearing themselves in an easy, careless manner, but remaining near the horses, ready to mount.

The colonel informed a rebel officer, who seemed to have some authority, that he was Colonel Clarkson, and that he had been doing duty on the Big Sandy river, and had been ordered to report in Richmond with one hundred cavalry. Soon the command was beyond Centerville, on route for Peters' mountain...

...This expedition commanded by Colonel Paxton was not only extremely hazardous, but one of great exposure and intence [sic] suffering from deep snows and cold weather. These incursions (and I state it emphatically) so far into the enemy's country with a small force, were very dangerous, and usually resulted in little loss or damage to the foe, while imposing upon the men who made them the greatest hardship.[224]

It was a cold afternoon and the snow was very deep, making the roads nearly impassable. A blinding snowstorm arose and the guide became lost, leading the detachment several miles off course. The men had only frozen rations from their haversacks to eat and there was no food for the horses. Paxton thought it best to return to Camp Piatt. To avoid the Confederate cavalry who were in pursuit of the Colonel Clarkson impersonator, the Federal cavalrymen took a route through Flat Top Mountain and Raleigh Court House. The men arrived back at Camp

Piatt by January 15th.[225] What a week! The remainder of the winter was spent patrolling for, and capturing, bushwhackers in Kanawha, Boone, Fayette, Wyoming, Wood, and Raleigh counties, and recruiting local men for service.[226]

As winter turned to spring, Confederate Brigadier General A.G. Jenkins was once again on the move. He harassed U.S. troops at Hurricane Bridge (now Hurricane) and Point Pleasant before heading south.[227] On the evening of April 3rd, Captain David Dove led over 140 members of the Second West Virginia Cavalry from Camp Piatt on a three-day expedition in search of Jenkins. Dove learned that Jenkins had too much of a head start, but part of another cavalry battalion was nearby. Dove wrote:

After a sharp skirmish, we drove them from their position, when a very exciting and hazardous chase ensued, the enemy scattering in every direction...The result of the expedition was: Killed, 1; captured, 3 commissioned officers and 31 enlisted men and 30 horses, and destroyed between 75 and 100 stand of arms. No one hurt on our side. I cannot close this report without saying that all the officers and men acted nobly.[228]

A Wheeling newspaper reported:

On Sunday last Jenkins and his guerrillas on their way back into Dixie, after the Point Pleasant raid, were attacked by the 2d Virginia Cavalry upon the Mud Fork, not far from the Falls of Guyan. Two rebels were killed, twenty-eight were captured and about the same number of horses and guns were taken. The prisoners are now on their way to this city.

When Gen. Scammon, who commands at Charleston, Kanawha, heard of the arrival of Jenkins at Point Pleasant he sent the 2d Virginia Cavalry around on the North side of the Kanawha towards Ripley, supposing that Jenkins would go out the same route by which he came in on the occasion of his former raid. Instead of doing so, however, the guerilla chief struck up the south side of the Kanawha. The 2d Virginia therefore, had to go back to Charleston and by hard marching managed to overtake Jenkins' rear at the place above indicated.[229]

It was not uncommon for officers' families to join the officers in camp during the war. Mrs. Hayes and her two oldest sons, Birch and Webb, spent the winters of 1861-1863 in camp with Colonel Hayes. On nicer days, the boys enjoyed outdoor activities such as fishing and riding horses. Mrs. Hayes visited the infirm. Rutherford B. Hayes wrote home on April 10, 1863 with news of Dove's expedition:

General Jenkins and about eight hundred men left the railroad at Marion, Smith County, southwestern Virginia, and crossed the mountains to the head waters of Sandy River and so across towards the mouth of Kanawha. They reached our outpost twenty-four miles from here and demanded a surrender. Captain Johnson with four companies of the Thirteenth Virginia declined to surrender and, after a good fight, repulsed General Jenkins. He then crossed Kanawha twenty miles from the mouth or less and attacked Point Pleasant at the mouth. Captain Carter and one company of the Thirteenth Virginia occupied the court-house. They could not keep the whole town clear of Rebels but defended themselves gallantly until relieved from Gallipolis. General Jenkins then retreated. Colonel Paxton and Captain Gilmore followed by different routes, worrying him badly and getting about forty prisoners...Does Birch remember Captain Waller, a cavalry captain who took care of Colonel Paxton and sat opposite us at table often? Perhaps he recollects his little boy. Well, he, the boy, rode with his father in the pursuit and captured two armed men himself![230]

Unfortunately, Wallar's "little boy" is not named but I suspect it was Wallar's oldest, Lafayette, or Fay. According to Fay Wallar's obituary:

He ran away from home when the civil war broke out and joined a Union regiment as bugle boy. The regiment happened to be the one in which his father, Capt. J.L. Waller, was an officer, and the first knowledge Capt. Waller had that his son had run away from home was when he saw the boy of 13 in the ranks.[231]

In April 1863, the Hayes boys were nine and seven years old. Fay Wallar was fourteen, Charles Wallar was eight, and Harry was six years old. While it's likely that the younger Wallar boys played with the Hayes boys if they were in camp, it seems unlikely that a six- or eight-year-old would have set out on a cavalry expedition.

In late April, Colonel Paxton left Camp Piatt with the Second West Virginia Cavalry regiment on a reconnaissance expedition. The destination was Lewisburg, a journey of about one hundred miles south and east. There were a few skirmishes with bushwhackers along the way, but nothing unexpected. Learning that some Confederate cavalrymen were camped near Lewisburg and remembering the glorious Sinking Creek Raid five months earlier, Paxton hoped to surprise and rout the rebel cavalry.

Shortly after midnight on May 2nd, Captain David Dove and Company H were sent in advance and met the enemy's picket in a wooded area two miles northwest of Lewisburg. The rebels escaped, and the element of surprise was lost. Dove returned to Paxton and informed him of the encounter. Paxton drunkenly ordered the advance under Dove to proceed. Not aware that the enemy was in close proximity, the advance made their way up a winding road, talking and laughing. They were surprised by the rebels and a bloody battle ensued. By dawn, the Second West Virginia Cavalry had withdrawn. Paxton sent a message to Confederate Lieutenant Colonel George M. Edgar asking for a truce to tend to the wounded and gather the dead. Four Union soldiers were killed, eight wounded, four missing, and twenty-eight horses were killed. Four rebel soldiers were taken prisoner. The regiment returned to Camp Piatt on May 5th. This skirmish is referred to as the Battle of Tuckwiller's Hill.[232]

Battle of Tuckwiller's Hill marker[233]

Because of Paxton's poor decision, Major General Robert C. Schenck sent a message on May 7th to the Assistant Adjutant-General:

Brigadier-General Scammon telegraphs me that he sent Colonel J. C. Paxton, of Second Virginia Volunteer Cavalry, to Lewisburg, to attack the enemy and create a diversion. He got drunk, and failed, and General Scammon asks his immediate dismissal. In this request I urgently concur.[234]

Colonel Paxton was dismissed on May 8th and Lieutenant Colonel William H. Powell was commissioned as Colonel of the Second West

Virginia Cavalry. This was generally a popular choice. Colonel Powell had joined the Second West Virginia Cavalry as the Captain of Company B, and was a "brave, fearless, and efficient officer." Private Joseph J. Sutton recalled in his regimental history:

While the command severely criticised, and did not excuse the conduct of Colonel Paxton in permitting the surprise and making the sacrifice possible, yet, the very high esteem in which both officers and men regarded him for his many admirable qualities as a gentleman, his kindly interest in and attention to the wants of his command, his genuine and undoubted loyalty to the flag, and devotion to the union, made all deeply sympathize with Colonel Paxton. He truly and sincerely loved his "boys" (as he called them) and was frequently the central figure of a group, pleasantly taking part in such conversation as might be general about the camp.[235]

The remainder of May and most of June were spent scouting and drilling. On June 20, 1863, West Virginia was recognized as the thirty-fifth state by the United States government. Later that month, companies B and I of the Second West Virginia Cavalry headed to Loup Creek on an excursion to save the wharf boat there, and in July, seven companies (B, C, D, E, F, H, I) participated in a raid of Wytheville, Virginia. Company A was at this time stationed at Gauley Bridge and did not participate in these engagements.

In the summer of 1863, Confederate General John Hunt Morgan led a daring cavalry raid into Indiana and Ohio, distracting Union forces, disrupting supply lines, capturing the nation's attention and spreading panic among the civilian population, likely including the Wallar family in Racine.

Morgan and his two thousand men crossed the Ohio River into southern Indiana near Mauckport on July 8th. The rebels spent five days destroying railroads, warehouses, and bridges, and taking horses from civilians. Five days later, the raiders entered Ohio at Harrison. After bypassing Cincinnati, General Morgan and his men headed east on what is now Ohio State Routes 32 and 124. They encountered local militia groups who took shots at them, and felled trees to barricade the road. There were a few skirmishes with Federal troops as well.

On July 18th, the Confederate raiders planned to cross the Ohio River into West Virginia using the ferry at Middleport in Meigs County, but they encountered a very determined force of Middleport and Pomeroy militia, supported by several companies of Union infantry and cavalry. The townspeople used trees, fence posts, and anything else that could be used to barricade the roads to the river. The militiamen waited in the woods to ambush the passing rebel cavalry, and an old cannon that had recently been used to celebrate the Fourth of July was filled with scrap metal and aimed at the road. Noticing smoke coming from the direction of Pomeroy, the rebels correctly deduced that there were Union gunboats unloading troops at the dock there, and decided the quickest way to cross the Ohio River was to continue east toward Buffington Island.

This was not an easy task, however. The road a mile north of Pomeroy passed through a narrow valley, and the militia and the arriving Union troops put up a fierce fight. It took three hours for Morgan's cavalry to travel the four miles through this pass. Weary after the long skirmish, Morgan and his men rested in the town of Chester. When they arrived at Portland on the Ohio River around 9 p.m. and looked at the Buffington Island ford, Morgan's advance was shocked to find a Union redoubt and two large cannons. Adding to their dismay, the Ohio River, which had been thirty inches deep a week prior, was now five or six feet deep and moving fast. Meanwhile, Union troops under Brigadier General Henry M. Judah marched through Racine, ten miles away, toward Buffington Island.[236] Once more, the Civil War arrived at the Wallar family's doorstep. The Wallar boys, I can imagine, were excited to see the Union troops march through Racine. Perhaps they walked the fifty yards from their home to the main road through town to cheer the men in blue on their way to Buffington Island to the east. Frances and the girls may have offered water and food to the men while thinking of James one hundred miles away.

At the Battle of Buffington Island early on the morning of Sunday, July 19th, Morgan was soundly defeated. The Confederates were tired and their spirits broken. Fifty of Morgan's men were killed, 100 wounded, and nearly 1000 missing or captured. Morgan and several hundred of his men escaped to the north without crossing the Ohio River. On July 26th, Morgan surrendered near Salineville, Ohio, about 175 miles north of Buffington Island. The Battle of Buffington Island was the only Civil War battle fought in Ohio.[237]

Battle of Buffington Island Memorial[238]

While Federal troops were pursuing Confederate General John H. Morgan in Ohio, Company A was ordered from Gauley Bridge to Division Headquarters in Charleston for duty by Commander of the 3rd Brigade Lieutenant Colonel Freeman E. Franklin.[239] They would remain stationed there until November.[240]

As cavalry units proved their value as effective fighting forces, more training was needed. On September 24th, the mercurial General Alfred Napoleon Duffié was assigned to train cavalry units in West Virginia. Duffié was a native of France who had moved to the United States before the Civil War and enlisted in 1861. He'd recently erred in his command of First Rhode Island Cavalry at the Battle of Middleburg in northern Virginia and thus was sent to the relatively unimportant theatre of West Virginia, where it was expected he could do less harm.[241]

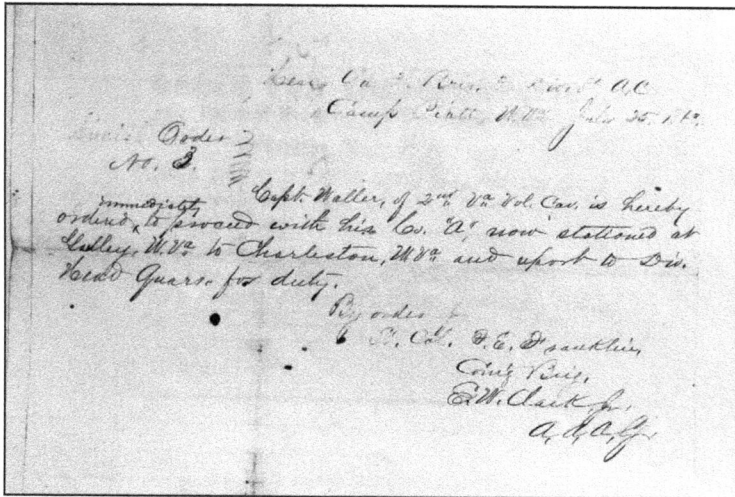

Special Order #3 Sending Company A to Charleston[242]

The historical sketch of the Second West Virginia Cavalry recounted:

On the 24th Gen A. N. Duffie (a frenchman) had been assigned the command of a mounted Brigade ordered the regt to be removed to Camp Toland Charleston WVa. We at once began to form his brigade and perfect them in drill, they having previously drilled in single rank once changed it to double rank formation and effectually drilled this regt in that form. Great credit is due the General for his mode of Educating the troopers, his severity was on officers instead of the men. As soon as he had his brigade formed to his ideas, he was then ready for action, and the 2d Va soon grew to be his special favorite.[243]

In late fall 1863, Union Brigadier General William W. Averell was ordered to destroy the Virginia and Tennessee Railroad and capture Lewisburg. He left Beverly, West Virginia with nearly 5000 men on November 1st and headed southwest toward Lewisburg, 100 miles away. The men marched south to Huntersville and then took the road through Hillsboro to Lewisburg.[244] In support of Averell, nine companies of the Second West Virginia Cavalry (including Company A) left Camp Toland in Charleston at 6:00 a.m. on November 3rd.[245] Under the command of Major Hoffman and Brigadier General Duffié, the men moved eastward on the James River and Kanawha Turnpike toward Lewisburg, marching some thirty miles before setting up camp.[246]

The following day, the men marched to Sewell Mountain, some twenty-two miles east. The trip was arduous, requiring the soldiers to build bridges, remove obstacles, or build roads to reach their destination. The men were rewarded with a tasty dinner that evening when they camped at the farm of a secessionist and raided his chicken coop and apple orchard![247]

By 2:00 p.m. on November 6th, Duffié's battery, including the Second West Virginia Cavalry, were eighteen miles west of Lewisburg. They skirmished with rebel pickets on Little Sewell Mountain and captured prisoners, who informed Duffié that there was only one cavalry regiment left in Lewisburg and the remainder of the Confederate soldiers had departed.[248]

While Averell's command distracted the Confederate Army, drawing them away from Lewisburg, Duffié and his men, including Wallar's Company A, entered the town with little resistance on the morning of November 7th. The cavalry, in advance, charged into Lewisburg but found no Confederate troops present. They captured the Confederate camps and, having no transportation to haul all they found, destroyed large quantities of food, tents, knapsacks, clothing, and other supplies. The Union cavalry were destructive toward the townspeople as well. A church and several houses were burned by the marauding soldiers. General Averell, upon learning of the looting, sent his advance to Lewisburg to restore order.[249]

Averell, meanwhile, engaged the Confederate troops under General John Echols in the Battle of Droop Mountain. The Confederate Brigadier General Echols learned of Averell's approach and fell back to Droop Mountain about twenty-five miles northeast of Lewisburg on November 5th. Here, a decisive battle was fought on November 6th.

At Droop Mountain, the Confederate troops occupied the top of the mountain and shot at the Union troops as they stormed up the mountain. After an afternoon of vicious fighting, the Union army was victorious. Echols began to retreat toward Lewisburg. Learning that Duffié and his men were at the top of Little Sewell Mountain, eighteen miles west of Lewisburg, Echols did not stop and continued his retreat south to the Virginia border. Averell's main objective of destroying the Virginia and Tennessee Railroad was unfulfilled.[250]

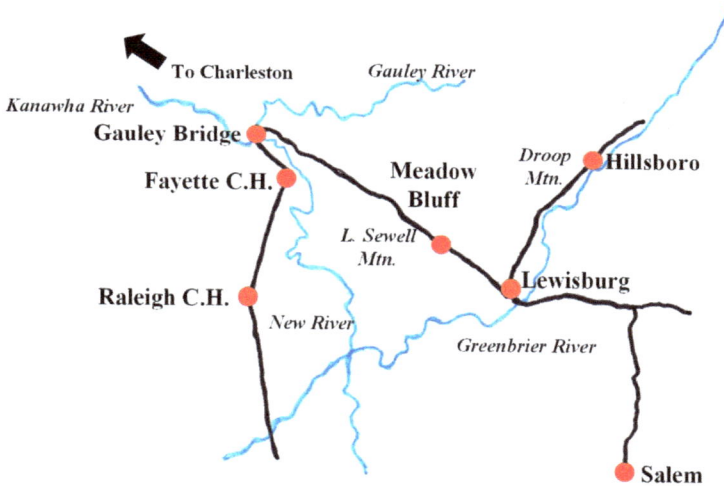

Droop Mountain Campaign, 1863

Private J. J. Sutton recalled:

On the 3rd of November the command marched thirty miles and camped for the night. On the 4th it marched to Gauley, and crossed the river by means of a small ferry boat, and went forward on the Lewisburg pike. The march was much delayed by blockades in the road. This was unexpected, and the obstacles presented themselves for a distance of eight miles, so that in some places a new road had to be dug around them. The force went into camp for the night at the Hamilton farm, eight miles from Gauley. On the 5th it marched to Tyree's, a distance of twenty-two miles, being delayed again by blockades. At this place the command was joined by Col. White, with detachments of infantry. On the 6th the whole command marched to Meadow Bluff, about eighteen miles from Lewisburg. The enemy's pickets were encountered on Little Sewell mountain, and our advance succeeded in capturing two of them. On the morning of the 7th the force started for Lewisburg, the object being to intercept the rebel forces that had fought General Averell at Droop mountain. On the 7th of November at 9 a.m. the cavalry occupied Lewisburg, and learned that General Averell had badly defeated the enemy at Droop mountain, and that they had passed through in the direction of Union. We gave pursuit, but they could not be brought to bay, although the 2d West Virginia captured 110 head of cattle, 2 caissons and a few prisoners.

At Lewisburg we captured the rebel camps and a considerable quantity of stores, which we destroyed; also the knapsacks of the 22d Virginia infantry and the regimental tents.

On the return march the command found five inches of snow on Sewell mountain, which made it very difficult to move artillery and trains. However at 10 a.m. on the 13th the command reached Charleston, having been absent eleven days and marched 250 miles.

The result of this expedition, summed up, is as follows: —Prisoners captured, 34; horses captured, 50; cattle captured, 110; small arms, 102. The above were brought away. Besides this 350 small arms, a large quantity of ammunition, tents for a regiment, knapsacks for a regiment, with the clothing in them, 2 artillery caissons, 10 wagons, and some quartermaster's stores were destroyed.[251]

A rainy and foggy day at the summit of Droop Mountain[252]

With roughly 5000 Federal troops and 1700 Confederate troops participating, the Battle of Droop Mountain was the largest and last major Civil War battle in West Virginia. It was not until the following month that Averell destroyed the railroad at Salem, Virginia.[253] Some of the Second West Virginia Cavalry left Charleston for Lewisburg on the afternoon of December 8th to help Averell in this quest. Accompanying the cavalry was a section of battery. The troops carried hard bread, salt, sugar, and coffee for three days. Similar rations for seven days were provided by the division quartermaster.[254]

The men reached Gauley Bridge on the afternoon of the 9th and camped at Gauley Mount. It took three more days to travel to Lewisburg. The Second West Virginia stayed in Lewisburg until December 15th and protected Averell's troops from any Confederate movement from the north. After a round-trip of 200 miles, the cavalry returned to Charleston on December 19th.[255]

8

DISSATISFACTION

While most of the Second West Virginia Cavalry overwintered in Charleston, scouting throughout the state and perfecting their drills, Captain Wallar spent the months of January and February 1864 on recruiting leave. There was a continual need for more soldiers. On January 2nd, General A.N. Duffié sent Wallar on detached service, recruiting for thirty days. Again, on January 28th, Duffié signed an order for Wallar to continue his recruiting. Amongst the papers in James Wallar's service record is an order for transportation, requesting that the B&O Railroad provide transportation for Wallar on his recruiting mission between Wheeling and New Creek in eastern West Virginia.[256]

Wallar also took advantage of the time away from camp and presumably visited Frances and the children. A letter from James to Lieutenant Colonel Dove, dated March 2, 1864, was written in Mason, West Virginia, less than ten miles from Racine. In this letter, Wallar explained to Dove that he had a great idea for recruiting and asked if he might stay on recruiting duty longer.[257] Whether or not he was able to implement his idea on his recruiting trip is unknown, but he reunited with his company in Summersville on March 12th.

It likely was frustrating for James to watch so many of his fellow captains be promoted. At the formation of the Second West Virginia Cavalry, W.H. Powell was a captain alongside Wallar, and by this time in 1864 Powell was a Colonel and a Medal of Honor recipient. Other officers promoted over Wallar include Charles E. Hambleton, promoted from First Lieutenant to Captain. Major James Allen started the war as a Second Lieutenant, was promoted to Captain and, later, to Major. John McMahan was promoted from Captain to Major, and David Dove was promoted from Captain to Lieutenant Colonel.[258] Meanwhile, from April 1861-March 11, 1864, Wallar remained a captain.

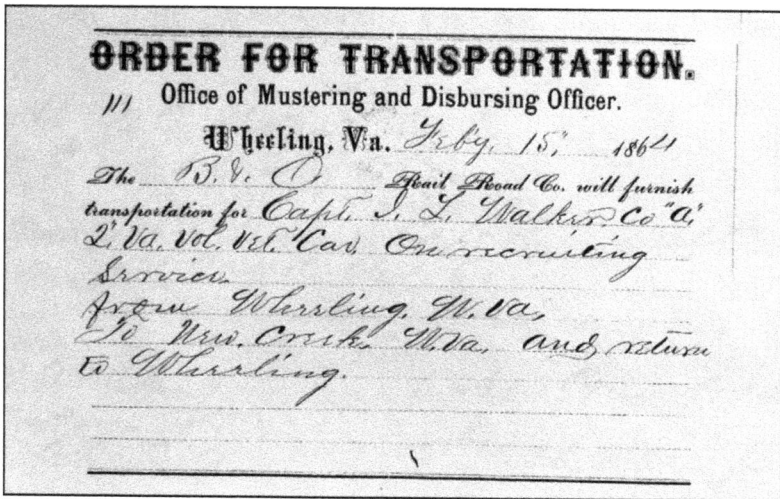

Wallar's Transportation Order[259]

On March 11, 1864, Wallar was commissioned as a Major.[260] Why did it take so long for him to earn a promotion? Was he generally ineffective? Did he have a drinking problem? It's easy to assume that Captain Wallar was sent on recruiting missions because of his charisma, charm, and previous success. But maybe Powell just didn't like Wallar and was happy to be rid of him for a while.

Months earlier, Lieutenant Colonel Powell, in a letter to H.J. Samuels, Assistant Adjutant General in Wheeling wrote:

I am determined as I said to Genl S. [Scammon] to change the entire character of the Regiment and to rid it of every inefficient and drunken officer. The Regiment during my absence from duty (some 3 mo) became very much demoralized and it will require nerve, energy and close application to build it up to what it ought to and must be under my administration. If I am spared, we will need field officers soon. I am

determined to ask the promotion of none upon any other ground than
meritorious conduct and trust you will grant my requests, that I may be
enabled to make the Regiment <u>Efficient</u> and creditable to my self to you,
a benefit to the service and a terror to Rebels. I will do this or die in the
attempt.[261]

It would soon become apparent that Wallar wasn't fond of Powell. Despite his promotion, James L. Wallar's military career was coming to an abrupt end. In his military service record at the National Archives, there are three letters of affidavit from soldiers recounting what seems to have been a drunken tirade on the part of Wallar. One of the letters is reproduced and transcribed here:

Before the subscriber James Allen Capt and Provost Marshal 3rd Div
Dept West Va.
This day came Serg't C.E. Brigden, Co. B. 23rd Reg. O.V. Inf. and
made oath to the following:
On or about the 25th day of April 1864 I heard Capt Jas L. Wallar say
that Col Powell the one eyed son of a b_h had (murdered) him (Wallar),
that he (Wallar) had no country, no wife, or family, said he disowned them.
And that in future he would be an adventurer. He (Wallar) also said he
was as good as a Rebel as he was a Union Man. And said he would have
revenge if he had to raise a company of partisan rangers and seek it on the
battle field. —C.E. Brigden, Serg't Co. B 23d Regt. O.V. Inf.

James was really in hot water this time. While true that Powell lost "practical use" of his right eye on his twenty-first birthday while working at the Iron Works in Wheeling,[262] James clearly overstepped his bounds by speaking so disparagingly of Colonel Powell and the Union army.

Affidavit of Sergeant C. E. Brigden[263]

According to the United States Army regulations, "Any officer or soldier who shall behave himself with contempt or disrespect toward his commanding officer, shall be punished, according to the nature of his offense, by the judgement of a court-martial."[264] Aside from alcohol, what was the cause of the outburst? How did Colonel William H. Powell "murder" or "ruin" Wallar? Powell had recently returned to his duties after a few weeks at home after being a prisoner of the Confederate army for six months. Was there deep-seated animosity between Wallar and Powell with Powell's return pushing Wallar over the edge?

Again from the U.S. Army regulations:

The original proceedings of all general courts-martial, after the decision on them of the reviewing authority, and all proceedings that require the decision of the President under the 65th and 89th Articles of War, and copies of all orders confirming or disapproving, or remitting, the sentences of courts-martial, and all official communications for the Judge Advocate of the army, will be addressed to "The Adjutant-General of the Army, War Department..."[265]

and,

...neither shall any sentence of a general court-martial, in the time of peace, extending to the loss of life, or the dismission of a commissioned officer, or which shall, either in time of peace or war, respect a general officer, be carried into execution until after the whole proceedings shall have been transmitted to the Secretary of War, to be laid before the President of the United States for his confirmation or disapproval, and orders in the case.[266]

Because of these regulations, it seems likely that a court-martial occurred at the camp. On April 26, 1864, Wallar, now demoted to Captain, was dishonorably discharged from the Union Army by Major General Franz Sigel. Sigel ordered Wallar to Harper's Ferry on his own recognizance to await the decision of President Lincoln as to his fate. I don't think these two events would've happened had Wallar not been court-martialed. Checks of the Harper's Ferry court-martial index at the National Archives, the *Papers of Abraham Lincoln* at the Abraham Lincoln Presidential Library and the *Abraham Lincoln Papers* at the Library of Congress did not reveal Wallar's name, nor did research at the West Virginia Archives and History Library and the West Virginia and Regional History Center.

Order sending Wallar to Harper's Ferry[267]

Head Quarters 3d Division, Department West Va., Charleston, West Va, Apr. 30 1864

Sir: I have the honor to transmit herewith affidavits in the case of Capt. James L Waller 2d Regt Va Cav Vols who since his dismissal from the United States Service has been making threats for which he was placed in close arrest. Not having a guard to send with him, he – Waller—is released and ordered to report at Harper's Ferry.

Respectfully, Your Obt Servt., George Crook, Brig. Gen.

VIEW OF "HARPER'S FERRY," VA. NOVEMBER 18TH, 1863.
Photographed by B. Shunk.

Harper's Ferry, 1863[268]

Did James Wallar go to Harper's Ferry on his own recognizance? Harper's Ferry, a strategic location at the confluence of the Potomac and the Shenandoah Rivers, changed hands many times during the Civil War. In the spring of 1864, the town was again in the hands of the Union army and served as a headquarters and supply depot. Had James gone to Harper's Ferry, he likely would have visited the Provost Marshal's office which has been restored and is now part of Harpers Ferry National Historical Park.

If Wallar went to Harper's Ferry, he may have been dismissed immediately, but it seems unlikely he went because there are no records of him being there. It is this author's opinion that the disgraced Captain James L. Wallar was unwilling to face his fate and ran home to his family.

Provost Marshal's Office, Harpers Ferry National Historical Park, Harpers Ferry, West Virginia[269]

270

*Hd. Qrs. Dept West Va, Woodstock
VA, May 14, 1864
Respectfully referred to Brg. Gnl.
Max Weber, Harper's Ferry Va for
his information. This officer, with
two others of 2d Va Cavalry was
dismissed from service by Genl orders
from there Hd Qrs subject to the
approval of the President, and has
been ordered to Harpers Ferry there
to await the decision of the President.
By order Major Genl Sigel,
T. Melvin A.A.G.*

Sigel's order[271]

In the final year of the Civil War, the Second West Virginia Cavalry, minus Captain Wallar, would see more battle action than they had previously. They fought in the Battle of Cove Mountain in Wythe County, participated in the Lynchburg campaign, fought several battles in the Shenandoah Valley, and battled in Dinwiddie County south and west of Richmond, Virginia. From Dinwiddie, the Second West Virginia Cavalry traveled west, fighting at Sailor's Creek. In the Third Division under General George Armstrong Custer, the Second West Virginia Cavalry were at Appomattox when Lee surrendered to Grant, ending the Civil War. General Custer's Third Division led the Grand Review of the Armies in Washington D.C. on May 23, 1865, with all men wearing red neck ties in honor of General Custer.[272]

Company Muster-out Roll Card[273]

Civil War Photograph of James L. Wallar[274]

9

BEHOLD, I STAND AT THE DOOR AND KNOCK

I n late April or early May 1864, it seems that James hurried home to Ohio, gathered up the wife and children he had disavowed only days earlier, and moved west. Only five weeks after being ordered to Harper's Ferry, Lots 4, 5, and 6 of the Hopkins Addition to the town of Racine were sold by James L. Wallar and his wife Frances Wallar on June 6, 1864 to William and Mary A. Alexander for $700.00.[275]

Nine days later, on June 15th, James L. Wallar purchased forty acres of land in northwest Richland County, Illinois from Abraham and Frances Davis for the sum of $800.00. This land, located ten miles northwest of Olney, is the northeast quarter of the northwest quarter of Section 32, Township 5 North, Range 9 East.[276]

The Wallar family was enumerated the following year in the 1865 Illinois state census in Denver Township, immediately after Abraham Davis and his family. The census taker wrote "Walten" for James' surname. In addition to being adjacent to Abraham Davis on the list of names, all the known Wallar family members are accounted for in this census—two males under age ten (William and Harry), two males between ten and twenty (Charles and Lafayette), one male between forty and fifty (James), one female under ten (Lillie), one female between ten and twenty (Lauretta), and one female between thirty and forty (Frances), for a total of eight people. The family had livestock worth $125.00 and reported three pounds of wool.[277]

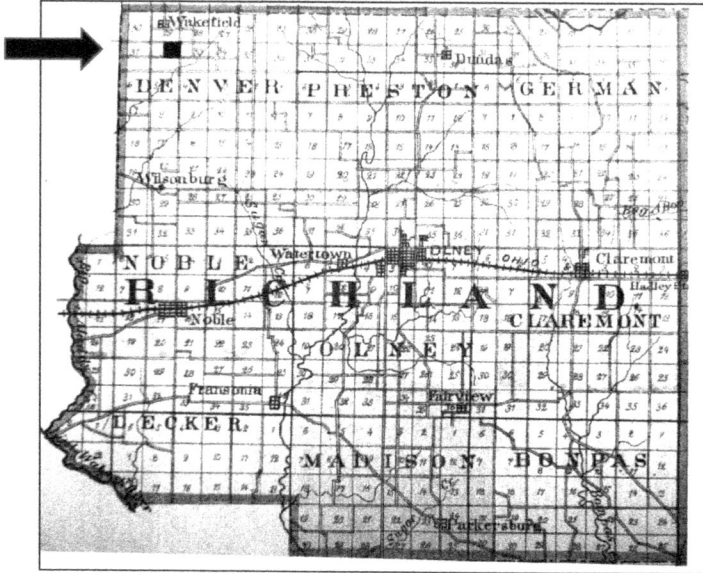

Location of Wallar's land in Richland County, Illinois[278]

James quickly realized that a farmer's life was not satisfying to him. On September 21, 1866, at the annual meeting of the Southern Illinois Conference of the Methodist Episcopal Church held in Centralia, James was admitted on trial into the ministry. To be admitted on trial, James would've received the recommendation of his local circuit that he could "give satisfactory evidence respecting his knowledge of those particular subjects which have been recommended to his consideration."[279] Shortly afterwards, the family moved to Georgetown, Illinois in northern Clay County for James' first preaching appointment.[280] James and Frances sold back their farmland to Abraham Davis for $900.00 on October 26, 1866.[281]

The guidelines for a preacher's conduct were spelled out quite clearly in *The Doctrines and Disciplines of the Methodist Episcopal Church*. A preacher was instructed to use his time wisely and be diligent, to use caution when speaking to women, to speak earnestly and not joke, to be punctual, and to not be scornful or speak ill of others. Sermons were to be serious and solemn, and preachers were asked to speak plainly and not ramble. A preacher was told to eliminate awkward, distracting gestures or pronunciations, and to "always avail yourself of the great festivals by preaching on the occasion."[282]

J.L. Wallar was "continued on trial" in the Methodist Episcopal Church in 1867. A two-year trial period was the norm. This allowed the Bishop and Presiding Elder time to evaluate his work, and for the prospective preacher to decide if the ministry was the right fit for him. He was stationed at Newton in Jasper County, Illinois in 1867 and the first part of 1868. On September 13, 1868, he was received into "full connection." A majority of the members of the Annual Conference elected James L. Wallar a deacon and he was ordained by Bishop E. S. Janes by "the laying on of the hands" at the annual meeting in DuQuoin, Illinois.[283] A deacon could preach sermons, organize and lead Sunday School classes, perform marriages and funeral rites, and:

assist the elder in divine service. And especially when he ministereth the holy communion, to help him in the distribution thereof, and to read and expound the Holy Scriptures; to instruct the youth, and to baptize. And furthermore, it is his office to search for the sick, poor, and impotent, that they may be visited and relieved.[284]

By 1869, Reverend Wallar was involved with committee work in the Annual Conference. In this year he was on the Periodicals committee, and was preaching in Robinson, Illinois, in Crawford County.[285] Making himself at home, in March 1870, he opened the Crawford County Teachers' Institute with an invocation.[286] James and his older daughter Etta served on a Grand Army of the Republic post committee to make arrangements to decorate the graves of Union soldiers on the upcoming Decoration Day, later to be called Memorial Day.[287] Reverend Wallar also spoke at the Independence Day celebration in 1870.[288]

On September 14, 1870, James Wallar was ordained an elder by the esteemed Bishop Matthew Simpson who, five years earlier, preached President Abraham Lincoln's funeral sermon in Springfield.[289] As an elder, Reverend Wallar was now permitted to administer communion.[290]

The Wallars' young daughter Lillie May died on February 9, 1871. She is buried in the Old Robinson Cemetery. Oddly, no dates are inscribed on the grave marker. She was enumerated as an eight-year-old in the 1870 census on June 13th of that year, so we can assume she was eight or nine years old at the time of her death. It was reported in the same newspaper that "Rev. J.L. Wallar was confined to his home with an attack of pneumonia." Perhaps pneumonia was the cause of young Lillie's death.[291]

Lillie May Wallar's grave marker, Robinson, Illinois[292]

In March 1871, Reverend J.L. Wallar unsurprisingly chaired an ad hoc committee to nominate candidates to the Robinson town board who were against licensing the sale of "intoxicating liquors as a beverage." James L. Wallar undoubtedly knew the dangers of excessive alcohol consumption.[293]

That year in September at Annual Conference held in Cairo, Illinois, James was listed as serving on the Sunday Schools and the Conference Tabernacle committees.[294] On the final day of the conference, it was announced that J.L. Wallar would leave Robinson for Sumner, Illinois, a small, unincorporated town in western Lawrence County.[295] He preached his last sermon in Robinson on September 17, 1871,[296] and the family moved to Sumner on October 10th.[297] The Methodist Episcopal church at Sumner was a relatively new building on the south side of town. It was built in 1868-1869 and was described as "a neat building with a steeple," with a foundation of 70 by 36 feet.[298]

At this time, a preacher was not to serve more than three years in one location. He was in Sumner for only one year, and was then moved to Carmi, Illinois for one year, from September 1872 to September 1873. As pastor of the recently built Carmi Methodist Episcopal Church, James was true to his work as a minister, supplying the citizenry with bibles through the White County Bible Society.[299] The present-day First United Methodist Church in Carmi is located on the same corner of Main and Church Streets as the "handsome white frame church house with a steeple overlooking the town" where James L. Wallar preached that year.[300] On Tuesday, July 17, 1894, Reverend J. L. Wallar returned to Carmi to address the crowd at the ceremony to lay the cornerstone of the current church building.[301]

During the time the Wallar family lived in Carmi, the little town was consumed by a cholera epidemic. Fifty-five cases were reported in White County, with thirty-four deaths. The quintesessential benevolent minister, Reverend Wallar assisted an unfortunate family in their time of need. Perhaps he was thinking of his little Lillie May at this time.

But it was in the spring of 1873 that we had our best opportunity to study this great and good man, one of nature's noblesmen, for in that year the city was visited by a dreadful plague; cholera was claiming its victims in all parts of the city, and it mattered not how high or low the person stricken down. Dr. Wallar was found at their bedside soon after they were taken sick. At the grave it was Dr. Wallar who performed the last sad rites, and no person who fell under that dread disease but what was given a church burial, no matter what their church; in one case a widow died who was leaving behind two little girls, and it was a sad sight to see Dr. Wallar performing the last rites at the grave, while the two little girls and the two gravediggers were the only other persons in attendance, and later see him taking the little girls to his own home, where he left them until quarantine regulations allowed them to be sent to an uncle, while the rest of us stood aloof, leaving the victims of the scourge to get along as best they might with the hired men employed by the city. Dr. Wallar could not have done more had each been members of his own family. No man that has ever lived had a bigger heart than Dr. Wallar.[302]

In October 1873, the family moved to Cairo, Illinois for Reverend Wallar's next station. Cairo was a river town, located at the confluence of the Mississippi and Ohio Rivers. The town housed an important training camp and supply depot for the Union Army during the Civil War, and General Ulysses S. Grant was headquartered in Cairo for a time. After the war, the population and commerce decreased, but by the mid-1870s, the population was about 6300 people and was rapidly growing. Several railroads branched out of Cairo, and the brand-new Customs House would serve to collect tariffs on goods travelling on the Mississippi River. The building was also used for Federal court purposes and housed the post office.[303]

The Methodist Episcopal church in Cairo was located on the corner of Walnut (now Dr. Martin Luther King Avenue) and Eighth Streets.[304] James preached his first sermon there on October 19th. Church was an all-day affair for Reverend Wallar. The following week, for example, he preached at 11:00, held Sunday School at 3:00 in the afternoon, and then preached again at 7:30 in the evening.[305] The newspaper invited, "the public generally, and strangers, especially."[306]

10

THE KNIGHTS TEMPLAR

At some point before this time, James became involved with the Freemasons, specifically the Knights Templar, the pinnacle of the York Rite. One of his many obituaries suggests that he joined the A.F. and A.M. Lodge No. 196 in Louisville, Illinois.[307] This likely was sometime between 1864 and 1867, when he was living in northwest Richland County and stationed at Georgetown in Clay County. He was instrumental in the formation of a Royal Arch Mason chapter in Robinson, Illinois, serving as its first High Priest in December 1870.[308] At an Ascension Day ceremony held May 14, 1874, "Rev. Sir Knight Wallar" addressed the attendees and led them in prayer. After the services, the Commandery marched through the city in their resplendent garb before disbanding.[309]

Freemasonry is a men's social and philanthropic fraternity with a strong spiritual component. The late 19th century was a time of high interest in fraternal societies, and James, being a charismatic, outgoing person, likely would have enjoyed the camaraderie of such a group. Within Freemasonry, degrees are conferred on members based on their knowledge of Masonic stories. While Freemasonry is open to any man who believes in God, membership in the Knights Templar is open only to Christians. This was certainly a fitting group for a Methodist minister! The Knights Templar wore elegant, military-style uniforms and prided themselves in their parade drills. Even today, Knights Templar wear similarly styled uniforms and participate in marching drills.[310]

Knights Templar uniform of the mid- to late 19th century[311]

The following Friday, May 22, 1874, a group of over one thousand "excursionists" from Sunday schools in the Humboldt, Tennessee area arrived in Cairo. They rode on trains to Columbus, Kentucky, then took steamers up the Mississippi River to Cairo. The Cairo newspaper reported the purpose of the trip was "to get acquainted with our people and view our city." Reverend J.L. Wallar was on a committee to make the visit a pleasant one.[312] These Sunday school excursions were quite common at the time, but this one was especially large. The goal was a day or two of leisure for the participants and was a successful fundraiser for the host.[313] Often, as in the case of the Humboldt, Tennessee excursion, many churches would combine forces to make the outing even more grand. An 1875 Methodist excursion to Paducah, Kentucky was organized in Cairo to raise money for Reverend Wallar's salary. Church repairs had been necessary, and the money earmarked for the pastor's salary had been used for repairs.[314]

The account of an 1874 excursion took nearly two full columns in the following day's newspaper. Reverend Wallar, other clergymen, and a few community leaders boarded a tug and met the steamer *Gracey* at the confluence of the Ohio and Mississippi Rivers. They boarded the *Gracey* and accompanied the excited excursionists the short distance to the Cairo landing. Church bells were rung to call the Cairo Sunday School attendees to the meeting point at Tenth and Washington Streets. From there the group marched down to the landing on the Ohio River at Sixth Street, led by the town's cornet band. The excited visitors from Tennessee disembarked around 2:00 p.m. and proceeded through the ranks of the Cairo participants until they arrived at the National Bank a couple of blocks away. "The programme was a little defective—just a little—and the marching; of the procession did not at first move as smoothly as was desirable. The marshals found the handling of two thousand children an onerous task…" The grand marshal of the day, a Colonel Gamble, addressed the cheerful throng, as did the mayors of both Cairo and Humboldt. The men spoke of unity and friendship, alluding to the difficult times after the Civil War. A quartet of singers from the Odd Fellow Female College in Humboldt sang a splendid hymn, and then it was time for the excursionists to leave. The Illinoisians and Tennesseans bade each other farewell and the group from Humboldt paraded back through town to the waiting steamer for their trip home.[315]

By spring of 1874, eldest son Lafayette was employed as a physician, possibly in Crawford County, Illinois.[316] Daughter Lauretta "Etta" Reeder's life was mirroring that of her mother's—life as a minister's wife meant the family moved frequently. Sons Charles Millard Wallar and Harry Herbert Wallar were finishing their school year at Union Christian College, a college preparatory school and undergraduate college in Merom, Indiana. Charles was in his third and last year, and Harry was finishing his first and only year at the school. Cousins Eva, Ida, and William C.A. Wallar, children of James' brother Elijah, also attended Union Christian College.[317]

That left fourteen-year-old Willie as the only child still living at home in the spring of 1874. Education was important to Willie, and he had a bright future. On May 22nd, Willie Wallar was named to the Roll of Honor in Room 3 of the Thirteenth Street School.[318] The Thirteenth Street School was built in 1864 on the corner of Thirteenth and Walnut Streets. It was a three-story school building with two classrooms on each of the first and second floors, and one classroom on the third floor.[319] Willie walked a quarter mile to the school from the parsonage.

In June of that year, Reverend Wallar became seriously ill. It was reported in the newspaper that he was, "...much better and is no longer in danger."[320] The following week he was, "rapidly improving and is now able to be up and about. It is not certain, however, if he will undertake to conduct services to-morrow."[321] There is no indication in the newspapers of what ailed him. Fortunately, on June 30th, James was well enough to accompany son Charles on the train to the Normal School at Carbondale, sixty miles to the north.[322]

Having presumably regained his full health, just before midnight on Wednesday November 25, 1874, the Rev. Sir Knight Wallar boarded the *Thompson Dean* to travel to New Orleans for the Grand Encampment of the Knights Templar.[323] The Cairo Commandery No. 13 chartered the three-hundred foot long, two-thousand-ton steamer to transport them down the Mississippi River.[324] Built in 1872, the *Thompson Dean* was one of the finest steamboats on the Mississippi and Ohio Rivers. Like other post-Civil War steamers, the *Thompson Dean* had a large, splendidly decorated social hall that also served as a dining room. This hall was nearly 250 feet in length, 18 feet wide, and 17 feet in height. Plush carpeting, ornate draperies, a grand piano, mirrors, and fine furniture added to the opulent experience for the guests.[325] On its regularly scheduled trips between Cincinnati or Memphis and New Orleans, the steamer would stop many times along the way to load cotton, cottonseed, sugar cane, and other commodities to be shipped to ports around the world and to take on more coal to power the massive steam engines necessary for the journey.[326]

For this special trip the *Thompson Dean* was decorated inside and out with colorful signs, flags, and buntings. In addition to the twenty-seven Knights Templar from Cairo, many wives and daughters accompanied the Knights. James' wife Frances was not among them.[327] The happy group was joined by other commanderies and their guests, namely those of Centralia, Illinois and Terre Haute, Indiana, the Grand Officers of the Grand Commandery of Illinois, and a twenty-seven-piece band.[328]

From a painting in the Louisiana State Museum, New Orleans.

The steamer *Thompson Dean* [329]

In Memphis, Tennessee on Friday, November 27th, the *Thompson Dean* took on coal and departed at ten a.m. for New Orleans along with the steamer *Idlewild* and the flotilla's flagship, *The Great Republic*. A large crowd at the landing cheered and waved and cannons were fired in salute as the convoy headed south on the Mississippi River.[330]

The steamers arrived at Vicksburg, Mississippi early Sunday morning, and Baton Rouge around noon on Monday, November 30th, where the passengers were allowed an hour to stroll along the waterfront. Back onboard, James Wallar and the other excursionists likely discussed amongst themselves the scenery—sugar plantations, stately live oaks, and cypress trees covered with Spanish moss—sights not seen in the Midwest! [331]

While Monday's weather was nearly summerlike, fog earlier in the trip delayed the arrival of the convoy in New Orleans by several hours. The gaily adorned *Thompson Dean* finally appeared at the Canal Street landing between four and five o'clock in the afternoon on Monday. Because of the delay, the wharf had filled again with other boats. It had been an exceptionally busy day, with nearly 120 ships loading and unloading cargo throughout the day. After some shuffling, the *Thompson Dean* was able to dock, and the excited Knights from Illinois and Indiana were greeted by the Knights of Orleans Commandery No. 3 and a crowd of enthusiastic New Orleanians. Two twelve-pound cannons from the Louisiana Field Artillery fired a "salute of a hundred guns" to welcome the steamer and her passengers.[332] After the passengers departed, 83 bales of cotton and 1927 sacks of cotton seed were off-loaded from the *Thompson Dean*.[333]

> *It was a scene of excitement; mules, drays and people were thrown together in indistinguishable confusion. Cotton was piled so high that it formed defiles and gorges, through which the commanderies had to find their way to the city. Altogether there were some 6000 or 7000 persons on the Levee, and the largest amount of freight for many a day.*[334]

To kick off the Grand Encampment, the Knights Templar processed in military fashion through the streets of New Orleans, which were lined with townspeople and decorated with banners and wreaths. The parade of nearly two thousand Knights dressed in their splendid uniforms with swords by their side was led by the Grand Commandery of Louisiana on horseback. The other commanderies followed on foot. The Cairo Commandery and their band led the third section of the parade, serving as escorts to the Grand Commandery of Illinois. The final entry in the parade was the national leaders of the Knights Templar, also on horseback. The procession ended outside the Masonic Hall, where the meeting was called to order.[335]

The Masonic Hall on the corner of St. Charles and Perdido Streets was decorated both inside and out with evergreens and flowers. Tents and flags lined the inside of the hall, and the stage "was filled with rare plants, ornamental trees, flowers and the banners of the order."[336] A triangle enclosing a large red cross hung over St. Charles Street closer to the equally resplendent Exposition Hall, a five-minute walk from the Masonic Hall. This cross was illuminated by gas and must have been a sight to see! No expense was spared in welcoming the visitors to New Orleans.[337]

In addition to the business meetings of the Grand Encampment, the visiting Knights and their families were invited to various events throughout the city. For example, the United States Army invited the visitors to the barracks for a demonstration of the Gatling gun, with the note that, "a most delightful time will be had." Conversely, the *Thompson Dean* welcomed a set of esteemed New Orleanians for a dinner party on at least one evening.[338]

After a week of meetings, the Knights Templar concluded their conclave with a Grand Parade on Friday, December 4th. The day was treated as a holiday in New Orleans, with the public schools and courts closed for the day. The parade began at 11:30 in the morning, "with waving plumes and glistening sabres, formed such a spectacle as is seldom witnessed in any city, and never before in New Orleans." Curious and enthusiastic onlookers cheered as the Knights marched by, showing:

...an unexpected proficiency of drill...On the march they formed crosses, triangles, and squares, broke from single into lines of threes, fours, and sizes, wheeled by fours and into line again, kept sabres at the shoulder, aport, crossed from hand to hand, and at a present, all with the precision of machinery.[339]

Still basking in the revelry of the week's activities, James and his fellow Knights boarded the *Thompson Dean* for their scheduled Friday 5:00 p.m. departure.[340] Along with the passengers, the steamer carried 800 tons of miscellaneous freight headed for ports to the north.[341] Arriving in Memphis in the evening of Tuesday December 8th, the ladies of the Knights Templar presented the *Thompson Dean* captain with a gold-headed cane in appreciation of the fine and safe journey.[342] At last, the weary Knights of Cairo Commandery No. 13, their families, and friends arrived in Cairo at 3:00 a.m. on Thursday December 10th after a busy, productive, and fun-filled visit to New Orleans.[343]

Lectures were frequently presented in Cairo at this time by both men and women. In the time before radio and television this was a welcome form of entertainment. Reverend Wallar was a popular speaker. In February 1875, his lecture entitled *The Natural and the Supernatural* was so popular, he repeated it to an overflowing crowd at the Methodist church. Admission was twenty-five cents.[344] The following month he lectured on *The Point of Power* and *What is Man?*[345] A lecture on temperance at the Methodist church prompted the community to create an organization called "United Friends of Temperance." Reverend J.L. Wallar was elected as chaplain of the society.[346]

The Southern Illinois Annual Conference was held in Centralia in September 1875. At this conference, Wallar was ordered to take over the Methodist Episcopal church in Mount Carmel, Illinois later that month. Mount Carmel was a thriving town of close to 2000 people located 140 miles northeast of Cairo at the confluence of the Wabash and White Rivers. Wallar's last sermon in Cairo was on September 19th, and his first sermon in Mt. Carmel was on September 26th. The Cairo newspaper sent him on his way with these kind words:

During Rev. Mr. Wallar's stay in Cairo, he acquired by his unbiased mind and kind heart the friendship and good will of all. He has done much good in the cause of Christianity during his labors here, and the members of his congregation have become much attached to him, and will regret to see him go from among them.[347]

11

CYCLONE!

The family quickly settled in Mount Carmel, living in the parsonage adjacent to the Methodist Episcopal church, also called Beauchamp Chapel. The church, completed in 1851, was located on Fourth Street across from the Wabash County courthouse and jail. The church building was reported to be "the finest in Southern Illinois."[348] The former church was later used as the offices and print shop for the Mount Carmel *Register*, and currently is an antiques shop.[349] Some say the building is haunted by Caesar, the playful spirit of an African American man who worked at the church as a janitor.[350] Did James and his family know Caesar, or perhaps his spirit?

J.L. Wallar had assumed leadership responsibilities in the Southern Illinois Annual Conference by 1876, serving this year as an Examiner of Local Deacons for Elder's Orders, and as a Trier of Appeals. He served as Secretary of the Church Extension committee and presided over sessions of the Freedmen's Aid and Ministerial Education Societies.[351] Reverend Wallar also had the honor of officiating the marriage of oldest son Fay K. Wallar and Miss Kate McClure near Sumner in Lawrence County, Illinois on May 15, 1877.[352]

Monday June 4, 1877 was a rainy day. Farmers unable to work in their soggy fields came to town and chatted about the anticipated wheat harvest. Their wives brought fresh strawberries for sale. Children skipped down the streets to school, anxious to see their friends again after the weekend. Homemakers ran errands and tended to chores, and the county court was in session. Mount Carmel was bustling!

Around 3:30 in the afternoon the skies to the west turned an ominous dark. Lightning could be seen in the clouds and thunder rumbled in the distance. Before many of the residents of Mount Carmel could take shelter, a large tornado took shape and bore down upon the town.

With the lightning speed of a race horse the tempest came onward and leaping over the wood that skirted the prairie, rushed upon the ground and swept toward the city with the unearthly shriek of a fiend. The groans of the wounded, and the shrieks of the women and children mingled with the roaring of the storm. Pen cannot depict or describe the wild confusion of that fearful calamity.

For less than two minutes, winds estimated to be in excess of 150 miles per hour blew through Mount Carmel from southwest to northeast, damaging or destroying most buildings and homes between Third and Fifth Streets, including the courthouse. The air was thick with dust and debris such as uprooted trees, roofs, doors, demolished fences, carts, and signs.

Townspeople took refuge wherever they could as the torrential rain fell and the winds swirled. The cupola of the courthouse landed four miles away. The Methodist Episcopal church was heavily damaged, as was the parsonage next door. The front of the church and the roof were destroyed.[353] The steeple, spire vane, and gilded ball were blown nearly ten miles, landing in a farmer's field near Decker's Station, Indiana.[354] A fire began in the adjacent Parkinson building, one of three large, three-story warehouses located near the corner of Fourth and Main streets. Mount Carmel did not have fire-fighting equipment. A message was telegraphed to Vincennes, Indiana, twenty-four miles away: "Our town is in ruins and in flames. Send us aid." Within an hour, firemen and engines arrived on a special train. It took nearly six hours to contain the raging fire.[355]

Beauchamp Chapel as it looked before the tornado

The former Beauchamp Chapel in 2022. The inset shows the arched windows on the west side of the building where stained glass once was.[356]

Unfortunately, James and Frances Wallar's youngest son, Willie, took shelter from the storm in the Parkinson building, likely on his way home from school. He was trapped under the collapsed wall of the warehouse and burned to death. Reverend Wallar was slightly injured. A newspaper in neighboring Indiana gruesomely sensationalized seventeen-year-old Willie's death:

[The tornado] had now reached the best buildings in town, and right here the greatest loss of life occurred. The top of the courthouse, which occupied one corner, was blown off and the county offices, which were in the same building, presented a gutted and desolate appearance. Just across Fourth street stood the three large brick store rooms, known as the Edgar buildings, which burned after they fell, and from the ruins of which a majority of the dead bodies were taken, some of them crushed and mangled by the debris and afterwards burned to a crisp. From the ruins we saw them take out the body of Willie Waller, the minister's son, whose body was yet roasting when removed. His skull crumbled away like dust, leaving his brain exposed and perfectly charred, while his father stood near by looking at the sight in silent anguish.[357]

"The Courthouse"[358]

The storm made national news, with a New Orleans newspaper reporting this about the Wallar family:

Rev. Mr. Waller, of the Methodist Episcopal Church, was with his family in the parsonage, and succeeded in getting them into a safe place. He dwelt upon the stifling atmosphere which preceded the storm, and agreed with others in the impression that it did not last more than a minute. He marked the time by thirty steps taken after he had looked out of a window and warned his family of the impending danger. There was one, alas! of that beloved circle who was beyond the hearing of admonition. His son, Willie Waller, was in Mr. Parkinson's store, on the corner, and in the moment of peril started out of the back door to the parsonage. As he ran, he was buried under the ruins of the falling wall.[359]

"Taking Out the Dead"[360]

Willie Wallar's grave marker, Mount Carmel, Illinois[361]

After the tornado, the devastated town became a macabre tourist destination. On Sunday June 10th, less than a week after the storm, the Southeastern Railroad ran an excursion:

...leaving Evansville at 9 a.m., and Mt. Vernon at 9:50 a.m. Returning, the train arrives at Mt. Vernon at 5:20 p.m. and at Evansville at 6:10 p.m. The fare for the round trip will be $2 from Evansville and $1.50 from Mt. Vernon. The proceeds of this...will be given entire to the destitute, and will afford all an opportunity of witnessing the wreck made by a vengeful nature.[362]

The Cairo and Vincennes Railroad anticipated at least two hundred people would take advantage of an excursion from Cairo on the same day:[363]

...in order to give those of our people who are desirous of viewing the ruins of the unfortunate town. The train will leave the depot at six o'clock Sunday morning and return about eight o'clock in the evening, giving all who go between three and four hours among the ruins.[364]

The Cairo newspaper mentioned afterwards that, "The town of Mt. Carmel was packed on last Sunday by visitors from Evansville, Vincennes, Cairo and other cities, who were curious to view the ruins."[365]

The following Sunday, twenty-five passenger cars pulled by two engines arrived at the depot in Mount Carmel with people wanting to see the ruins.[366] While there is still to this day an obsession with disasters and natural phenomena, in the late nineteenth century, a train trip to the affected area would have been an entertaining way to spend the day and appreciate the devastation.

"The Mount Carmel Disaster—A View of the Ruins on Fourth Street"[367]

Sixteen people died in the June 4th tornado and fire, and approximately one hundred were injured. The property damage value was approximately $400,000,[368] and more than one hundred families were displaced from their homes.[369] The mayor of Mount Carmel appealed to other communities for help. The cities of Evansville and Vincennes each sent $500.[370] Nearby communities and those along the railroad lines collected money, clothing, and food for the citizens of Mount Carmel, including Carmi, Cairo, Grayville, Cincinnati, Chicago, Springfield, Robinson, and Carbondale. The editors of the *Mount Carmel Register* pleaded:

Now we ask our friends in the country to come up and show that their hearts are in the right place. Let every farmer bring in a sack of flour, a barrel of meal, two or three hams, shoulders, or sides of meat, butter, eggs, or anything that will answer to 'keep the gaunt wolf from the door.' Bedding of any kind will also be very acceptable.[371]

Reverend Wallar appealed to his friends in Robinson, having "lost everything he had" in the tornado. Several families there sent money to help the Wallar family.[372]

Life went on. Homes, schools, and businesses were repaired or rebuilt. Broken bones and spirits healed. By June 21st, the Methodist Episcopal church had a new roof and it was hoped that services could be held in the church basement on Sunday June 24th.[373]

12

A Preacher of More than Ordinary Ability

The year 1878 started out on a pleasant note. On January 27th, James and Frances' son Charles Wallar of Newton, Illinois married Miss Laura C. Townsend of Mount Carmel.[374] Charles was practicing law in Newton.[375] Son Fay K. Wallar graduated from the Miami Medical College in Cincinnati in February 1878.[376]

The remainder of the year was mostly uneventful. James tended to his flock, preaching weekly, and officiating over weddings and funerals. Staying true to his convictions, Reverend Wallar spoke at the temperance union meeting in Mount Carmel on April 18, 1878.[377] Sadly, son Fay's wife Katie died on August 22, 1878 at age 27. She is buried in Sumner Cemetery in Lawrence County, Illinois.[378] He would marry again to Martha M. Leeper on October 1, 1879 in Olney, Richland County, Illinois. She was the daughter of Methodist minister John Leeper.[379]On April 1, 1879, son Harry Herbert Wallar married Mary Melissa "Mollie" Ballew, a daughter of Peter and Frances (Ford) Bellew in Louisville, Clay County, Illinois.

Still living in Mount Carmel the following year, J.L. Wallar served on the Education committee of and as a Visitor to McKendree College. This appointment required him to attend the college examinations and report back to the Conference. He preached a sermon during this annual meeting and reported his missionary collections.[380]

"Brother Wallar was a preacher of more than ordinary ability," claimed Reverend John Leeper in Wallar's obituary.[381] At the 1879 Southern Illinois Conference, James L. Wallar was chosen to serve as Presiding Elder of the Mount Carmel District.[382] He would maintain this position until autumn 1883. As presiding elder, Wallar oversaw the district's pastors and churches. This position was a good fit for Wallar, with his excellent communication skills, knowledge, and charisma. Because of his new responsibilities, he was excused from the Committee to Examine Local Deacons for Elder's Orders and from the Board of Stewards, but was still a Visitor to McKendree College. He and Frances lived in Enfield, Illinois at this time.[383]

After his stint as Presiding Elder, James' next station was to serve as pastor of the Methodist Episcopal church in Effingham, Illinois. He served as the pastor there from 1883-1885.[384] The "substantial brick church" was built in 1866 and was named Centenary to honor the 100th anniversary of Methodism in America.[385]

Wallar was on hand to dedicate the Prairie Methodist Episcopal Church in Crawford County in 1881, a fitting occasion for the presence of a Presiding Elder. This was a frame church, 38 x 42 feet in area, and cost the congregation $1100 to build. It was located about five miles north of Stoy, Illinois at what is now the corner of East 1400th Avenue and North 525th Street.[386] The church is now demolished, but the cemetery is still extant. Coincidentally, I have many ancestors and relatives from my father's side of the family who worshiped and are buried there. Reverend Wallar also dedicated a new chapel south of Oblong in Crawford County in November 1883.[387]

Reverend Wallar continued to be busy in 1884. He was named a reserve delegate to the General Conference of the Methodist Episcopal Church, held in Philadelphia in May 1884, but based on newspaper mentions from around the time of the conference, I don't believe he attended.[388] On May 11th, he preached a thought-provoking sermon in Effingham. The subject was "The Sabbath was made for man, and not man for the Sabbbath:"

He [Wallar] *did not ask for the Puritan Sabbath, and severely condemmed* [sic] *the growing desecration of the modern sabbath. He believed in the complete cessation of the labor of the week, thereby giving a change of thought and furnishing rest. Those who labor in stores, shops, houses or offices need out-door scenes on the Sabbath, while the brawny muscle produced by severe physical labor needs to be inactive and quiet and use the mental powers to furnish needed rest. Above all and through all he urged the contemplation of the Creator and meditation on his goodness and his mercies. He showed conclusively that neither man nor beast can sustain health and secure best results and violate God's law requiring one day in seven for rest.*[389]

In August 1884, the Prohibition party held a ratification meeting to endorse the party's candidates. Reverend J.L. Wallar and others spoke, asking that the manufacture and sale of alcohol be prohibited, and denouncing both the Democrats and Republicans.[390] Shortly before the election Wallar stumped for the Prohibition party candidate in southern Illinois.[391]

At the Southern Illinois Conference in September of that year, he was a member of the Education committee, and a manager of the Missionary Society. In addition to being a Visitor to McKendree College, he was also one of two Visitors to Garrett Biblical Institute in Chicago, the first Methodist seminary in the Midwest. Founded in 1853, it is now called the Garrett-Evangelical Theological Seminary.[392] J.L. Wallar also conducted the devotional exercises for the Education Society and spoke at the Temperance Society meeting.[393]

Reverend J.L. Wallar was named a delegate to the Centennial Methodist Conference, held in Baltimore in December 1884. He left Effingham on Sunday November 30th and traveled to Zanesville, Ohio. Frances had been there some time visiting family. While there, the couple celebrated their 37th wedding anniversary with family and friends. Afterwards, he continued on to Baltimore.[394]

The conference in Baltimore was held at the grand Mount Vernon Place Methodist Episcopal Church from December 9-17, 1884. To celebrate the centenary of the Methodist Church, representatives from the Methodist Episcopal Church, Methodist Episcopal Church South, Methodist Protestant Church, African Methodist Episcopal Church, African Methodist Episcopal Zion Church, Colored Methodist Episcopal Church, and the Independent Methodist Church were in attendance. The usual business meetings and informative sessions were held, and the history of Methodism was celebrated. Moral questions such as temperance, the Lord's Day, divorce, Mormonism, and "popular amusements," such as theater, playing cards, and dancing were discussed at length.[395] Wallar later reported to the Vandalia District Methodist Episcopal Conference about "The Baltimore Centennial and its Results."[396]

The Wallars were back in Effingham before Christmas. This holiday season was especially fun for James and Frances, as son Herb, his wife Mollie, and two children, two-and-a-half year old Frances and six-week-old Harry Junior, visited from Fairfield, Illinois, sixty miles from Effingham.[397] This may have been the first time the elder Wallars met their new grandson, who was born in November 1884.[398]

Former president Ulysses S. Grant died on July 23, 1885. Communities throughout the United States held memorial services to honor the contributions of General Grant to the United States. On August 8th, Reverend J.L. Wallar spoke at a memorial service in Altamont, Illinois, about twelve miles from Effingham:

The address by Rev. J.L. Wallar, of Effingham, was to the point and listened to with marked attention. His theme throughout was that Gen. U.S. Grant was a common-sense man, a common-sense soldier, a common-sense General and a common-sense President. That in all his actions, whether private or official, he acted with common sense. In dealing with difficulties he always took a common-sense view. In all his answers to questions they were given in a plain, common way, was free from pretention or pomp, was a man of the people, was too large-hearted to think evil or do evil, even to his enemies; that he was truly of this great country, and belonged to every part, north, south, east and west. In his remarks he said that such tributes of respect and feeling had never been so universal as on

the present occasion; that there was at the same hour like services held in
every place of note in the United States—a concert of mourning...

The M.E. church here was very appropriately draped in mourning
on the occasion of the memorial services. Nearly 150 yards of black was
used. Back of the pulpit was black on which was letters of gold "Our
Hero is Dead," below was a portrait of Grant, to the side was a sword
sheathed in mourning with the name U.S. Grant in gold, then below all
was the moto "Let us have peace," surrounding all was the American flag
in mourning...[399]

The year 1886 began with welcome visits from daughter Etta Reeder
and her family, and son Charley from Fairfield, Illinois. By this time,
the Wallars had nine grandchildren and surely enjoyed watching them
grow.[400]

Once the children returned home, Reverend Wallar began
coordinating a series of lectures to be presented in February and March
to benefit the Methodist Episcopal church.[401] The cost for the entire
series of lectures was $1.00, and topics included "The Battle of Shiloh,"
"Christianity and Modern Civilization," and "Prison Life." [402]

James had many close friends in Effingham, including those from his
Masonic lodge. A February newspaper reported:

The Masonic lodge treated Rev. Wallar to a very agreeable surprise
Monday evening. The members with their wives and ladies assembled at
their hall in the evening, among whom was Rev. Wallar and wife, when
Mr. J.C. White in behalf of the lodge called Mr. Wallar to the East and
presented him with a handsome Knight Templar's suit. Rev. Wallar was
completely surprised, but with a very happy and feeling speech did justice to
the occasion. Mr. H.B. Kepley also made some appropriate remarks. Rev.
Wallar is now able to attend the Triennial Conclave of Knights Templars
at St. Louis this year.[403]

Though he had previously attended the New Orleans meeting in
1875, I suspect that his former Knights Templar uniform disappeared
during the tornado in Mount Carmel in 1877.

Unfortunately, it was soon determined that Frances Wallar was ill with cancer.[404] The newspaper reported that she was "dangerously ill" in early April.[405] The next year would be busy with visits from the Wallar children, Frances' sister, and well-meaning friends. By November, 1886, she was incapacitated by pain, and was taking "heavy doses of narcotics."[406]

It was nearly time for Reverend Wallar to be reassigned to a different church in a different town, and his friends in Effingham gathered for a garden party. Money was collected for the Wallar family.

The closing months of the three years' pastoral labors in our city of Rev. J.L. Wallar of the M.E. church were hallowed and made radiant Thursday evening by a lawn sociable at the residence of Mr. Phil. E. Crooker's, which was tendered to Rev. Wallar by some of our leading citizens and church people. Mr. Crooker's handsome residence and spacious grounds were crowded to their utmost capacity by the elite of our city who assembled without regard to religious creed to testify to the estimable Christian character and services of Mr. Wallar. By his able sermons, Christian faithfulness and kindly nature, Rev. Wallar has endeared himself to our whole city and it is with genuine regret that the conference regulations compel him to sever his pastoral connection with us. And we think we are not overestimating the quality of his gratitude when we say that in his recollections of happy pastoral and social relations the recollections of the congregation and citizens of Effingham will be among the brightest and the best. The net receipts were about $85. [407]

Another group of friends organized a:

...concert, musical and literary, [which] *will be given at The Temple next Monday evening, for the benefit of Rev. J.L. Wallar. A fine programme has been arranged. Admission ten cents. During the intermission refreshments, consisting of cream and cake, will be served. Mr. Sturdevant, a fine violinist of Casey, is expected to be present and give an exhibition of his skill with the bow.* [408]

Later in the summer J.L. Wallar was one of seven men chosen to be a delegate to the Prohibition party convention.[409] He wrote a letter to a newspaper editor stating that he "...expect[ed] to fight it out on this line until the traffic in strong drink is banished from the land."[410] He continued:

I am sorry you think the Methodist church is doing so little to secure prohibition. My opinion is, if you take the Methodist church out of the prohibition ranks there will not be enough left to frighten the enemy much...while I do preach prohibition, I do not denounce men for not voting with the prohibition party; neither do I urge them, in my sermons, to vote with that party, but I do urge them to vote and do everything else conscientiously. I would not sit and hear a Republican, or Democratic, party speech from the pulpit; therefore, I would not make a party speech of any kind from the pulpit myself. As an American citizen I have a right to talk party politics from the stump or platform. But as a preacher I have no right to preach party politics from the pulpit.[411]

13

CENTRALIA

In September 1886, Reverend Wallar learned that Centralia, Illinois would be his next station. He and Frances, who was well enough to travel on Monday October 4th, packed up their belongings and made the sixty-mile journey south and west to their new city.[412]

Centralia was a railroad town, named after the Illinois Central Railroad in the 1850s. Nearly 4000 people lived in the bustling town when the Wallars moved there. The Methodist Episcopal Church in Centralia at the time was built in 1854 and was located on the northeast corner of what are now Fifth and Poplar Streets.[413]

The Methodist Episcopal Church in Centralia, 1854-1903

Cornerstone on the current First United Methodist Church in Centralia, commemorating the church where Reverend Wallar preached.[414]

In mid-March 1887, Reverend Wallar became concerningly ill from "nervous prostration induced by over work in Sabbath services. He preached two very able and instructive services yesterday and taking a severe cold after the evening service was so prostrated this morning as to be unconscious. Dr. Hallam the physician says that serious results are not probable."[415] Two days later it was reported that, "Rev. J.L. Wallar is improving slowly, and was able to talk a little cheerfully, and pleasantly this morning,"[416] yet he was unable to preach the following Sunday.[417] It's likely he suffered from anxiety or depression, as the Effingham newspaper reported in April 1887:

We were in Centralia Monday and while there, in company with Virgil Wood, called on Rev. J.L. Wallar. Both Mr. Wood and ourselves were surprised when Rev. Wallar came to the door to receive us, for we supposed he was still bed-rid. He has, however, sufficiently recovered from his recent attack of nervousness to be up and about. We were glad to see him on the road to recovery. Mrs. Wallar, after having improved in health for three months, had just suffered a relapse. [418]

THE SWEET SINGERS!

A Senefit to the Dhoir of the Methodist
Episcopal Church will be
given at

Sadler's Opera House

WEDNESDAY EVENING,

May 6th

REV. J. L. WALLAR will de-
liver his Celebrated
Lecture on

PLUCK!

Which should be heard by all.

A FINE MUSICAL ENTERTAIN-
MENT has been prepared to delight
the audience.

Tickets for sale at the stores of
Z. T. Condit & Co., H. D. Buck,
Parkinson & Bailey's and
other places.

ADMISSION....25 CENTS.

ALL ARE INVITED.

Newspaper Advertisement[419]

Soon the Reverend was up and about, tending to ministerial duties such as preaching and performing weddings and funerals. In May of 1887, he participated in a fundraiser for the Methodist Episcopal Church choir, delivering a lecture on pluck. The following day's newspaper reported:

Rev. J.L. Wallar delivered his popular lecture on Pluck to a delighted audience. There was no show of pomp, demonstration or theoretical playing but a simple, energetic lecture which depended upon the substance for its merit. It was warmly applauded as elsewhere where it has been delivered. The audience was composed of about 250 to 300 of the best citizens of the city. A handsome sum of money was netted on the occasion for the benefit of the choir, for which they return their kindest thanks to the public.[420]

The next week, Wallar participated in a Grand Army of the Republic campfire, where he recounted his time in the army. The Grand Army of the Republic was a fraternal organization for Civil War veterans of the Union Army.

The camp fire held at the Grand Army Hall last night was a success in every respect, despite the hard and stormy weather in the early part of the evening. Rev. J.L. Wallar delivered a stirring address on army life, his experiences and thoughts before the war, and after the first shot was fired on Ft. Sumpter, on the men developed by the war from humble and unknown homes, &c. The latter part was devoted to scenes and incidents of the war which was humorous in the main and captivated the audience.[421]

Captain Wallar surely didn't tell *all* of his Civil War stories!

At the Centralia schools' commencement program on the following day, Reverend Wallar spoke to the students:

...and dealt forcibly and earnestly with subjects affecting them. The sermon displayed great depth of thought and presented ideas which deserved the careful consideration of all. His theme was that there is a point

of power within the reach of everyone, which is often not reached. His logic went to prove that those persons who are not making themselves felt in the affairs of the world, are out of their sphere. His discourse was replete with profound logic and was delivered with much force and earnestness. [422]

Reverend Wallar was certainly a dynamic and impactful speaker. Because of his impact on the Methodist community in southern Illinois, he was honored with a Doctor of Divinity degree at the 1887 commencement exercises at McKendree College in Lebanon, Illinois.[423] A preacher of more than ordinary ability, indeed.

While James kept busy with weddings, funerals, church benefits, weekly sermons, and commencements, his wife of nearly forty years remained at home benefitting from the loving care of family and friends. By early June, Frances was on her death bed, unable to eat.[424] On Sunday June 26, 1887 at 7:00 p.m., Frances Elizabeth (Gammon) Wallar died after suffering with cancer for fifteen months. An embellished obituary appeared on the front page of the Centralia Daily Sentinel the following day:

BEYOND THE VALE
Mrs. J. L. Wallar Sinks Quietly to Rest at Seven O'clock Yesterday Evening
Funeral From the M. E. Church, in This City at Three p.m. Tomorrow
"Beyond the smiling and the weeping I soon shall be"

For sometime past anxious friends have stood around the bedside of the late Mrs. J. L. Wallar, and tenderly ministered to her every want; anxious hearts have anticipated her wishes, and willing hands have supplied them. Each day, sympathizing friends have made inquiry, and it was with faces touched with sadness, that they turned away when assured that she was gradually sinking.

Yesterday evening, as the sun was slowly sinking to rest beneath the western horizon; at the time when the earth was bathed in a flood of mellow light, when the golden rays of the setting sun lit up the heavens, in their

*good night kiss to this world of ours, the spirit of Mrs. Wallar took its flight.
Softly and tenderly the watchers turned away and the living and the dead
were left together. A few moments later the deep and solemn tones of the
bell announced to our people that another of the tried and true had been
summoned to come up higher, and receive the glorious reward for a faithful,
well spent life.*

*There were moistened eyes and saddened hearts in many homes in this
city as the news was rapidly borne from house to house, that Mrs. Wallar
had been called away. While she had not lived many years among us, yet
she was possessed of friends, who felt, in her suffering, much of the pain that
was hers, and whose only consolation in the hour of grief is in the thought
that "as we suffer, so shall we rejoice".*

*To Mr. Wallar and bereaved family the SENTINEL extends its
deepest and tenderest sympathies, and can only hope that the sustaining
grace which was given to the departed one, will be given to them, and that
He, who tempers the wind to the shorn lamb, will fold about them the
protecting arms of love, and may they feel that by this sacrifice, made on
earth, they have a stronger tie to the upper and brighter kingdom. The
funeral will take place from the First Methodist church in this city at three
o'clock tomorrow afternoon. At the request of Mrs. Wallar, the services will
be conducted by the Rev. J. T. Pender, of Mt. Carmel.*

*Frances E. Gammon was born in Zanesville, Ohio, March 10th, 1830.
She was united in marriage with Rev. J. L. Wallar, Dec. 4th, 1847. She was
converted and united with the M. E. church, in January 1848. She came
to Illinois and settled on a farm in Richland county, in the fall of 1864.
Her husband joined the Southern Illinois Conference, in this city, and also
in this church, in 1866. She then entered upon the duties of an itinerant
preachers wife, going to the following appointments: Georgetown, Newton,
Robinson, Sumner, Carmi, Cairo, Mt. Carmel, Fairfield, Mt. Carmel
district, with residence at Enfield, Effingham, and last to Centralia, where
she died June 26th, 1887, aged 57 years, three months, and 16 days.*

*She was the mother of seven children, three of whom have preceded her
to the better land. Mrs. Wallar was an earnest christian and a faithful
worker in the cause. To her, old time, came round, each year bringing
whiter frosts to glint her hair; came with the changing scenes of day and*

*night; with winter's storms and summer's calm, came with sunny peace and
backward dreams of age, until one day the eye of the relentless old reaper
rested upon her, standing right in the swath, amid the golden corn, the sweep
of that noiseless scythe, that never turns its edge, and the cycle of a life was
ended.*[425]

Frances Wallar's funeral was held on Tuesday, June 28th:

*Long before the hour of three yesterday afternoon, the large auditorium
at the M.E. church was filled to its utmost capacity with residents of our city
who had gathered to witness the last sad rites over the remains of Mrs. J.L.
Wallar. To many in that throng, Mrs. Wallar had become endeared by the
never ending ties of Christian love and friendship, and it was noticeable
that, as they sat in that crowded church, tendering the last tribute of respect
from the living to the dead, their eyes grew dim with tears, and more
than one person was heard to give expression to the grief and sorrow that
burdened their hearts.*

*Rev. Mr. Pender delivered an interesting sermon, dwelling at length
upon the beauties of a true Christian character and referring, in well
selected language, to the exemplary life of Mrs. Wallar as had been
evidenced by her daily walks.*

*At the conclusion of the services at the church, that vast concourse of
people followed the remains to their temporary resting place in the vault
in the city cemetery, and as the sadly, solemn words of "earth to earth"
were spoken, turned away, feeling that one more of the faithful had been
gathered home.*[426]

The Centralia Democrat newspaper carried this fine tribute to Mrs.
Wallar:

*At her home in this city, Sunday afternoon, June 26, 1887, Mrs. J.L.
Wallar, aged fifty-seven years, three months and sixteen days.*

*For many long, weary months Mrs. Wallar has been an invalid
confined to her couch and compelled to bear the afflictions which often fall
to the lot of human beings. This affliction she bore with a Christian spirit*

of forbearance, patience and long suffering, which gave evidence to the fact that He who tempers the wind to the shorn lamb gives His followers strength to bear the burdens imposed upon them.

The kindly ministrations of her family and friends, whose every efforts was put forth to make her sufferings less painful and to add to her comfort, as well as the skill of the medical profession were unavailing to restore her health, and the only cure was in death. Her husband's family and friends, though overcome with grief at the loss of their wife, mother and friend, find sweet consolation in the assurance that her soul has found a haven of rest, where the sufferings of this life will meet their reward in eternal happiness.

Mrs. Wallar was a woman whose life was full of good works. She was an ideal wife and mother. Kind, thoughtful and considerate of the wishes of others, she made all those with whom she came in contact happier because they knew her.

She was married to Rev. J.L. Wallar Dec. 4, 1847, and since that time has helped him bear the strife and turmoil of life, and softened the hardships which fall to the share of every man. Seven children blessed their union, three of whom were awaiting to welcome their mother on the other shore, while three sons and one daughter gathered with their father at the grave to bid farewell for a brief period to their loving and beloved mother.

The assistance of sympathizing friends was offered with a generosity which betokened the esteem in which the deceased and the bereaved ones are held by their friends in Centralia.

The funeral services were held in the M.E. church Monday afternoon. The church was crowded with mourning friends who gathered to pay their last tribute to the one whom they loved in life and revered in death. Rev. J.T. Pender, of Mt. Carmel, conducted the services with the assistance of Rev. E.C. Evers of Effingham. The sermon was an eloquent and pathetic eulogy, offered in an earnest, heartfelt manner. Rev. Pender had been an old friend of Mrs. Wallar, and it was at her request that he delivered the funeral sermon.

At the conclusion of the services the remains were taken to the city cemetery, followed by a long line of mourners and friends. The body was placed in the vault, there to remain until some future time, when it will be removed to its permanent resting place.

Quite a number of relatives, ministers and friends from other cities came to Centralia to attend the funeral. [427]

Shortly after the death of Frances Wallar, James and his niece Belle Shaw traveled to Enfield to visit friends.[428] Whether Belle had relocated from Marietta, Ohio to care for her Aunt Frances during her illness, or to keep house for James after Frances' death is unknown. Belle, the oldest daughter of James' half-sister Rebecca, lived with her Uncle James until her untimely death on April 14, 1888.[429]

Oddly, the health of Miss Belle Shaw was a matter of community interest. On February 2, 1888, a Centralia newspaper printed a notice that the regular Methodist church service would be held, but the church bell would not be rung "on account of the serious illness of Miss Shaw." [430] The following day, Reverend Wallar asked that his friends not call at the parsonage to ask about Miss Shaw, her nervous system not being able to handle the stress. Instead, notices were "displayed on the gate morning, noon and night" updating the public on Belle's condition.[431]

Reverend Wallar's health was also a matter of public importance. The February 6, 1888 Centralia Sentinel reported:

Rev. J.L. Waller was taking supper with Prof. Gay Waters, Saturday evening, and while there received word that his son at Belmont, was dangerously sick. The news, connected with his own recent sickness, and the present condition of Miss Shaw, was too severe a strain on his nervous system and he completely gave way, and is now quite sick himself.[432]

The February 8th newspaper reported that both James and Belle were feeling better,[433] but the minister was still unable to return to the pulpit until after March 10th.[434] On February 23, 1888, a small statement in the newspaper announced that, "the jury decided that Miss Shaw is insane and should be sent to the asylum. It is believed that she can be restored to health in a short time."[435]

I don't think Belle went to the asylum. Her younger sister Jennie Rech cared for Belle for ten weeks before her death, and that timeline points to Jennie's arrival in Centralia in late February.[436] In mid-March, the *Centralia Daily Sentinel* noted that "Miss Shaw is reported as being on the road to a sure recovery. This will be news that will be hailed with joy by her many friends."[437] Sadly, it seems she quickly took a turn. On April 2nd, "Miss Belle Shaw is still in a very dangerous condition. She has not taken any nourishment, save by injection, for two weeks. She is not expected to live through the week."[438]

DIED—At the M.E. parsonage in Centralia, Ill., Saturday, April 14, 1888, at 11:20 p.m., Miss Bell Shaw, niece of Rev. J.L. Wallar, in the 29th year of her age. The funeral services were held at the M.E. church this forenoon at ten o'clock, the sermon being preached by Rev. V.C. Evars, of Effingham. The remains were followed to the cemetery by a large concourse of sorrowing and sympathetic friends. The casket containing the remains of Mrs. J.L. Wallar, which has been in the McCord-Clark vault since her death last summer, was taken out and the two caskets buried in a beautiful lot. Miss Shaw has been a sufferer for many long weeks, the particulars of which our citizens are well acquainted. The last few weeks, however, she refused to take food or nourishment of any kind, and gradually wasted away, and when death relieved her she passed away without a struggle or even the movement of a muscle; the heart ceased to beat; the breath stopped, and she was no more in this world.[439]

Shortly after Belle's death, Dr. Wallar accompanied his niece Jennie to her home in Marietta, Ohio.[440] James then spent several days visiting friends before traveling to the General Conference of the Methodist Episcopal Church, held, in part, at the Metropolitan Opera House in New York City from May 1st to May 31st. At this conference, James was one of three ministerial delegates from the Southern Illinois Conference.[441]

THE METROPOLITAN OPERA HOUSE
1884

The Metropolitan Opera House[442]

It's unlikely that Reverend Wallar had ever seen a place as magnificent as the Metropolitan Opera House. Completed just five years earlier, the Metropolitan Opera House was the largest opera house in the world, spanning the entire block between 39th and 40th Streets along the west side of Broadway. The Metropolitan Opera House was funded by nouveau riche New York families such as the Roosevelts, Morgans, and Vanderbilts who had been snubbed by the existing Academy of Music patrons in a Gilded Age opera house war. By 1886, the Metropolitan Opera House had become the place to see and be seen, and the Academy of Music was forced to resort to vaudeville shows to keep the doors open.[443]

The General Conference was held every four years, with delegates from all over the world in attendance. While general sessions were held on the main floor of the opera house each morning, nearby churches were used for afternoon committee sessions, as the opera house was not large enough to accommodate all the meetings. The election of bishops, temperance, and the role of women in the church were some of the business items addressed at the Conference.[444] Reverend Wallar was back in Centralia on Friday, June 1st and preached the next Sunday.[445]

July 1888 started with wedding bells, as James Wallar married Mrs. Jeannette McCord, a well-to-do Centralia widow, in St. Louis, Missouri.

Yesterday it broke loose in this city that the minister [Wallar] *and Mrs. McCord had "gone off and got married," but it was some time before our people would believe the report, but nevertheless that did not hinder the news from spreading and in one hour's time it was all over the city, and was crowding some portions of the country rather briskly. The following, clipped from today's* St. Louis Republic, *explains itself:*

Despite the heat and all-pervading atmosphere of "Independence" yesterday a love-lorn couple were found willing to defy the one and renounce the other in the persons of Rev. Dr. J.L. Wallar, pastor of the First Methodist church of Centralia, Ill., and Mrs. Jeannette E. McCord, also of the strawberry emporium of Egypt. The ceremony took place yesterday afternoon at 3 o'clock at the Planters' House, Rev. Dr. B. St. James Fry officiating. Mrs. E.S. Condit, of Centralia, accompanied the bridal party to this city and gave the bride away. The young couple is expected home tonight, and no doubt will be given a cordial reception. The Sentinel *says "Glory, we're glad it's true," and wishes them many happy 4th of Julys...*[446]

The newlyweds quickly adapted to their new life together. Sermons were written and preached, weddings and funerals performed, and the new Mrs. Wallar managed the household. She owned a residence and leased storefronts to businesses on the northeast corner of Broadway and Locust streets in Centralia.[447] The couple may have lived in her home, or perhaps they lived in the parsonage. Luckily for James, his son Herb lived in Centralia with his wife and four children. The youngest, Florence Jeanette Wallar, was born on August 11, 1889, and was likely named for her step-grandmother.[448] James' sons Fay and Charley lived in Bellmont and Fairfield, respectively, and daughter Etta lived in Newton, so none of the children were too far away. The newspaper often mentioned that James was visiting a child, or a child was visiting Centralia.

James L. Wallar was Grand Chaplain of the Grand Royal Arch Chapter of Illinois from 1887-1889.[449] He was also busy with district church meetings and his Knights Templar work, even travelling to Terre Haute, Indiana, Washington, D.C., New York, and Chicago in 1889.[450]

On his way home from the East Coast in October 1889, James passed through Johnstown, Pennsylvania, which only five months earlier had been destroyed by floodwaters from the failed South Fork dam. The Centralia newspaper reported, "Rev. Wallar has presented us with a piece of concrete brick, picked up by him at Johnstown. He says that the newspapers never exaggerated the desolation wrought there."[451]

Later in October, at the annual meeting of the Southern Illinois Conference of the Methodist Episcopal Church, James Wallar was made supernumerary, meaning he retired from active, full-time ministry.[452] He was in his mid- to late-sixties. If James and Jeannette were living in the parsonage, they would have moved out since a new minister would have been assigned to the Centralia church at this time. James' retirement proved to be temporary, however; in November of 1889, Reverend Wallar agreed to preach on the Sabbath at McLeansboro, Illinois "until other arrangements can be made."[453] The McLeansboro Methodist Episcopal church in Hamilton County, Illinois was a 46 by 80 feet, two-story brick church, built in 1870.[454] Reverend Wallar travelled the 45 miles from Centralia to McLeansboro on Saturdays by train and returned home on Mondays. His ministerial status was changed from supernumerary to effective (meaning again a regularly assigned preacher) at the Southern Illinois Conference in September 1891.[455]

James kept busy in his semi-retirement. Until his death in 1900, the *Centralia Sentinel* was littered with tidbits regarding his and Mrs. Wallar's health, their travels, marriages and funerals officiated by the Reverend, guest preaching stints, motivational speeches given, and the social activities of Mrs. Wallar.

In December 1889, Dr. J.L. Wallar was elected Generalissimo of the Cyrene Commandery, No. 23, Knights Templar.[456] This position was second in command, assisting the Commander and presiding if the Commander was absent.[457]

The August 8, 1890 Centralia *Daily Sentinel* reported that, "Dr. J.L. Wallar is a candidate for State Senator instead of the Legislature. He don't run for small offices. He leaves them for the little fellows,"[458] but he must have had a change in heart, because later in the month it was reported that, "Dr. J.L. Wallar declines to accept the nomination for State Senator on the Prohibition Ticket.[459]

Attesting to his charisma, wit, and popularity, the Centralia newspaper published this amusing anecdote:

The other day Dr. Wallar was passing along the street and met an Irishman. Before he reached the emigrant from the Emerald Isle, the latter squared himself in the center of the sidewalk, lifted his hat and made a most graceful bow.

The Doctor saw that he was a tramp but fairly well dressed and duly sober, and hesitated a moment to see what he had to say.

The Irishman, with many gestures and facial expressions, said, "'Tis said that intelligence and goodness are stamped upon the human countenance."

"Yes," replied Mr. Wallar, "that is what they say," and started to pass on, but the Irishman says, "Hold, that is not all I have to say."

Then he hesitated a moment, and, eying Mr. Wallar very closely, remarked:

"I am busted. I want to go to Du Quoin."

"Well," replied the Doctor, "that is a very unhandy condition to be in, but as I am not operating the railroad I can't get you to Du Quoin."

The Irishman gave the Doctor another optical survey, and very cooly replied:

"I was right in the intelligence part, but I am afraid I was mistaken as to the goodness."

That was too rich for Mr. Wallar, so he handed the fellow a nickel. He held the coin in the palm of his hand, and, after another of his momentary studies said:

"And how far do you think that nickle [sic] will take me?"[460]

In the late winter and spring of 1891, Reverend J.L. Wallar lectured in several locations in Southern Illinois, sharing his thoughts supporting the woman's right to vote.[461] Not all Methodists supported suffrage, but the Methodist church, in general, was a leader in allowing women to participate in the works of the church as lay members.[462] Wallar was publicly thanked by Centralia's Equal Suffrage Association for his "very able lecture."[463] The next year, at Southern Illinois Conference, J.L. Wallar was appointed Counsel for the Church.[464]

The crowd at the Chicago World's Fair, July 4, 1893[465]

From May through October 1893, Chicago hosted the World's Columbian Exposition in honor of Christopher Columbus' 1492 visit to North America. This exposition, also called the Chicago World's Fair, featured cultural and scientific attractions from over forty countries, amusements such as the first Ferris wheel, and full-sized replicas of the *Niña*, the *Pinta*, and the *Santa Maria*. The exposition buildings were constructed in Jackson Park and on Midway Plaisance, south of downtown Chicago. The exposition's Palace of Fine Arts currently houses Chicago's Museum of Science and Industry and the exposition's amusements were on the Midway Plaisance, lending the word "midway" to our current use for a group of carnival rides and games at a fair. James and Jeanette Wallar spent three weeks in Chicago in the summer of 1893 and attended the Chicago World's Fair. A Centralia newspaper reported: "He was there on the 4th [of July], and while all was grand, it was particularly so when 200,000 voices joined in singing "America" and other National airs."[466]

In 1893, Reverend Wallar was still preaching part time in McLeansboro. He was on the Conference Sabbath Observance committee and addressed the Temperance Society. He was also appointed to a committee relative to Wesley Hospital.[467] Wesley Hospital opened in Chicago in 1888, and after a series of consolidations and mergers became what is now known as Northwestern Memorial Hospital in 1972.[468]

In 1894, J.L. Wallar served on the Public Worship committee, a committee on the "Moral and Religious Condition of the Army and Navy," and was a Visitor to Garrett Biblical Institute. He was listed as a new Supernumerary Preacher, meaning he was again retired from full-time preaching.[469]

Not willing to let grass grow under his feet, James Wallar and a partner started a new business venture. For many weeks, the Centralia newspaper ran an ad for this new business: "Wallar & Noleman is the name of a new real estate firm in this city, Dr. J.L. Wallar and F.F. Noleman having formed a co-partnership for the purpose of buying and selling real estate and loaning money. That is a firm that speaks for itself."[470] In the course of this work, "Dr. Wallar is learning to manipulate the typewriter. He can manip all right, but his speed is not yet sufficiently swift to heat the bearing of the machine."[471] The last notice in the newspaper for this real estate and mortgage business appeared in the December 31, 1896 *Centralia Daily Sentinel*.[472]

I can imagine James walking uptown every morning and chatting with passersby and making the rounds of the various shops and offices in Centralia. Perhaps daily visits to the newspaper office are why so many anecdotes about his life appear in print. The newspaper mentions, "You will find in the park almost every day the following gentlemen engaged in philosophical discussion: Rev. Dr. J.L. Wallar, Prof. Gay Waters, Elder Clark and Prof. Patrick. These gentlemen are in the habit of receiving visitors from time to time at their meetings."[473] One day in July 1895, James kept busy directing pedestrians away from the newly set pavement on Broadway Street, lest they leave their footprints![474]

James' thirty-four-year-old daughter-in-law, Mollie, husband of Herb Wallar, died on June 20, 1895 in Albion, Illinois of tuberculosis.[475] James became ill while in Albion for the funeral and nearly died. Mrs. Wallar, who was preparing for a pleasure trip to Carlsbad, was telegraphed for, and she hurried to Albion.[476] James was able to return home to Centralia in early July. [477]

In autumn 1895, Reverend Wallar was continued in the Supernumerary relation.[478] In 1896, he was changed from supernumerary to superannuated.[479] He remained in superannuated status in 1899.[480] A superannuated minister is one who is no longer able to preach by reason of impaired health.

In October 1895, James was chosen to be chaplain of the Order of High Priesthood at the Masonic conference in Chicago.[481] Two years later, Reverend and Mrs. Wallar were still healthy enough for travel and again attended the Masonic convention in Chicago.[482]

At a celebration held at the Methodist Episcopal church in honor of the birthday of Abraham Lincoln, James gave a short address in which he "claimed that Lincoln was a greater man than Washington, and gave the reason of this opinion that Lincoln was preeminently and wholly an American product, whereas Washington was reared under British influences and surroundings."[483]

Summary of Reverend James L. Wallar's pastoral assignments

1	Georgetown, IL	1866
2	Newton, IL	1867-1868
3	Robinson, IL	1869-1870
4	Sumner, IL	1871
5	Carmi, IL	1872
6	Cairo, IL	1873-1874
7	Mount Carmel, IL	1875-1877
8	Fairfield, IL	1878
	Presiding Elder	1879-1882
9	Effingham, IL	1883-1885
10	Centralia, IL	1886-1888
11	McLeansboro, IL	1889-1891

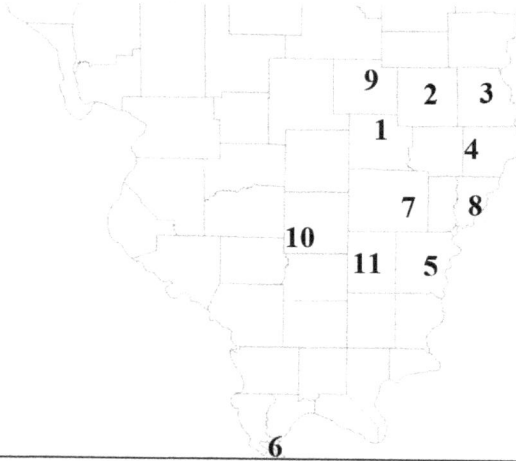

Map of Wallar's pastoral assignments[484]

In mid-July 1898, William Jennings Bryan, former candidate for the U.S. presidency and Marion County, Illinois native, passed through Centralia with his newly formed regiment of soldiers on their way to Florida to fight in the Spanish-American War. Not unexpectedly, James Wallar had a hand in the reception:[485]

Grand, patriotic old Centralia, she did herself proud in showing honor to the boys who have answered their country's call and announced a willingness to give up their lives if need be for the defense of that glorious emblem of liberty, the most beautiful of all flags.

As in the days of the sixties, so today Centralia is second to no city in showing her respect for the soldier boys, as was demonstrated last night as never before. Never on so short a notice and with so little advertising was such a monster crowd got together and held so patiently in spite of the long delayed train that brought the first detachment in. It was originally expected that the first train would arrive not after than 7 o'clock, but later the hour was fixed at 8:15, only to be put off from time to time, as the train lost time at every move, until 10:30, but when it did get here finally the crowd was well repaid for their waiting, and those who went home were not missed at all.

Every available place near the Central depot was not only covered, but crowded; at least 5,000 persons being present. And when it came to the reception it mattered not that the boys were led by one that Centralians as a majority did not see fit to honor with their votes in '96, it was the idea now championed by their leader and the boys that caught the people, and in honoring the Bryan regiment we but showed that when it comes to the interests of our country we know no Democrats or Republicans—it was not Bryan, but a Marion county boy who was leading to the front a brave and gallant command.

Such gatherings as that of last night do honor to a city and have a greater tendency than all else to help to build up a country's greatness and to instill in the minds of all a love for the flag.

As early as six o'clock the crowd commenced to gather at the depot, and it steadily increased till nine o'clock rolled around, though the crowd was distributed along the streets near by till train time. As it was impossible to get any idea of what time the train would stay, and it was known that part of that time must be taken up with supper, few arrangements were perfected. The band had been hired, the anvils and powder got out to do the heavy noise work, and a floral offering secured with Dr. Wallar's services to make the presentation and there the arrangements ended. Col. Bryan was hurried from the car to the dining room and then brought out on the platform arranged for the presentation, and made a short talk that was to the point and was heartfelt. After that in some well chosen remarks Dr. Wallar presented the flowers, and the Col. was taken in to supper.

It was impossible for near all the crowd to hear much of the talks, but all will now say that Dr. Wallar voiced the sentiments of all when he said that Centralia wished Col. Bryan and his regiment all the good luck possible and that every man of them might return home when the war is over, all bringing fresh honors. After supper the Col. went to his car and for quite a while stood on the steps and shook hands with those who could manage to get close enough to reach him. It was near twelve o'clock when the train pulled out and another pulled up, but still the crowd was a dense one.

Col. Bryan was in good health and fine spirits, and he has a fine body of men with him. Had the train been here in daytime the crowd would have been larger and the sightseers would have enjoyed the occasion more.

The health of the Wallars continued to be a concern, and was often mentioned in the newspaper. In February 1900, it was noted that,

Chas. M. Wallar was over to Centralia Sunday to visit his father, Dr. J.L. Wallar, who is in poor health and it is not expected that he will recover. Dr. Wallar is now in his eighty-third year and his many friends here will regret to learn that his health is so poor and that he is not likely to live much longer.[486]

By summer, James had recovered, and he and Jeannette traveled to Chicago, planning to "visit some of the northern resorts," and intended to return to Centralia in early October.[487] One of their stops was Sturgeon Bay, Wisconsin, a resort area in Door County.[488] James was home by September 24th, but Jeannette became ill on the vacation and did not accompany her husband back to Centralia. James returned to Chicago on October 8th to be with Jeannette until she was able to travel home a week later.[489]

Sadly, the couple's time together was nearing its end. Two months later, James would be dead.[490]

14

DEATH

After lunch on Saturday, December 15, 1900, James left his home on Broadway Street and strolled down Locust Street, admiring the shop windows which were decorated for Christmas. Noticing that his friend Jacob Severns was working in his insurance agency, he entered the office and took a seat. Sadly, this would be his final stop.

Dr. J.L. Wallar dropped dead at 3:30 this afternoon, while sitting in a chair in Jacob Severns' office, on south Locust street. He was talking in his usual way and fell over and expired in a moment. He has seemingly been in his usual health for the last few days, but has been subject to attacks for some time, and this proved to be the fatal one.[491]

The *Centralia Democrat* published this obituary:

REV. DR. WALLAR
Mechanic, Farmer, Lawyer, Soldier, Minister, and Mason

The sudden death of Dr. James Lee Wallar took from Centralia a man who was universally respected and liked by all who knew him. A great man of the old school, always liberal in his views and courteous to all with whom he came in contact, an honorable man who had completed an honorable career and who took great interest in the affairs of to-day.

Dr. Wallar was born near Burlington, Vt., November 24, 1817, and spent his early days on the New England farm and learning his trade as a marble cutter. In 1836 he moved to Zanesville, Ohio, where he took up the study of law and was admitted to the bar and gained an enviable reputation as an attorney. In 1847 he was married to Frances Elizabeth Gammon and to them were born seven children, four of whom are still living. Mrs. Wallar died in this city June 26, 1887.

In the first call for troops for the civil war Mr. Wallar enlisted and was elected captain of Co. B, 18th Ohio Vol. Inf., and served in this capacity through three month's service. Then he organized Co. A., Second West Virginia Cavalry and before the three years' service had expired he had been made a Major and on re-enlisting for the veteran service he reached the rank of Lieutenant Colonel and was mustered out in this rank. He was a member of Wallace Post No. 55, G.A.R.

At the close of the war he came to Illinois and engaged in farming for a few years and then entered the ministry of the M.E. church.

In Masonic circles Dr. Wallar gained considerable prominence but he held no membership in the local lodges. His membership was as follows: Louisville Lodge, No. 196 Louisville A.F. and A.M.; Fairfield Chapter, Fairfield R.A.M.; Cairo Commandery No. 13, Cairo K.T. He was Past Grand Prelate of the Grand Commandery of Illinois and had filled offices in the Grand Chapter of Illinois.

Mr. Wallar went into the service of the M.E. church in 1866. He was admitted on trial and sent to Georgetown. In 1867 he was sent to Newton and in 1868 was admitted to full connection. In '69 he was sent to Robinson and the next year made an elder. Then he was assigned as follows: 1871 Sumner; '72 Carmi; '73 Cairo; '76 Mt. Carmel; '77 Fairfield; '78 Presiding Elder of the Mt. Carmel district; '82 Effingham; '86 Centralia.

After three years here he went on the retired list but continued to preach at McLeansboro for five years, making his home in this city. During his pastorate here his first wife died and July 4, 1888, he was married to Mrs. Jeanette E. McCord, who survives him.

Four children survive him. They are: Dr. F.K. Wallar, Mt. Carmel; Herbert Wallar, Robinson; Charles M. Wallar, Fairfield and Mrs. Etta Reeder, Edgewood.[492]

The Southern Illinois Conference of the Methodist Episcopal Church eulogized James Wallar at their next conference:

James L. Wallar was born near Burlington, Vermont, November 24, 1819, and died at Centralia, Illinois, December 15, 1900. His early life was spent on a farm in Vermont, and in learning the trade of a marble cutter.

In 1836 he moved to Zanesville, Ohio, where he read law, and was admitted to the bar. He practiced his profession until the beginning of the Civil War.

He was married in January, 1847, to Frances Elizabeth Gammon. Seven children were born of this union. His wife died at Centralia, Ill., June 26, 1887. On July 4, 1888, he was married to Mrs. Jeannette E. McCord, of Centralia, Ill. At the first call for troops at the beginning of the Civil War he enlisted in the three months' service. He was elected Captain of Company H, Eighteenth Ohio Volunteer Infantry. In August 1863, he raised Company A of the Second West Virginia Cavalry for three years. He was promoted to the rank of Major. As a veteran he was re-elected and promoted to the rank of Lieutenant Colonel, which he held to the close of the war.

Soon after the close of the war he moved to Illinois and settled in Richland County, where he engaged in farming. In a few years he entered the ministry; was received on trial in the Southern Illinois Conference at Centralia, in 1866; he was received into full connection at DuQuion, Ill., in 1868, and ordained by Bishop E. S. Janes. He was ordained elder in 1870 by Bishop Simpson. Brother Wallar served the following charges: Georgetown, Newton, Robinson, Sumner, Carmi, Cairo, Mt. Carmel and Fairfield. At the session of the Conference at Salem in 1879 he was appointed presiding elder of the Mt. Carmel district, which he served for four years. In 1883 he was appointed pastor of Effingham station, which he served for three years, and Centralia the following three years. At the close of his pastorate at Centralia he received a supernumerary relation, which he held to the close of his life. By the appointment of the presiding elder he was pastor at McLeansboro for five years.

He was a delegate to the General Conference, which was held in New York City in 1888. McKendree College honored him by the degree of Doctor of Divinity. Brother Wallar was a preacher of more than ordinary ability. He was especially helpful to young men. He was a true man and a faithful servant of the church. He rests from his labors and his works follow him. Peace to his memory.[493]

In McLeansboro, his last preaching post, a memorial service was held. "A large picture of him was appropriately draped and hung on the pulpit, and the service was very largely attended."[494]

The Mascoutah Herald called James Wallar, "one of the widest known divines in central southern Illinois."[495]

James Wallar's funeral was well attended by family, friends, and Southern Illinois ministers. The funeral was held at 2:00 p.m. on December 20, 1900 at the Methodist Episcopal church in Centralia. The attendees sang hymns, prayed, and listened to readings and eulogies from other ministers. Businesses in Centralia closed in honor of James' funeral. A search for an official record of James Wallar's death in the Marion County, Illinois Death Register books was unproductive.[496]

The "suitable tombstone over his grave" in Elmwood Cemetery in Centralia was generously paid for by wife Jeannette Wallar. The couple chose to be buried by their first spouses—she with Dr. David H. McCord after her death on September 30, 1908, and James with Frances.[497] According to cemetery records on the City of Centralia website, James Wallar purchased eight plots here on April 17, 1888. [498]This was only days after the death of niece Florence Belle Shaw.

While keen to embellish or alter facts about his early life, he was an outstanding minister and productive member of his various communities—towns, churches, and social organizations. It's almost as though he lived two lives—one before April 26, 1864—the date of his dismissal from the United States Army—and one afterward. He was generally well-liked and highly regarded. Undeniably intelligent and well-read, James was a passionate life-long learner, willing to listen, contemplate, and reconsider. He was a helper—there for anyone in need. His was a life well lived.

DIED.

Rev. James Lee Wallar, D. D.

Born November 24th, 1817.
Died in Centralia, Illinois December 15th, 1900.
Aged 83 years and 21 days.

The funeral services will be held from the M. E. church Monday,
December 17th, 1900, at two o'clock p. m.

Friends of the family are invited.

GReat GRaNDaD WallaR

Death notice for James Lee Wallar[499]

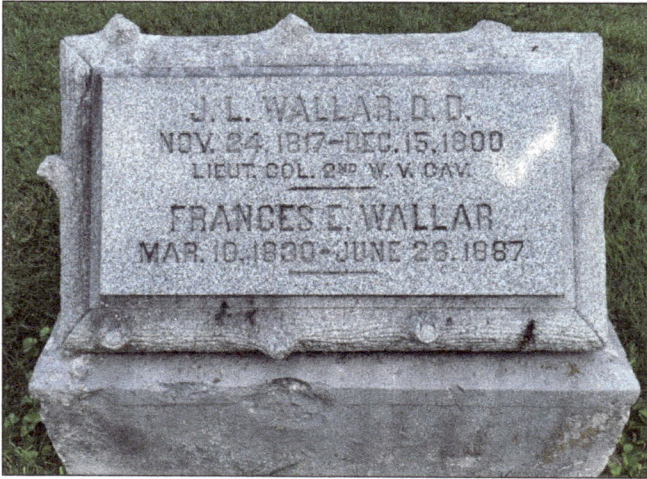

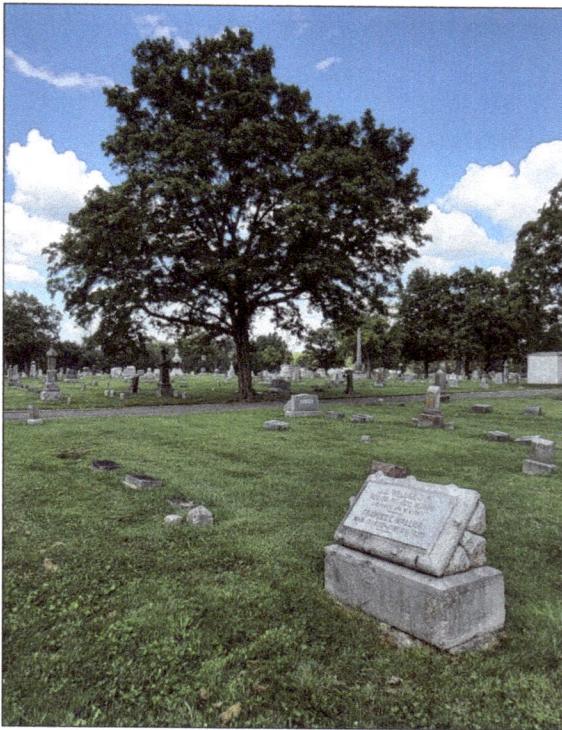

**Grave marker of J.L. Wallar and Frances E. Wallar,
Elmwood Cemetery, Centralia, Illinois**[500]

Undated photo from obituary in Methodist Episcopal journal[501]

THE AGED CHRISTIAN.

BY DR. J. L. WALLAR.

The vigor of youth has departed
  The strength of my manhood has fled;
The silvery touch of time's finger
  Has placed a white wreath on my head.

I am nearing the bank of the river,
  I can hear the dark waters roll;
But I'm happy and shall be forever,
  For Jesus abides in my soul.

I linger again in the twilight
  To press once again to my heart
The form of one whom I promised
  To love until death shall us part

I must bid adieu to my loved ones—
  This thought fills my moments with gloom,
But I shall hail them again on the morrow
  Where flowers eternally bloom.

There, undimmed by mists of earth's sorrows,
  Their faces with glory shall shine;
For all that is earthly shall perish
  And that which endures be divine.

There, on pinions immortal, together
  We'll join with the sanctified host
In worshipping Him who hath bred us
  And died to redeem us when lost.

Together we'll seek the solution
  Of the infinite problem of love;
Together we'll join in the anthems
  Which ring through the arches above.

No, I fear not to enter the river,
  Though its dark waters threateningly roll,
For Jesus is walking beside me:
  Praise the Lord, praise the Lord, oh, my soul.

Presented by H. H. Wallar.

WRitten By GReat GRanDaD
  WaLLaR.

Poem written by J.L. Wallar[502]

THE AGED CHRISTIAN, by Dr. J.L. Wallar

The vigor of youth has departed,
The strength of my manhood has fled;
The silvery touch of time's finger,
Has placed a white wreath on my head.
I am nearing the bank of the river,
I can hear the dark waters roll;
But I'm happy, and shall be forever,
For Jesus abides in my soul.
I linger a while in the twilight,
To press once again to my heart;
The form of one whom I promised,
To love until death shall us part.
I must now bid adieu to my loved ones,
This thought fills my moments with gloom;
But I shall hail them again on the morrow;
Where flowers eternally bloom.
There, undimmed by the mists of earth's sorrows,
Their faces with glory shall shine;
For all that is earthly shall perish,
And that which endures be divine.
There, on pinions immortal, together,
We'll join with the sanctified host;
In worshiping Him who hath bred us,
And died to redeem us when lost.
Together we'll seek the solution,
Of the infinite problem of love;
Together we'll join in the anthems,
Which ring through the arches above.
No, I fear not to enter the river,
Though its dark waters threateningly roll;
For Jesus is walking beside me,
Praise the Lord, praise the Lord, O, my soul.

15

Some Descendants of James Lee Wallar

The following information is taken from readily available sources such as *Ancestry.com*, *FamilySearch.org*, and historic newspaper websites. While I did not rely on personal family trees, it is nevertheless likely there are omissions and errors.

James Lee Wallar was likely born in Harrison County, Ohio in about 1829 to **Verden** and **Edith (Layport) Wallar**.[503] He married **Frances Elizabeth Gammon** on December 5, 1847 in Muskingum County, Ohio.[504] Frances was born on March 10, 1830 in Zanesville, Muskingum County, Ohio.[505] She was the daughter of **Robert** and **Elizabeth (Bailey) Gammon**.[506] According to Frances Wallar's obituary, she was the mother of seven children.[507] I found record of six. Frances Elizabeth (Gammon) Wallar died on June 26, 1887 in Centralia, Marion County, Illinois and was buried in Elmwood Cemetery in Centralia on June 28, 1887.[508]

SON OF JAMES AND FRANCES WALLAR:

Lafayette "Fay" K. Wallar was born in Zanesville, Ohio on October 2, 1848.[509] He married **Catherine S. McClure** on May 15, 1877 in Lawrence County, Illinois.[510] She died on August 22, 1878.[511] He later married **Martha M. Leeper**, daughter of Reverend John Leeper, on October 1, 1879 in Olney, Richland County, Illinois.[512] Fay K. Wallar died at the Odd Fellows Home in Mattoon, Coles County, Illinois on November 24, 1915.[513] He was buried at Brown's Chapel Cemetery in Coles County.[514]

Fay and Martha (Leeper) Wallar had the following children:

Glen Leeper Wallar was born on October 4, 1881 in Lancaster, Wabash County, Illinois.[515] He married **Grace Tanquary** on November 8, 1900 in Bellmont, Wabash County, Illinois.[516] A later marriage to **May Allen** was solemnized on January 15, 1919 in Joliet, Will County, Illinois.[517] Glen died at home in Saint Louis, Missouri on January 27, 1955.[518] He was buried at Resthaven Memorial Cemetery in Louisville, Kentucky.[519]

Orla L. "Jack" Wallar was born on February 13, 1883 in Lancaster, Wabash County, Illinois.[520] He married **Anna L. (Ware) Krueger** in Saint Louis, Missouri on April 22, 1914.[521] Jack Wallar died September 6, 1950 in New Brunswick, New Jersey and is interred at Mount Hope Cemetery Mausoleum in Lemay, Saint Louis County, Missouri.[522]

Children of Fay and Martha Wallar, continued

Herbert Earl Wallar was born July 7, 1884 in Lancaster, Wabash County, Illinois.[523] He married, first, to **Margaret Ankenbrandt** on October 18, 1906 in Saint Louis, Missouri,[524] and second, to **Mary Alice Parks** in Deer Lodge, Powell County, Montana on August 5, 1921.[525] Earl Wallar died on October 7, 1957[526] and is buried in Silverton, Marion County, Oregon.[527]

Paul Sabine Wallar was born in Bellmont, Wabash County, Illinois on February 28, 1886.[528] He married **Clara Elsie Jungclaus** in Saint Louis, Missouri on September 9, 1925.[529] Paul Wallar died on April 8, 1959 in Granite City, Illinois[530] and is buried in the Sunset Hill Cemetery in Glen Carbon, Illinois.[531]

Cornelia Fay Wallar was born April 10, 1893.[532] She was living in Saint Louis, Missouri when she married **Chester Butler Hyde** on November 8, 1911 in Joplin, Jasper County, Missouri.[533] they were divorced before 1930, and Cornelia Hyde married **William Lella** in New Jersey in 1931[534]. Cornelia Lella died on August 7, 1981. She is buried in Our Lady of Seven Dolors Catholic Cemetery in Welsh, Jefferson Davis Parish, Louisiana.[535]

DAUGHTER OF JAMES AND FRANCES WALLAR:

Lauretta May "Etta" Wallar was born in Zanesville, Ohio on June 10, 1851.[536] She married **John D. Reeder** in Crawford County, Illinois on May 26, 1870.[537] Etta Reeder died in Cleveland, Cuyahoga County, Ohio on January 4, 1920.[538] She was buried in Crown Hill Cemetery in Indianapolis, Indiana.[539] I found record of ten children.

John D. and Lauretta (Wallar) Reeder had the following children:

William Clyde Reeder was born in Coffeyville, Montgomery County, Kansas on March 3, 1871.[540] He was married first to **Nettie Davis** in Charleston, Coles County, Illinois on March 7, 1893.[541] William later married **Mabel Edna Watkins** on December 23, 1925 in Champaign County, Illinois.[542] William died in Danville, Vermilion County, Illinois on May 18, 1941.[543] He is buried in Spring Hill Cemetery in Danville.[544]

Arthur Lee Reeder was born in DeSoto, Jackson County, Illinois on January 3, 1875.[545] His first marriage was to **Adda L. Sampson** in Caldwell, Moultrie County, Illinois on November 6, 1896.[546] Arthur's second marriage took place on September 2, 1905 in Clay County, Illinois to **Mrs. Stella (Edwards) Mulquin**.[547] Arthur died in Grass Valley, Nevada County, California on June 10, 1945.[548] He is buried in Saint Mary's Cemetery, Oakland, Alameda County, California.[549]

Children of John and Etta Reeder, continued:

Cary Kent Reeder was born on October 14, 1876 in Illinois.[550] He married **Esther Crews** on February 12, 1896 in Edgewood, Effingham County, Illinois.[551] Cary died in Wood River, Madison County, Illinois on March 6, 1931[552] and is buried in Mount Hope Cemetery, Belleville, Saint Clair County, Illinois.[553]

May Reeder was born in November 1879 in Illinois[554]. She married first to **John A.L. Edwards** in Clay County, Illinois on May 9, 1899.[555] Her second marriage took place on July 16, 1903 to **Everett Osman** in Effingham, Effingham County, Illinois.[556] I was unable to confirm a death date or location for May. She was not listed as a survivor in her father's 1933 obituary.[557]

Merrill Clark Reeder was born in Flat Rock, Crawford County, Illinois on September 14, 1881.[558] He married **Myrtle Hackney** on April 22, 1901[559] and **Lillie Pauley** in Saint Charles County, Missouri on August 22, 1942.[560] Merrill Reeder died on April 13, 1953 in Effingham, Effingham County, Illinois. He is buried in the Beecher City Cemetery, Effingham County, Illinois.[561]

Children of John and Etta Reeder, continued:

Wilbur Verden Reeder was born in Mount Erie, Wayne County, Illinois on October 9, 1883.[562] He married **Jane Ruth Burbank** in Cuyahoga County, Ohio on May 22, 1926.[563] Wilbur died on January 22, 1957 in San Diego, San Diego County, California[564] and is buried in Greenwood Memorial Park there.[565]

Louetta "Lula" Reeder was born in Mount Erie, Wayne County, Illinois on March 26, 1885.[566] She was first married to **Isaac "Ike" Adams** in Clay County, Illinois on August 18, 1905.[567] Lula's second marriage was to **Earl Brown**. They were married on August 31, 1910 in Effingham County, Illinois.[568] Lula married a third time to **John Hitt** in Madison County, Indiana on June 11, 1929.[569] Lula Reeder died on February 2, 1973 in Monterey Park, Los Angeles County, California and is buried in Montecino Memorial Park in Colton, San Bernardino County, California.[570]

Warren Fergis Reeder was born on January 1, 1887 in Newton, Jasper County, Illinois.[571] He married **Julia Thorp** in Jackson County, Illinois on September 19, 1910.[572] Warren Reeder died on December 7, 1922 in Taylorville, Christian County, Illinois and is buried in Brown Cemetery, Edgewood, Effingham County, Illinois.[573]

Children of John and Etta Reeder, continued:

Bessie Jean Reeder was born in Illinois on March 27, 1889.[574] She married **Claude Everett Battrelle** in Saint Louis, Missouri on December 8, 1913.[575] Bessie died in Monterey Park, Los Angeles County, California on December 10, 1973.[576] She is buried in Montecino Memorial Park in Colton, San Bernardino County, California.[577]

Roy Raymond Reeder was born on December 3, 1890 in Fairfield, Wayne County, Illinois.[578] He married **Dora Ellen Hackney** on August 25, 1915 in Edgewood, Effingham County, Illinois.[579] Roy died on November 8, 1972 in Shelbyville, Shelby County, Illinois.[580] He is buried in Red Bank Cemetery, Lakewood, Shelby County, Illinois.[581]

SON OF JAMES AND FRANCES WALLAR:

Charles Millard Wallar was born on September 9, 1854 in Washington County, Ohio. He received his education at McKendree College, Lebanon, Illinois and read law in Mount Carmel and Cairo, Illinois. He first practiced law in Newton, Illinois, beginning in 1876. He married **Laura C. Townsend** on January 28, 1878 in Mount Carmel, Illinois.[582] Charles died in Wayne County, Illinois on February 3, 1908.[583]

Charles M. and Laura (Townsend) Wallar had the following children:

James L. Wallar was likely born in Fairfield, Wayne County, Illinois in June 1879. He died there at age 3 months in September 1879 of "cholera infantum."[584]

Charles Burgess Wallar was born on January 20, 1881 in Fairfield, Wayne County, Illinois.[585] He married **Grace Harpole** in Fairfield, Wayne County, Illinois on May 14, 1902.[586] The couple divorced in December 1912.[587] Charles died sometime after October 20, 1947, when he as living in East Saint Louis, Illinois.[588]

Edmond Neal Wallar was born on July 16, 1889 in Fairfield, Wayne County, Illinois. He died sometime after April 27, 1942, the date he signed a World War II Draft Registration card in Edwards County, Illinois.[589] He is not named as a survivor in his mother's October 21, 1947 obituary.[590]

SON OF JAMES AND FRANCES WALLAR:

Harry Herbert "Herb" Wallar was born on April 29th, probably in 1857, in Ohio. He was three years old in the 1860 census, so I don't believe the 1860 birthdate on his death certificate and grave marker is correct. His first wife was **Mary Melissa "Mollie" Bellew**. They married in Louisville, Clay County, Illinois on April 1, 1879.[591] Mollie died in Edwards County, Illinois on June 20, 1895 of tuberculosis.[592] Her death notice read, "Mrs. Herbert Wallar after a lingering illness died last night, leaving a husband and a family of helpless little children." She is buried in the Old Albion Cemetery in Albion, Edwards County, Illinois.[593] On November 9, 1895, Herb married for a second time, to Mrs. **Cora (Firman) Coats** in Crawford County, Illinois.[594] None of the children from Herb's first marriage were living with Herb and Cora in 1900.[595] Sadly, these children were separated after the death of their mother and raised separately but seemed to remain in contact as adults. The two sisters, Fannie and Florence, married brothers and were close throughout their lives, and brother Harry listed his older sister, Mrs. W.C. Bashears (Fannie), on his World War I draft registration card as someone who would always know where he was living.[596] The author's mother, Dorothy "Betty" (Bashears) Wiseman recalled seeing a photo which included her grandmother Florence's brother Clarence as an adult. Harry Herbert Wallar died on June 21, 1915 in Lewistown, Fulton County, Illinois[597] and is buried in the Oak Hill Cemetery in Lewistown.[598]

Harry Herbert and Mary Melissa (Ballew) Wallar had the following children:

unknown Wallar born before July 2, 1882.[599]

Children of Herb and Mollie Wallar, continued:

Anna Francis (later Frances Lee) "Fannie" Wallar was born in Albion, Edwards County, Illinois on July 2, 1882.[600] Fannie married **William Clarence "Tuckie" Bashears** in Crawford County, Illinois on November 26, 1901.[601] Fannie died in Springfield, Sangamon County, Illinois on April 17, 1974.[602] She is buried in the Robinson New Cemetery, Robinson, Crawford County, Illinois.[603]

Harry Herbert Wallar was born on November 18, 1884.[604] He married Mrs. **Josie E. (Brown) Cann** on July 6, 1912 in East Saint Louis, Saint Clair County, Illinois.[605] They separated on September 6, 1912[606] and the divorce was granted on March 7, 1913 in Saint Clair County, Illinois.[607] Harry and Mrs. **Della McRoy** were married in Saint Louis, Missouri on May 16, 1914.[608] **Myrtle McBride** married Harry Wallar after January 10, 1920, when they were neighbors on Fifth Street in East Saint Louis, Illinois.[609] A marriage license was issued to Harry Wallar and **Helena "Lena" B. Treece** in Monroe County, Illinois in May 1930.[610] Lena Wallar obtained a divorce from Harry for desertion in Omaha, Nebraska in 1938.[611] Harry Wallar died in Indianapolis, Marion County, Indiana on June 11, 1940. He is buried at New Crown Cemetery in Indianapolis.[612]

Children of Herb and Mollie Wallar, continued:

Clarence L. Wallar (later Clarence McCredie) was born in Albion, Edwards County, Illinois on May 2, 1887.[613] After the death of his mother and abandonment by his father, Clarence was adopted by Peter and Annie McCredie of Warsaw, Hancock County, Illinois. Thereafter he used the name Clarence McCredie. This adoption occured before June 7, 1900, the date he was enumerated in the family of Peter T. McCready in the 1900 federal census.[614] Clarence first married **Rita E. Rhodes** on June 12, 1912 in Adams County, Illinois.[615] His second marriage was to **Mamie Adams** on December 27, 1929 in East Saint Louis, Saint Clair County, Illinois.[616] Clarence L. McCredie died on May 9, 1972 in Belleville, Saint Clair County, Illinois and is buried at Lake View Memorial Gardens, Fairview Heights, Saint Clair County, Illinois.[617]

Florence Jeanette Wallar was born in Centralia, Marion County, Illinois on August 11, 1889. The year 1889 is contrary to that on her marriage record (1886) and death certificate (1888), but it's likely correct because in the Centralia newspaper on August 15, 1889 there is a small note, "Herb Wallar is wearing his Sunday clothes all the time now. It is a girl and looks just like its pap..."[618] This seems to indicate the birth of a daughter and no child is known to be born in this family after Florence. After the death of her mother, she was adopted by George W. and Annie D. Wilkin and was living in Jefferson townhsip, Fayette County, Pennsylvania on June 7, 1900.[619] By 1906, Florence had returned to the Midwest, where she was living in Terre Haute, Vigo County, Indiana and was employed as a milliner. It was there on July 18, 1906, that sixteen-year-old Florence married **Earnest Winfield Bashears**, the younger brother of her sister Fannie's husband.[620] Florence died in Robinson, Crawford County, Illinois on March 27, 1968. She is buried in Robinson New Cemetery, Robinson, Crawford County, Illinois.[621]

Harry Herbert and Cora Wallar had the following children:

Ella B. Wallar was born in Robinson, Crawford County Illinois on July 26, 1896.[622] She married **John Patrick O'Neal** on June 15, 1916 at Lewistown, Fulton County, Illinois.[623] Ella died on June 26, 1920 in Beardstown, Cass County, Illinois and is buried in the Saint Alexius Catholic Cemetery there.[624]

Clinton Harold Wallar was born on October 16, 1899 in Robinson, Crawford County, Illinois.[625] He married **Nellie Mae West** in Davenport, Scott County, Iowa on October 24, 1925.[626] Clinton Waller died in September 1965 and is buried in Oak Hill Cemetery, Lewistown, Fulton County, Illinois.[627]

Esther R. Wallar was born in Batesville, Independence County, Arkansas[628] on October 2, 1905.[629] Her first husband was a Mr. **Rowley**.[630] She married her second husband, **Gerald T. Graves**, on November 1, 1939 in Burlington, Des Moines County, Iowa.[631] Esther Graves died in Galesburg, Knox County, Illinois on November 3, 2000 and is buried in Oak Lawn Memorial Gardens in Galesburg.[632]

SON OF JAMES AND FRANCES WALLAR:

William C. (or G.) "Willie" Wallar was born on August 26, 1859[633] in Ohio,[634] likely Racine. Willie was killed when a tornado hit Mount Carmel, Wabash County, Illinois on June 4, 1877.[635] He is buried in Rose Hill Cemetery in Mount Carmel.[636]

DAUGHTER OF JAMES AND FRANCES WALLAR:

Lillie May Wallar was born about 1862 in Ohio,[637] likely Racine. She died on February 9, 1871 in Robinson, Crawford County, Illinois,[638] and is buried in the Old Robinson cemetery.[639]

ENDNOTES

1. *Minutes and Journal of the Southern Illinois Annual Conference of the Methodist Episcopal Church Held at Alton, Ills., Sept. 18-23, 1901* (St. Louis, Missouri: Perrin & Smith Ptg. Co., 1901), 73; imaged, *Divinity Archive* (http://divinityarchive.com/handle/11258/4404 : accessed 10 June 2023).

2. *The History of Henry and St. Clair Counties, Missouri* (St. Joseph, Missouri: National Historical Company, 1883), 600; imaged, *Internet Archive.* (https://archive.org/details/historyofhenryst00nati/page/600/mode/2up : accessed 12 June 2019).

3. "Ohio, County Marriages, 1789-2016," database with images, *FamilySearch* (https://www.familysearch.org/ark:/61903/1:1:2QQR-87G : accessed 15 January 2019), James L. Waller and Frances Gammon marriage license, 4 December 1847.

4. 1830 U.S. census, Harrison County, Ohio, population schedule, town of Cadiz, page 162, Verden Waller; imaged, "1830 United States Federal Census," *Ancestry.com* (https://www.ancestry.com/search/collections/8058/ : accessed 27 August 2021); citing National Archives microfilm publication M19, roll 133.

5. 1840 U.S. census, Tuscarawas County, Ohio, population schedule, Eastport township, town of Uhrichsville, Virden Wallar; imaged, "1840 United States Federal Census," *Ancestry.com* (https://www.ancestry.com/search/collections/8057/ : accessed 27 August 2021); citing National Archives microfilm publication M704, roll 430.

6. 1850 U.S. census, Pickaway County, Ohio, population schedule, town of Circleville, page 196 (stamped), dwelling 395, family 408, James L. Waller; imaged, "1850 United States Federal Census," *Ancestry.com* (https://www.ancestry.com/search/collections/8054/ : accessed 27 August 2021); citing National Archives microfilm publication M432, roll 720.

7. 1860 U.S. census, Meigs County, Ohio, population schedule, town of Racine, page 232 (stamped), dwelling 591, family 571, James L. Waller; imaged, "1860 United States Federal Census," *Ancestry.com* (https://www.ancestry.com/search/collections/7667/ : accessed 27 August 2021); citing National Archives microfilm publication M653, roll 1008.

8. Charles S. Waller, Sr., *The Chesapeakers: Waller Descendants from the Chesapeake Bay, Old Somerset Co., Md. 1654-1985* (Baltimore, Maryland: Gateway Press, Inc, 1985), pages 40-41.

9. *Pomeroy [Ohio] Weekly Telegraph*, 3 May 1861, page 3, column 1; imaged, *Newspapers.com* (https://www.newspapers.com/image/171437868 : accessed 28 November 2021).

10. "The Centralia House," *Centralia [Illinois] Daily Sentinel*, 13 November 1890, page 2, column 4, imaged, NewspaperArchive (https://access-newspaperarchive-com.carmel.idm.oclc.org/us/illinois/centralia/centralia-daily-sentinel/1890/11-13/page-2 : accessed 26 May 2017).

11. 1870 U.S. census, Crawford County, Illinois, population schedule, town of Robinson, page 174A, dwelling 288, family 282, James L. Waller; imaged, "1870 United States Census," *Ancestry.com* (https://www.ancestry.com/search/collections/7163/ : accessed 27 August 2021); citing National Archives microfilm publication M593, roll 214.

12. 1880 U.S. census, White County, Illinois, population schedule, town of Enfield, enumeration district [ED] 151, 318C (stamped), dwelling 62, family 63, J.L. Waller; imaged, "1880 United States Census," *Ancestry.com* (https://www.ancestry.com/search/collections/6742/ : accessed 27 August 2021); citing National Archives microfilm publication T9, roll 258.

13. 1900 U.S. census, Marion County, Illinois, population schedule, city of Centralia, ward 3, enumeration district [ED] 0019, page 70A (stamped), dwelling 562, family 585, James L. Waller; imaged, "1900 United States Federal Census," *Ancestry.com* (https://www.ancestry.com/search/collections/7602/ : accessed 27 August 2021); citing National Archives microfilm publication T623, roll 327.

14. *Combined History of Edwards, Lawrence and Wabash Counties, Illinois* (Philadelphia, Pennsylvania: J.L. McDonough & Co., 1883), 309; imaged, *Internet Archive* (https://archive.org/details/combinedhistoryo00phil/page/n379/mode/2up : accessed 6 September 2024).

15. 1850 U.S. census, Pickaway Co., Ohio, pop. sch., p. 196 (stamped), dwell. 395, fam. 408, James L. Waller.

16. 1900 U.S. census, Clay County, Illinois, population schedule, Larkinsburg Township, enumeration district [ED] 0007, page 13 (handwritten), dwelling 275, family 281, John D. Reeder; imaged, "1900 United States Federal Census," *Ancestry.com* (https://www.ancestry.com/search/collections/7602/ : accessed 27 August 2021); citing National Archives microfilm publication T623, roll 243.

17. "Branch of the Vermont Marble Works," *Davenport [Iowa] Gazette*, 14 July 1853, page 5, column 5; imaged, *GenealogyBank* (https://genealogybank.com: accessed 17 February 2019). Note: Rock Island Street is now called Pershing Avenue.

18. "Davenport IA Population," database, *Population.US* (https://population.us/ia/davenport/ : accessed 28 Aug 2021).

19. *The History of Henry and St. Clair Counties, Missouri*, 600.

20. Fulton County, Illinois, death certificate no. 30 (1915), Henry H. Waller; Office of the County Clerk, Lewistown.

21. 1860 U.S. census, Meigs County, Ohio, population schedule, town of Racine, page 232 (stamped), dwelling 591, family 571, Harvey Waller; imaged, "1860 United States Federal Census," *Ancestry.com* (https://www.ancestry.com/search/collections/7667/ : accessed 27 August 2021); citing National Archives microfilm publication M653, roll 1008.

22. 1870 U.S. census, Crawford County, Illinois, population schedule, town of Robinson, page 174A, dwelling 288, family 282, Harry H. Waller; imaged, "1870 United States Federal Census," *Ancestry.com* (https://www.ancestry.com/search/collections/7163/ : accessed 27 August 2021); citing National Archives microfilm publication M593, roll 214.

23. 1880 U.S. census, Edwards County, Illinois, population schedule, town of Albion, enumeration district [ED] 7, 393B (stamped), dwelling 16, family 16, H.H. Wallar; imaged, "1880 United States Federal Census," *Ancestry.com* (https://www.ancestry.com/search/collections/6742/ : accessed 27 August 2021); citing National Archives microfilm publication T9, roll 204.

24. "For the Telegraph," *Meigs County [Ohio] Telegraph*, 22 April 1856, page 1, columns 2-3; imaged, *GenealogyBank* (https://genealogybank.com: accessed 3 July 2022).

25. "New Advertisements," *Meigs County [Ohio] Telegraph,* 20 July 1858, page 3, column 7; imaged, *GenealogyBank* (https://genealogybank.com: accessed 17 February 2019).

26. George W. Hawes, *Geo. W. Hawes' Ohio State Gazetteer, and Business Directory, for 1860-'61* (Indianapolis, Indiana: George W. Hawes, 1860), 524.

27. *Collections of Bits & Pieces of Sutton Township History* (Pomeroy, Ohio: Meigs County Pioneer and Historical Society, undated), spiral notebook available at the Meigs County Historical Society and Museum, Middleport, Ohio, accessed July 2022.

28. "Racine," *Pomeroy [Ohio] Weekly Telegraph*, 17 August 1858, page 3, column 2; imaged, *GenealogyBank* (https://genealogybank.com: accessed 3 July 2022).

29. *Meigs County [Ohio] Telegraph*, 30 March 1858, page 4, column 1; imaged, *GenealogyBank* (http://www.genealogybank.com: accessed 17 February 2019).

30. Silas Allen Burnap grave marker in Mound Cemetery near Pomeroy, Meigs County, Ohio photograph, September 2019; privately held by Nancy E. Wiseman, Carmel, Indiana.

31. "Racine Correspondence," *Meigs County [Ohio] Telegraph*, 6 July 1858, page 3, column 4; imaged, *GenealogyBank* (https://genealogybank.com: accessed 17 February 2019).

32. "County Fair," *Meigs County [Ohio] Telegraph*, 20 September 1859, page 4, column 2; imaged, *GenealogyBank* (https://genealogybank.com: accessed 17 February 2019).

33. Meigs County, Ohio, "Deed Record 22, Meigs County," pages 181-182, David O. Hopkins to James L. Wallar; imaged, *FamilySearch* (https://www.familysearch.org/ark:/61903/3:1:3Q9M-C37P-L3Q7-7 : accessed 13 January 2022), digital film #008585242, "Deeds, v. 21-22, 1858-1860," images 447-448 of 666.

34. Meigs County, Ohio, 1910 Plat Book of Racine, portion of Hopkins Addition, accessed 29 June 2022; County Recorder's Office, Pomeroy.

35. *Find a Grave*, database with images (http://www.findagrave.com : accessed 29 March 2020), memorial 12690408, William G. Wallar; Rose Hill Cemetery, Mount Carmel, Wabash County, Illinois; grave marker photographed by Find a Grave user Brenda Priddy Jenkins.

36. 1860 U.S. census, Meigs Co., OH, pop. sch., Racine, p. 230 (stamped), dwell. 591, fam. 571, James L. Waller.

37. House at 201 Fifth Street, Racine, Ohio photograph, June 2023; privately held by Nancy E. Wiseman, Carmel, Indiana.

38. "Attachment Notice," *Pomeroy [Ohio] Weekly Telegraph*, 22 Nov 1859, page 3, column 7; imaged, *Newspapers.com* (https://www.newspapers.com/image/171443332/ : accessed 3 July 2022).

39. Hawes, *Geo. W. Hawes' Ohio State Gazetteer, and Business Directory, for 1860-'61*, 524. Note: At the Ohio History Connection Archives in July 2022, a thorough search of the Ohio Supreme Court Order Books for the years 1852-1864 did not show James Wallar being admitted to the Bar. Ohio, Supreme Court, Order Book vol. 1, 1852-1857, BV 02084, Ohio History Connection Archives, Columbus; and Ohio. Supreme Court, Order Book vol. 2, 1858-1864, BV 02085, Ohio History Connection Archives, Columbus; and Ohio. Supreme Court, Order Book vol. 3, 1863-1869, BV 02086, Ohio History Connection Archives, Columbus.

40. "The Meeting on Last Thursday Night," *Pomeroy [Ohio] Weekly Telegraph*, 17 Jul 1860, page 3, column 2; imaged, *GenealogyBank* (https://genealogybank.com: accessed 3 July 2022).

41. "Republican County Convention," *Pomeroy [Ohio] Weekly Telegraph*, 31 Jul 1860, page 4, column 2; imaged, *GenealogyBank* (https://genealogybank.com: accessed 17 February 2019).

42. *Pomeroy [Ohio] Weekly Telegraph*, 14 August 1860, page 4, column 1, imaged, *GenealogyBank* (https://www.genealogybank.com : accessed 17 Feb 2019).

43. Meigs County Courthouse in Pomeroy, Ohio photograph, July 2022; privately held by Nancy E. Wiseman, Carmel, Indiana. Note: The Meigs County Courthouse was built in 1848 and is still in use today.

44. "Marble Works," *Pomeroy [Ohio] Weekly Telegraph*, 23 November 1860, page 1, column 4; imaged, *GenealogyBank* (https://genealogybank.com: accessed 3 July 2022).

45. George W. Hawes, *G.W. Hawes' Commercial Gazetteer and Business Directory of the Ohio River, Embracing the Towns, Cities and Villages on the River from Pittsburg, Pennsylvania, to Cairo, Illinois, with an Extensive Classification* (Indianapolis: G.W. Hawes, 1861), 117, 397.

46. Meigs County, Ohio, "Deed Record 23, Meigs County" page 498, James L. Wallar to Hiram L. Sibley; imaged, *FamilySearch* (https://www.familysearch.org/ark:/61903/3:1:3Q9M-C37P-PSDX-C : accessed 13 January 2022), digital film #008585243, "Deeds, v. 23-24, 1860-1863," image 280 of 703.

47. Meigs County, Ohio, "Deed Record 24, Meigs County," pages 415-416, David O. Hopkins to Frances E. Wallar; imaged, *FamilySearch* (https://www.familysearch.org/ark:/61903/3:1:3Q9M-C37P-PSCT-F : accessed 13 January 2022), digital film #008585243, "Deeds, v. 23-24, 1860-1863", images 578-579 of 703.

48. Meigs County, Ohio, "Deed Record Book 24, Meigs County," page 415, Hiram L. Sibley to James L. Wallar; imaged; *FamilySearch* (https://www.familysearch.org/ark:/61903/3:1:3Q9M-C37P-PSCT-F : accessed 13 January 2022), digital film #008585243, "Deeds, v. 23-24, 1860-1863", image 578 of 703.

49. American Battlefield Trust, *Fort Sumter,* website (https://www.battlefields.org/learn/civil-war/battles/fort-sumter : accessed 5 October 2022).

50. "Public Meeting," *Pomeroy [Ohio] Weekly Telegraph*, 19 April 1861, page 3, column 2; imaged, *Newspapers.com* (https://www.newspapers.com/image/171437225/ : accessed 28 November 2021).

51. *Pomeroy [Ohio] Weekly Telegraph*, 03 May 1861, page 3; imaged, *Newspapers.com* (https://www.newspapers.com/image/171437868/: accessed 28 November 2021).

52. "The Meigs County Rangers," *Pomeroy [Ohio] Weekly Telegraph*, 3 May 1861, page 3, column 1; imaged, *Newspapers.com* (https://www.newspapers.com/image/171437868 : accessed 28 November 2021).

53. Compiled Military Service Record, James L. Waller, Captain, Company H, 18 Ohio Infantry, Civil War; Carded Records, Volunteer Organizations, Civil War; Record Group 94, Records of the Adjutant General's Office, 1780s-1917; National Archives, Washington, D.C.

54. "The Volunteers," *Pomeroy [Ohio] Weekly Telegraph*, 10 May 1861, page 4, column 2, *Newspapers.com*, (https://www.newspapers.com/image/171438122/ : accessed 17 Feb 2019).

55. "The Volunteers," *Pomeroy Weekly Telegraph*, 10 May 1861. Note: Of the 106 Meigs County Rangers listed, 56 enlisted for three months in the Eighteenth Ohio Infantry Volunteer Regiment, 52 of whom served in Wallar's Company H. Twenty-nine of 98 Pomeroy Guards also signed up for three months in the 18th Ohio Volunteer Infantry. Men from this list also served in other Ohio military units.

56. *Ohio History Central* (https://www.ohiocivilwarcentral.com/camp-wool/ : accessed 29 November 2021), "Camp Wool."

57. "Removal of Troops," *Pomeroy [Ohio] Weekly Telegraph*, 31 May 1861, page 3, column 1; imaged, *Newspapers.com* (https://www.newspapers.com/image/171439034/ : accessed 28 November 2021).

58. Monument to Meigs County Civil War Soldiers photograph, 2023; privately held by Nancy E. Wiseman, Carmel, Indiana. This monument stands outside the Meigs County Courthouse in Pomeroy, Ohio.

59. United States War Department, *The War of the Rebellion: A Compilation of the Official Records of the Union and Confederate Armies,* Series I. 53 vols., (Washington, D.C.: Government Printing Office, 1880), vol. 2: page 47, 26 May 1861 letter to Colonel J. Irvine from Major General George B. McClellan; imaged, *HathiTrust Digital Library* (https://babel.hathitrust.org/cgi/pt?id=coo.31924077730186&view=1up&seq=63 : accessed March 2022), image 63 of 1118.

60. United States War Department, *The War of the Rebellion: A Compilation of the Official Records of the Union and Confederate Armies,* Series I. 53 vols., (Washington, D.C.: Government Printing Office, 1880), vol. 2: page 48, 26 May 1861 Proclamation to the People of Western Virginia from Major General George B. McClellan; imaged, *HathiTrust Digital Library* (https://babel.hathitrust.org/cgi/pt?id=coo.31924077730186&view=1up&seq=64 : accessed March 2022), image 64 of 1118.

61. "Letter from Camp Union," *Pomeroy [Ohio] Weekly Telegraph*, 7 June 1861, page 3, column 2; imaged, *Newspapers.com* (https://www.newspapers.com/image/171439318/ : accessed 28 November 2021).

62. *History of Washington County, Ohio, with Illustrations and Biographical Sketches* (Cleveland, Ohio: H.Z. Williams & Bro., 1881), 148.

63. "Letter from Camp Union," *Pomeroy [Ohio] Weekly Telegraph*, 7 June 1861.

64. "Letter from Camp Union," *Pomeroy [Ohio] Weekly Telegraph*, 7 June 1861.

65. Camp Putnam historical marker photograph, June 2022; privately held by Nancy E. Wiseman, Carmel, Indiana. This marker is in Marietta, Ohio, south of the racetrack at the Washington County fairgrounds.

66. "Landing of U.S. Troops at Parkersburg, Western Virginia," *Frank Leslie's Illustrated Newspaper*, 24 August 1861, page 228.

67. H. E. Matheny, *Wood County, West Virginia, in Civil War Times with an Account of the Guerrilla Warfare in the Little Kanawha Valley* (Parkersburg, West Virginia: Trans-Allegheny Books, Inc., 1987), 6.

68. H. S. Graham and E. Hergesheimer, *Map of Virginia: showing the distribution of its slave population from the census of 1860.* (Washington: Henry S. Graham, 1861); digital image, *Library of Congress Geography and Map Division* (https://www.loc.gov/item/2010586922/ : accessed 9 September 2021).

69. "Inaugural Address of Governor Arthur I. Boreman, June 20, 1863," *West Virginia Archives and History* (https://archive.wvculture.org/history/government/governors/boremania.html : accessed 17 February 2022).

70. Matheny, *Wood County, West Virginia*, 15-17.

71. "A Row in Parkersburg," *Wheeling [Virginia] Daily Intelligencer*, 20 April 1861, page 3, column 1; imaged, *Newspapers.com* (https://www.newspapers.com/image/171192088/ : accessed 20 February 2022).

72. *History of Washington County, Ohio,* 148.

73. Matheny, *Wood County, West Virginia*, 88, 101.

74. Archie A Biggs, "File□: Stephenson House, Parkersburg, West Virginia.Jpg," *Wikimedia Commons*, September 18, 2012 (https://commons.wikimedia.org/wiki/File:Stephenson_House,_Parkersburg, _West_Virginia.jpg), marked as public domain, more details on Wikimedia Commons: https://commons.wikimedia.org/wiki/Template:PD-US. This file comes from the Historic American Buildings Survey. File HABS WV-46. This is a program of the National Park Service established for the purpose of documenting historic places. This image contains material based on a work of a National Park Service employee, created as part of that person's official duties. As a work of the U.S. federal government, such work is in the public domain in the United States.

75. "Letter from Camp Union," *Pomeroy Weekly Telegraph*, 7 June 1861.

76. "Letter from a Volunteer," *Pomeroy [Ohio] Weekly Telegraph*, 21 June 1861, page 3; imaged, *Newspapers.com* (https://www.newspapers.com/image/171440216/ : accessed 28 November 2021.

77. *Washington Fayette County [Ohio] Herald*, 6 June 1861, page 5; imaged, *NewspaperArchive.com* (http://www.newspaperarchive.com : accessed 31 December 2021).

78. "Bridge Burners," *Pomeroy [Ohio] Weekly Telegraph*, 28 June 1861, page 2, column 5; imaged, *Newspapers.com* (https://www.newspapers.com/image/171440405/ : accessed 28 November 2021.

79. Bell Irvin Wiley, *The Life of Billy Yank: The Common Soldier of the Union* (Baton Rouge: Louisiana State University Press, 1992 printing), 32.

80. Jewett Palmer, *A Historical Sketch of Company "B," Eighteenth Regiment, Ohio Volunteer Infantry, Three Months Service* (publisher not named, 1911), 8.

81. Henry Haymond, *History of Harrison County, West Virginia, From the Early days of Northwestern Virginia to the Present* (Morgantown, West Virginia: Acme Publishing Company, 1910), 318-319; imaged, *Google Books* (https://www.google.com/books/edition/History_of_Harrison_County_West_Virginia/J4QFK5LO-boC : accessed 10 March 2022).

82. United States War Department. *The War of the Rebellion*, Series I, 2:49.

83. "Communicated," *Pomeroy [Ohio] Weekly Telegraph*, 14 June 1861, page 3, column 2; imaged, *Newspapers.com* (https://www.newspapers.com/image/171439863/ : accessed 28 November 2021.

84. "Telegraphic," *Fremont [Ohio] Journal*, 14 June 1861, page 3, column 6; imaged, *GenealogyBank.com* (http://www.genealogybank.com : accessed 31 December 2021).

85. W.L. Nicholson, *Map of Western Virginia*, S.I.: Coast Survey Office, 1862; imaged, Library of Congress Geography and Map Division (https://www.loc.gov/item/2006629774 : accessed 21 December 2022). Placement of towns and lines denoting the railroad by this author.

86. "Letter from a Volunteer," *Pomeroy [Ohio] Weekly Telegraph*, 5 July 1861, page 2, column 5; *Newspapers.com* (https://www.newspapers.com/image/171440782/ : accessed 28 November 2021).

87. Historic American Engineering Record, creator. *Northwestern Virginia Railroad, Grafton Bridge, Spanning Tygart Valley River, Grafton, Taylor County, WV*; photograph. *Library of Congress Prints and Photographs Division* (https://www.loc.gov/resource/hhh.wv0106.photos/ : accessed 28 November 2021).

88. 1850 U.S. census, Harrison County, Virginia, population schedule, town of Clarksburg, pages 743-764 (handwritten); imaged, "1850 United States Federal Census," *Ancestry.com* (https://www.ancestry.com/search/collections/8054/ : accessed 22 March 2022); citing National Archives microfilm publication M432, roll 1351.

89. City of Clarksburg, West Virginia, *Historical Facts* (https://www.cityofclarksburgwv.com/267/Historical-Facts : accessed 10 March 2022).

90. "To the Public," *Ashtabula [Ohio] Weekly Telegraph*, 27 July 1861, page 1, column 6; imaged, *Newspapers.com* (https://www.newspapers.com/image/145269261/ : accessed 31 December 2021).

91. B & O Railroad historical marker photograph, 2022; privately held by Nancy E. Wiseman, Carmel, Indiana. The marker is located on Main Street, just east of Barrett Street/County Route 9 in Grafton, West Virginia.

92. "Our Army Correspondence," *Washington Fayette County [Ohio] Herald*, 4 July 1861, page 3, columns 2-3; imaged, *NewspaperArchive.com* (http://www.newspaperarchive.com: accessed 31 December 2021).

93. "Our Army Correspondence," *Washington Fayette County [Ohio] Herald*, 11 July 1861, page 1, columns 6-7; imaged, *NewspaperArchive.com* (http://www.newspaperarchive.com: accessed 31 December 2021).

94. Palmer, *A Historical Sketch of Company "B,"* 13.

95. United States War Department. *The War of the Rebellion*, Series I, 2:228.

96. United States War Department. *The War of the Rebellion*, Series I, 2:228.

97. Palmer, *A Historical Sketch of Company "B,"* 14-15.

98. "Military Orders," *Cleveland [Ohio] Plain Dealer*, 5 August 1861, page 2, column 2; imaged, *GenealogyBank* (http://www.genealogybank.com : accessed 31 December 2021).

99. "Soldiers Returned," *Pomeroy [Ohio] Weekly Telegraph*, 9 August 1861, page 3, column 3; imaged, *Newspapers.com* (https://www.newspapers.com/image/171442463 : accessed 31 December 2021).

100. Compiled Military Service Record, James L. Waller, Capt., Co. H, 18 Ohio Inf., Civil War.

101. "Payment of Volunteers," *Pomeroy [Ohio] Weekly Telegraph*, 30 August 1861, page 3, column 1; imaged, *Newspapers.com* (https://www.newspapers.com/image/171443595/ : accessed 31 December 2021).

102. *Pomeroy [Ohio] Weekly Telegraph*, 16 August 1861, page 3, column 1; imaged, *GenealogyBank* (http://www.genealogybank.com : accessed 17 February 2019).

103. "Killing our Horses—The Truth," *M'arthur [Ohio] Democrat*, 15 August 1861, page 2, column 3; imaged, *Newspapers.com* (https://www.newspapers.com/image/80055110/ : accessed 3 January 2021). Note: This newspaper article refers to an article in the *Wheeling Press*. I was unable to locate the original article.

104. Compiled Military Service Record, James L. Waller, Capt., Co. H, 18 Ohio Inf., Civil War.

105. *Pomeroy Weekly Telegraph*, 16 August 1861.

106. Compiled Military Service Record, James L. Wallar, Captain, Company A, 2 West Virginia Cavalry, Civil War; Carded Records, Volunteer Organizations, Civil War; Record Group 94, Records of the Adjutant General's Office, 1780s-1917; National Archives, Washington, D.C.

107. J.J. Sutton, *History of the Second Regiment West Virginia Cavalry Volunteers During the War of the Rebellion* (Portsmouth, Ohio: n.p., 1892), 48-50.

108. *Pomeroy [Ohio] Weekly Telegraph*, 13 September 1861, page 4, column 1; imaged, *GenealogyBank* (http://www.genealogybank.com : accessed 17 February 2019).

109. Compiled Military Service Record, James L. Wallar, Capt., Co. A, 2 WV Cav., Civil War.

110. Stephen Z. Starr, *The Union Cavalry in the Civil War,* 3 volumes (Baton Rouge, Louisiana: Louisiana State University Press, 1979), 1: 131-132.

111. Monument to Civil War Horses photograph, 2023; privately held by Nancy E. Wiseman, Carmel, Indiana. This statue is in the circle drive at the National Sporting Library & Museum, Middleburg, Virginia.

112. Laurence D. Schiller, "The Evolution of the Federal Cavalry 1861-1865," *Essential Civil War Curriculum*, Virginia Center for Civil War Studies at Virginia Tech, 2017 (https://www.essentialcivilwarcurriculum.com/the-evolution-of-union-cavalry-1861-1865.html : accessed 16 September 2020.)

113. Schiller, *The Evolution of the Federal Cavalry*, 6.

114. T.F. Dornblaser, *Sabre Strokes of the Pennsylvania Dragoons, in the War of 1861-1865* (Philadelphia, Pennsylvania: Lutheran Publication Society, 1884) 39-40; imaged, *Google Books* (https://www.google.com/books/edition/Sabre_Strokes_of_the_Pennsylvania_Dragoo/gGkx7djVR0UC : accessed 16 September 2020).

115. T.F. Dornblaser, *Sabre Strokes of the Pennsylvania Dragoons*, 39-40.

116. United States War Department, *Atlas to Accompany the Official Records of the Union and Confederate Armies* (https://commons.wikimedia.org/w/index.php?curid=13265621 : accessed 16 September 2023), Plate 172; Public Domain. Note: the rightmost image is of a Captain of the Artillery. On the adjacent image in the atlas, a Major of the Cavalry is wearing a double-breasted jacket, trousers with a gold stripe on the seam, with a curved sabre instead of a straight sword. I chose to show a captain's uniform here instead of a major's uniform.

117. United States War Department, *Atlas to Accompany the Official Records of the Union and Confederate Armies*.

118. Sutton, *History of the Second Regiment*, 49.

119. Starr, *The Union Cavalry in the Civil War*, 1: 132-139.

120. Compiled Military Service Record, James L. Wallar, Capt., Co. A, 2 WV Cav., Civil War.

121. "Southern West Virginia", website, *North American Forts* (http://www.northamericanforts.com/East/wvsouth.html#boreman : accessed 17 January 2022), Fort Boreman.

122. Jacob D. Cox, General Order No. 13, box 3, record group Ar382, West Virginia Adjutant Generals' Papers, Union Regiments 1861-1865; West Virginia Archives and History Library, Charleston.

123. A. Hoen & Co., *Parkersburg* (Baltimore, Maryland?, 1861) Map. *Library of Congress Geography and Map Division* (https://lccn.loc.gov/75696688 : accessed 28 November 2021).

124. Starr, *The Union Cavalry in the Civil War*, 1: 89-192.

125. Starr, *The Union Cavalry in the Civil War*, 1: 189-192.

126. The confluence of the Ohio and Kanawha Rivers at Parkersburg, West Virginia photograph, 2022; privately held by Nancy E. Wiseman, Carmel, Indiana.

127. Janet B. Hewett, editor. *Supplement to the Official Records of the Union and Confederate Armies*, Part II, Record of Events, vol. 73, Serial no. 85, (Wilmington, North Carolina: Broadfoot Publishing Company, 1998), 738.

128. Joe Geiger, Jr., "The Tragic Fate of Guyandotte," *West Virginia History*, vol. 54 (1995): 28-41.

129. *Historical Sketch of 2nd WVC,* page 2; folder 87: "Historical Sketch of the 2nd West Virginia Cavalry," box 3, record group Ar382, West Virginia Adjutant Generals' Papers, Union Regiments 1861-1865; West Virginia Archives and History Library, Charleston.

130. Hewett, *Supplement to the Official Records,* 738.

131. "Ceredo," *e-WV: The West Virginia Encyclopedia* (https://www.wvencyclopedia.org/articles/1040 : accessed 13 September 2024).

132. Hewett, *Supplement to the Official Records,* 738.

133. Camp Pierpont historical marker photograph, 2022; privately held by Nancy E. Wiseman, Carmel, Indiana. This marker is located on B Street in Ceredo, West Virginia between the Ceredo City Hall and the Ceredo Police Department.

134. Hewett, *Supplement to the Official Records,* 729, 739.

135. Rutherford B. Hayes and Charles Richard Williams, editor, *Diary and Letters of Rutherford Birchard Hayes, Nineteenth President of the United States,* 2 volumes (The Ohio State Archaeological and Historical Society, Columbus, 1922), 2: 210-213.

136. Sutton, *History of the Second Regiment,* 56.

137. Terry Lowry, *The Battle of Charleston and the 1862 Kanawha Valley Campaign* (Charleston, West Virginia: 35th Star Publishing, 2016), 4.

138. *Historical Sketch of 2nd WVC,* 3.

139. *Pomeroy [Ohio] Weekly Telegraph,* 4 April 1862, page 4, column 1; imaged, *GenealogyBank* (http://www.genealogybank.com : accessed 17 February 2019).

140. Camp Jones historical marker photograph, 2022; privately held by Nancy E. Wiseman, Carmel, Indiana. The marker is located about 1.5 miles southwest of Flat Top, Mercer County, West Virginia on U.S. 19.

141. Robert W. Black, *Cavalry Raids of the Civil War* (Mechanicsburg, Pennsylvania: Stackpole Books, 2004), 6-7.

142. "Camp at East River," *Pomeroy [Ohio] Weekly Telegraph,* 30 May 1862, page 3, columns 4-5; imaged, *GenealogyBank* (https://genealogybank.com : accessed 17 February 2019).

143. Hayes and Williams, *Diary and Letters of Rutherford Birchard Hayes*, 2: 238-240. Note: The commissary sergeant of the Twenty-Third Ohio was a young William McKinley, the future 25th president of the United States.

144. "Camp at East River," *Pomeroy Weekly Telegraph*, 30 May 1862.

145. J. Nep. Roesler, *Thunder-storm*, (Chicago: Ehrgott, Forbriger & Co., 1862); imaged, *Library of Congress Prints and Photograph Division* (http://hdl.loc.gov/loc.pnp/pga.10438 : downloaded 2 October 2022).

146. Hayes and Williams, *Diary and Letters of Rutherford Birchard Hayes*, 2: 246.

147. "Camp at East River," *Pomeroy Weekly Telegraph*, 30 May 1862.

148. Hayes and Williams, *Diary and Letters of Rutherford Birchard Hayes*, 2: 243.

149. Hayes and Williams, *Diary and Letters of Rutherford Birchard Hayes*, 2: 243-246.

150. *Pomeroy [Ohio] Weekly Telegraph*, 18 April 1862, page 2, column 6, imaged, *GenealogyBank* (https://genealogybank.com : accessed 3 July 2022); and "For the Soldiers," *Pomeroy [Ohio] Weekly Telegraph*, 23 May 1862, page 3, column 2; imaged, *GenealogyBank* (https://genealogybank.com : accessed 3 July 2022).

151. "Camp at East River," *Pomeroy Weekly Telegraph*, 30 May 1862.

152. Hayes and Williams, *Diary and Letters of Rutherford Birchard Hayes*, 2: 262-263.

153. "Camp at East River," *Pomeroy Weekly Telegraph*, 30 May 1862.

154. Hayes and Williams, *Diary and Letters of Rutherford Birchard Hayes*, 2: 266-268.

155. Hayes and Williams, *Diary and Letters of Rutherford Birchard Hayes*, 2: 268-270.

156. Hayes and Williams, *Diary and Letters of Rutherford Birchard Hayes*, 2: 269-270.

157. "Camp at East River," *Pomeroy Weekly Telegraph*, 30 May 1862.

158. "Camp at East River," *Pomeroy Weekly Telegraph*, 30 May 1862.

159. United States War Department, *The War of the Rebellion: A Compilation of the Official Records of the Union and Confederate Armies,* Series I. 53 vols., (Washington, D.C.: Government Printing Office, 1885), v. 12, pt. 1: 505-509, 21 May 1862 letter to Headquarters, Mountain Department from Brigadier General J.D. Cox; imaged, *HathiTrust Digital Library* (https://babel.hathitrust.org/cgi/pt?id=coo.31924077725921&view=1up&seq=521 : accessed March 2022), images 521-524 of 900.

160. Michael M. Meador, "Battle of Pigeon Roost." *e-WV: The West Virginia Encyclopedia* (https://www.wvencyclopedia.org/articles/1854, 22 October 2010 : accessed 16 September 2023).

161. United States War Department, *The War of the Rebellion: A Compilation of the Official Records of the Union and Confederate Armies,* Series I. 53 vols., (Washington, D.C.: Government Printing Office, 1885), v. 12, pt. 1: 513-517, 22 May 1862 report to General Robert E. Lee from Brigadier General Humphrey Marshall; imaged, *HathiTrust Digital Library* (https://babel.hathitrust.org/cgi/pt?id=coo.31924077725921&view=1up&seq=529 : accessed March 2022), images 529-533 of 900.

162. Battle of Pigeon's Roost historical marker photograph, 2023; privately held by Nancy E. Wiseman, Carmel, Indiana. The marker is located near Walgreens at 323 South Walker Street in Princeton, West Virginia.

163. 1870 U.S. census, Crawford County, Illinois, population schedule, Robinson Township, page 174A, dwelling 288, family 282, James L. Waller; imaged, "United States Census, 1870," *Ancestry.com* (https://www.ancestry.com/search/collections/7163/ : accessed 22 March 2020); citing National Archives microfilm publication M593, roll 214.

164. Compiled Military Service Record, James L. Wallar, Capt., Co. A, 2 WV Cav., Civil War.

165. Hayes and Williams, *Diary and Letters of Rutherford Birchard Hayes,* 2: 291.

166. Hayes and Williams, *Diary and Letters of Rutherford Birchard Hayes,* 2: 206.

167. Compiled Military Service Record, James L. Wallar, Capt., Co. A, 2 WV Cav., Civil War.

168. Hewett, *Supplement to the Official Records,* 739.

169. Compiled Military Service Record, James L. Wallar, Capt., Co. A, 2 WV Cav., Civil War.

170. United States War Department, *The War of the Rebellion: A Compilation of the Official Records of the Union and Confederate Armies,* Series I. 53 vols., (Washington, D.C.: Government Printing Office, 1885), v. 12, pt. 2: 116-118, 12 August 1862 report of Colonel E. Siber; imaged, *HathiTrust Digital Library* (https://babel.hathitrust.org/cgi/pt?id=coo.31924077728222&view=1up&seq=118&q1=Siber : accessed March 2022), images 118-120 of 906.

171. United States War Department, *The War of the Rebellion*, Series I, v. 12, pt. 2: 116-118.

172. United States War Department, *The War of the Rebellion*, Series I, v. 12, pt. 2: 116-118.

173. J. Nep. Roesler, *Crossing to Fayetteville*, (Chicago: Ehrgott, Forbriger & Co., 1862); imaged, *Library of Congress Prints and Photograph Division* (http://hdl.loc.gov/loc.pnp/pga.10398 : downloaded 2 October 2022).

174. United States War Department, *The War of the Rebellion*, Series I, v. 12, pt. 2: 115-118.

175. Cox, *Military Reminiscences*, 1: 224-226.

176. United States War Department. *The War of the Rebellion: A Compilation of the Official Records of the Union and Confederate Armies,* Series I, 53 vols., (Washington D.C., 1887), v. 19, pt. 1: 1058-1059, 24 September 1862 letter from Colonel J.A.J. Lightburn to Major General Horatio G. Wright; imaged, *Hathitrust Digital Library* (https://babel.hathitrust.org/cgi/pt?id=coo.31924079609610&view=1up&seq=1074 : accessed 2 October 2022) images 1074-1076 of 1232.

177. J. Nep. Roesler, *Camp, Gauley Bridge*, (Chicago: Ehrgott, Forbriger & Co., 1862); imaged, *Library of Congress Prints and Photograph Division* (http://hdl.loc.gov/loc.pnp/pga.10393 : downloaded 2 October 2022).

178. J.H.J. Lightburn to Colonel E. Siber, letter, 24 August 1862; folder 6, "Field & Staff, Letters," box 3, record group Ar382, West Virginia Adjutant Generals' Papers, Union Regiments 1861-1865; West Virginia Archives and History Library, Charleston.

179. J. Rickard, "Skirmish at Gauley Bridge, 3 September 1861," *History of War* (http://www.historyorwar.org/articles/battles_gauley_bridge.html : accessed 9 April 2023.

180. Cox, *Military Reminiscences*, 1: 81-85.

181. J. Nep. Roesler, *Tompkin's Farm*, (Chicago: Ehrgott, Forbriger & Co., 1862); digital image, *Library of Congress Prints and Photograph Division* (http://hdl.loc.gov/loc.pnp/pga.10439 : downloaded 2 October 2022).

182. Ellen Wilkins Tompkins, "The Colonel's Lady Some Letters of Ellen Wilkins Tompkins, July – December 1861," *The Virginia Magazine of History and Biography*, 69:4 (October 1961): 387-419, particularly 415; imaged, JSTOR (https://www.jstor.org/stable/4246788 : accessed 2 August 2024).

183. United States War Department. *The War of the Rebellion* Series I, v. 19, pt. 1: 1058-1060.

184. United States War Department. *The War of the Rebellion: A Compilation of the Official Records of the Union and Confederate Armies*, Series I, 53 vols., (Washington D.C., 1885), v. 12, pt. 2: 757-761, 19 September 1862 letter from Brigadier General A.G. Jenkins to Lieutenant Colonel H.H. Fitzhugh; imaged, *Hathitrust Digital Library* (https://babel.hathitrust.org/cgi/pt?id=coo.31924077728222&view=1up&seq=759 : accessed 2 October 2022) images 759-763 of 906.

185. W.L. Nicholson, *Map of Western Virginia*, S.I.: Coast Survey Office, 1862; imaged, Library of Congress Geography and Map Division (https://www.loc.gov/item/2006629774 : accessed 21 December 2022). Placement of towns and lines denoting Jenkins' route by this author.

186. Dave Manuel, *Inflation Calculator* (https://www.davemanuel.com/inflation-calculator.php : accessed 21 November 2023); the calculator uses data from Oregon State University.

187. United States War Department, *War of the Rebellion*, Series I, vol. 12, pt. 2: 757-761.

188. First Ohio Invasion historical marker photograph, 2023; privately held by Nancy E. Wiseman, Carmel, Indiana. This marker is at the Buffington Island Battlefield Memorial Park near Portland, Meigs County, Ohio.

189. "News of the Week," *Pomeroy [Ohio] Weekly Telegraph*, 12 Sep 1862, page 2, columns 2-3; imaged, *Newspapers.com* (https://www.newspapers.com/image/171444615/ : accessed 4 Sep 2022).

190. United States War Department, *War of the Rebellion*, Series I, vol. 12, pt. 2: 757-761.

191. Jenkins' Raid historical marker photograph, 2023; digital image by Gina Tillis, Rutland, Ohio and sent to Nancy E. Wiseman, Carmel, Indiana. The marker is located on the northeast corner of Star Mill Park adjacent to a bench near Fifth Street in Racine, Ohio. Thank you, Gina!

192. Sutton, *History of the Second Regiment*, 59-61.

193. *Historical Sketch of 2nd WVC*, 7.

194. United States War Department. *The War of the Rebellion,* Series I, vol. 19, pt. 1: 1060.

195. United States War Department. *The War of the Rebellion, Series I,* vol. 19, pt.1: 1057.

196. United States War Department. *The War of the Rebellion: A Compilation of the Official Records of the Union and Confederate Armies,* Series I, 53 vols., (Washington D.C., 1887), v. 19, pt. 1: 1063-1068, 21 September 1862 report from Colonel Samuel A. Gilbert to Second Lieutenant B.D. Boswell; imaged, *Hathitrust Digital Library* (https://babel.hathitrust.org/cgi/pt?id=coo.31924079609610&view=1up&se q=1079 : accessed 2 October 2022) images 1079-1084 of 1232.

197. Dave Manuel, *Inflation Calculator.*

198. United States War Department. *The War of the Rebellion: A Compilation of the Official Records of the Union and Confederate Armies,* Series I, 53 vols., (Washington D.C., 1887), v. 19, pt. 1: 1070-1071, 14 September 1862 report from Major General W.W. Loring to George W. Randolph; imaged, *Hathitrust Digital Library* (https://babel.hathitrust.org/cgi/pt?id=coo.31924079609610&view=1up&se q=1086&q1=1,000,000 : accessed 2 October 2022) images 1086-1087 of 1232.

199. Lowry, *The Battle of Charleston*, 248-255, 265.

200. Sutton, *History of the Second Regiment*, 61

201. "The Retreat of Col. Lightburn," *Pomeroy [Ohio] Weekly Telegraph*, 19 September 1862, page 4, column 2-3; digital images, *GenealogyBank* (http://www.genealogybank.com : accessed 26 November 2023).

202. Meigs Co., Ohio, Deed Record Book 24: 415-416.

203. Hewett, *Supplement to the Official Records*, p. 730.

204. Lowry, *The Battle of Charleston*, 264-272, 323.

205. "From Western Virginia," *Richmond [Virginia] Dispatch*, 21 October 1862, page 1, column 4, imaged; *Newspapers.com* (https://www.newspapers.com/image/80616387/ : accessed 29 November 2023).

206. Lowry, *The Battle of Charleston*, 315-328.

207. Lowry, *The Battle of Charleston*, 336-377.

208. Sutton, *History of the Second Regiment*, 84-85.

209. Camp Piatt historical marker photograph, 2022; digital image, privately held by Nancy E. Wiseman, Carmel, Indiana. The marker is located across the street from 1617 West Dupont Avenue in Belle, West Virginia.

210. "Attention!," *Pomeroy [Ohio] Weekly Telegraph*, 5 December 1862, page 2, column 6; imaged, *Genealogy Bank* (https://genealogybank.com : accessed 17 February 2019).

211. Schiller, *The Evolution of the Federal Cavalry*, 6.

212. United States War Department, *The War of the Rebellion: A Compilation of the Official Records of the Union and Confederate Armies*, Series I. 53 vols., (Washington, D.C.: Government Printing Office, 1888), v. 21: 8-9, 13 December 1862 report from Brigadier General George Crook to Major G.M. Bascom; imaged, *HathiTrust Digital Library* (https://babel.hathitrust.org/cgi/pt?id=coo.31924077723017&view=1up&seq=24 : accessed March 2022), images 521-524 of 900.

213. Sutton, *History of the Second Regiment*, 67-68.

214. Black, *Cavalry Raids of the Civil War*, p. 79-85.

215. "Rebel Prisoners," *Wheeling [Virginia] Intelligencer*, 6 December 1862, page 5, column 2, *NewspaperArchive* (htps://www.newspaperarchive.com : accessed 6 November 2023).

216. "William Henry Powell: U.S. Civil War: U.S. Army: Medal of Honor Recipient;" Congressional Medal of Honor Society, 2023. (https://cmohs.org/recipients/william-h-powell : accessed 6 November 2023).

217. "Letter from Gauley," Cincinnati Commercial Tribune, 8 December 1862, page 2, column 4, *Genealogy Bank* (https://www.genealogybank.com : accessed 24 February 2019).

218. Sinking Creek Raid historical marker photograph, 2023; digital image, privately held by Nancy E. Wiseman, Carmel, Indiana. The marker is located near Trout, West Virginia.

219. Hewett, *Supplement to the Official Records*, p. 731, 739.

220. Roy Bird Cook, "The Civil War Comes to Charleston," *West Virginia History* 23 (January 1962): 153-167; imaged, *West Virginia Archives and History*. (archive.wvculture.org/history/journal_wvh/wvh23-1.html : accessed 3 December 2023).

221. United States Department of the Interior, National Park Service, National Register of Historic Places Inventory, *Nomination Form for Cedar Grove, Cedar Grove, Kanawha County, West Virginia* (https://wvculture.org/wp-content/uploads/2021/03/Cedar-grove.pdf : accessed 3 August 2024).

222. Sutton, *History of the Second Regiment*, 71-72.

223. *Historical Sketch of 2nd WVC*, 10.

224. Sutton, *History of the Second Regiment*, 72-73.

225. *Historical Sketch of 2nd WVC*, 10.

226. Sutton, *History of the Second Regiment*, 73.

227. *Historical Sketch of 2nd WVC*, 11.

228. United States War Department, *The War of the Rebellion: A Compilation of the Official Records of the Union and Confederate Armies,* Series I. 53 vols., (Washington, D.C.: Government Printing Office, 1889), v. 25, pt.1: 79-80, 3 April 1863 report from Captain David Dove to Colonel J.C. Paxton; imaged, *HathiTrust Digital Library* (https://babel.hathitrust.org/cgi/pt?id=coo.31924077730244&view=1up&seq=95 : accessed March 2022), images 95-96 of 1286.

229. "More of Jenkins Guerrillas Taken," *Wheeling [Virginia] Intelligencer*, 11 April 1863, page 3, column 2, imaged, *OCPL Digital Newspaper Archives*, Ohio County (West Virginia) Public Library (https://ohiocountywv.historyarchives.online/home: accessed 15 Oct 2022).

230. Hayes and Williams, *Diary and Letters of Rutherford Birchard Hayes*, 2: 404.

231. "Dr. F.K. Waller dies; was Civil War Veteran," *St. Louis [Missouri] Globe-Democrat*, 25 November 1915, page 7 column 6; imaged, *Newspapers.com* (https://www.newspapers.com/image/572142887/ : accessed 17 February 2019).

232. Sutton, *History of the Second Regiment*, 76-82.

233. Battle of Tuckwiller's Hill historical marker photograph, 2023; privately held by Nancy E. Wiseman, Carmel, Indiana. The marker is located about two miles northwest of Lewisburg, West Virginia on U.S. Route 60.

234. United States War Department, *The War of the Rebellion: A Compilation of the Official Records of the Union and Confederate Armies,* Series I. 53 vols., (Washington, D.C.: Government Printing Office, 1889), v. 25, pt.2: 446, 7 May 1863 report from Major General Robert C. Schenck to Colonel J.C. Kelton; imaged, *HathiTrust Digital Library* (https://babel.hathitrust.org/cgi/pt?id=coo.31924085376626&view=1up&seq=448: accessed March 2022), images 448 of 978.

235. Sutton, *History of the Second Regiment*, 81-82.

236. David L. Mowery, *Morgan's Great Raid: The Remarkable Expedition from Kentucky to Ohio* (Charleston, South Carolina: The History Press: 2013), 96-108.

237. American Battlefield Trust, *Buffington Island,* (https://www.battlefields.org/learn/civil-war/battles/buffington-island: accessed 11 December 2023).

238. Buffington Island Battlefield Memorial photograph.

239. Compiled Military Service Record, James L. Wallar, Capt., Co. A, 2 WV Cav., Civil War.

240. Hewett, *Supplement to the Official Records*, p. 733.

241. Arnold Blumberg, "Alfred Duffie: A 'Napoleon' in the Civil War," *Military Heritage* 14:2 (August 2012): unpaginated on the website; *Warfare History Network* (https://warfarehistorynetwork.com/issue/military-heritage-august-2011-issue/) : accessed 4 October 2024).

242. Compiled Military Service Record, James L. Wallar, Capt., Co. A, 2 WV Cav., Civil War.

243. *Sketch of 2nd WVC*, 15-16.

244. Terry Lowry, *Last Sleep: The Battle of Droop Mountain, November 6, 1863* (Charleston, West Virginia: Pictorial Histories Publishing Co., Inc., 1996), 64.

245. Hewett, *Supplement to the Official Records*, p. 733.

246. Sutton, *History of the Second Regiment*, 109-110.

247. Lowry, *Last Sleep*, 67, 88-90.

248. Lowry, *Last Sleep*, 178.

249. Lowry, *Last Sleep*, 193-194.

250. Lowry, *Last Sleep*, 193-194.

251. Sutton, *History of the Second Regiment*, 109-110.

252. Droop Mountain photograph, 2022; privately held by Nancy E. Wiseman, Carmel, Indiana. The Droop Mountain Battlefield is now a West Virginia State Park located about 25 miles northeast of Lewisburg.

253. United States War Department, *The War of the Rebellion: A Compilation of the Official Records of the Union and Confederate Armies,* Series I. 53 vols., (Washington, D.C.: Government Printing Office, 1890), v.29, pt.1: 920-923, 18 February 1864 report from Brigadier General B.F. Kelley to Brigadier General G.W. Cullum; imaged, *HathiTrust Digital Library* (https://babel.hathitrust.org/cgi/pt?id=coo.31924077699886&view=1up&seq=938 : accessed March 2022), images 938-941 of 1172.

254. United States War Department, *The War of the Rebellion: A Compilation of the Official Records of the Union and Confederate Armies,* Series I. 53 vols., (Washington, D.C.: Government Printing Office, 1897), v.51, pt.1, sect.2: 1133, 8 December 1863 report from Assistant Adjutant-General Jas. L. Botsford to Brigadier General Duffié; imaged, *HathiTrust Digital Library* (https://babel.hathitrust.org/cgi/pt?id=coo.31924079609636&view=1up&seq=409 : accessed March 2022), image 409 of 746.

255. Hewett, *Supplement to the Official Records*, 734.

256. Compiled Military Service Record, James L. Wallar, Capt., Co. A, 2 WV Cav., Civil War.

257. Compiled Military Service Record, James L. Wallar, Capt., Co. A, 2 WV Cav., Civil War.

258. Sutton, *History of the Second Regiment*, 5-9.

259. Compiled Military Service Record, James L. Wallar, Capt., Co. A, 2 WV Cav., Civil War.

260. James L. Wallar Muster Card; Box 3a, record group Ar382, West Virginia Adjutant Generals' Papers, Union Regiments 1861-1865; West Virginia Archives and History Library, Charleston.

261. W.H. Powell to H.J. Samuels, letter, 9 May 1863; folder 4: "2nd West Virginia Cavalry-Field and Staff Letters," box 3, record group Ar382, West Virginia Adjutant Generals' Papers, Union Regiments, 1861-1865; West Virginia Archives and History Library, Charleston.

262. William H. Powell, "Autobiography," 18.

263. Compiled Military Service Record, James L. Wallar, Capt., Co. A, 2 WV Cav., Civil War.

264. United States War Department, *Revised United States Army Regulations of 1861, with an Appendix Containing the Changed and Laws Affecting Army Regulations and Articles of War to June 25, 1863.* (Washington, D.C.: Government Printing Office, 1863), 486; imaged, University of Michigan Library Digital Collections (https://name.umdl.umich.edu/AGY4285.0001.001 : accessed 25 July 2024).

265. United States War Department, *Revised United States Army Regulations of 1861*, 126.

266. United States War Department, *Revised United States Army Regulations of 1861*, 495.

267. Compiled Military Service Record, James L. Wallar, Capt., Co. A, 2 WV Cav., Civil War.

268. B. Shunk, photographer. *View of Harper's Ferry, Va. November 18th, 1863*; photograph. *Library of Congress Prints and Photographs Division* (https://www.loc.gov/pictures/item/2022631311/ : accessed 28 November 2021).

269. Provost Marshal's Office, Harpers Ferry National Historical Park photographs, 2023; privately held by Nancy E. Wiseman, Carmel, Indiana.

270. Compiled Military Service Record, James L. Wallar, Capt., Co. A, 2 WV Cav., Civil War.

271. Compiled Military Service Record, James L. Wallar, Capt., Co. A, 2 WV Cav., Civil War.

272. Sutton, *History of the Second Regiment*, 237-244.

273. Compiled Military Service Record, James L. Wallar, Capt., Co. A, 2 WV Cav., Civil War.

274. Captain J.L. Wallar, Company A, 2nd Regiment, West Virginia Volunteer Cavalry, c. 1862. *U.S. Army Photo Archives*, Military History Institute, Carlisle Barracks, Pennsylvania. 8x10 reproduction sent to Nancy E. Wiseman, April 26, 2001. Note: This photo was enhanced using AI-based tools by Karl Zemlin of Zemlin Photo.

275. Meigs County, Ohio, "Deed Record 26, Meigs County," pages 340-341, James L. Wallar and Frances Wallar to W. Alexander and Mary A. Alexander; imaged, *FamilySearch* (https://www.familysearch.org/ark:/61903/3:1:3Q9M-CSLF-N9ZK-8 : accessed 20 June 2022), digital film #8193207, Deeds, v. 25-26, 1863-1865, image 540 of 710.

276. Richland County, Illinois, "Deed Records R, 1864-1866," page 101, Abraham Davis and Frances Davis to J.L. Wallar; imaged, *FamilySearch* (https://www.familysearch.org/ark:/61903/3:1:3Q9M-CSBL-VSJF-J : accessed 15 January 2019); digital film #1307958, "Land deed records v. R (p.32-end), 1864-1866," image 45 of 1290.

277. 1865 Illinois state census, Richland County, Denver Township, page 52, James Walten; imaged, "Illinois, U.S., State Census Collection, 1825-1865," *Ancestry.com* (https://www.ancestry.com/search/collections/1079/ : accessed 10 April 2022); citing Record Series 103.010, 18 rolls. Illinois State Archives, Springfield, Illinois.

278. *Map of Richland County, Illinois*, imaged. *Illinois Digital Map Library* (http://usgwarchives.net/maps/illinois/il1875/RICHLAND.JPG : accessed 5 April 2022). Location of purchased land noted by author.

279. Kenyon Reed, Illinois Great Rivers Conference, The United Methodist Church Archivist, Springfield, Illinois, [e-mail for private use], to Nancy E. Wiseman, e-mail, 23 April 2022, "Questions about a 19th century minister/ancestor"; privately held by Nancy E. Wiseman, [e-mail & address for private use], Carmel, Indiana.

280. *History of Wayne and Clay Counties Illinois* (Chicago: Globe Publishing Company, Historical Publishers, 1884), 464.

281. Richland County, Illinois, "Deed Records Book V, 1866-1867," page 142, J.L. Wallar and Frances Wallar to Abraham Davis; imaged, *FamilySearch* (https://www.familysearch.org/ark:/61903/3:1:3Q9M-CSBP-H9TD-N : accessed 15 January 2019); digital film #8397291, "Land deed records v. V, 1866-1867," image 435 of 1244.

282. Methodist Episcopal Church, *The Doctrines and Discipline of the Methodist Episcopal Church 1868* (New York: Carlton & Lanahan, 1868), 64-67; digital images, *Google Books* (https://books.google.kg/books?id=8r9JAQAAMAAJ : accessed 23 April 2022).

283. Methodist Episcopal Church, Southern Illinois Conference, *Minutes and Journal of the Southern Illinois Annual Conference of the Methodist Episcopal Church Held at Litchfield, Montgomery County, Illinois, September 25-28, 1867* (Alton, Illinois: S.V. Crossman & Co., 1867), 6, 7, 20, 23; imaged, *Divinity Archive* (https://divinityarchive.com/handle/11258/4381 : accessed 10 April 2022).

284. *The Doctrines and Discipline of the Methodist Episcopal Church 1868*, 215-216.

285. Methodist Episcopal Church, Southern Illinois Conference, *Journal and Minutes of the Eighteenth Session of the Southern Illinois Conference held at Vandalia, Fayette Co., Ill., September 15-21, 1869* (Cincinnati: Western Methodist Book Concern, 1869), 4, 22; imaged, *Internet Archive* (https://archive.org/details/minutesofsession101818611867meth/page/n361/mode/2up : accessed 10 April 2022).

286. "Teachers' Institute," *Crawford County [Illinois] Argus*, 3 March 1870, page 1, column 1, imaged, *Robinson History Archives Online* (https://robinson.historyarchives.online/home : accessed 28 January 2024).

287. *Crawford County [Illinois] Argus*, 26 May 1870, page 3, column 2; imaged, *Robinson History Archives Online* (https://robinson.historyarchives.online/home : accessed 28 January 2024).

288. *Crawford County [Illinois] Argus*, 14 July 1870, page 3, column 2; imaged, *Robinson History Archives Online* (https://robinson.historyarchives.online/home : accessed 28 January 2024).

289. Reed to Wiseman, e-mail, 23 April 2022; information on Bishop Matthew Simpson from "Bishop Matthew Simpson, University's First President, Eulogizes President Lincoln." DePauw University, 2022 (https://www.depauw.edu/news-media/latest-news/details/21685/).

290. Reed to Wiseman, e-mail, 23 April 2022.

291. "Local News Recorded a Half Century Ago," *Robinson [Illinois] Argus*, 16 February 1921, page 5, column 2; imaged, *Robinson History Archives Online* (https://robinson.historyarchives.online/home : accessed 28 January 2024).

292. Lillie May Wallar grave marker in Old Robinson Cemetery, Robinson, Illinois, photograph, 2022; privately held by Nancy E. Wiseman. No dates are inscribed on any side of this marker. The worn inscription reads, "LILLIE MAY daughter of J.L. & F.E. WALLAR."

293. "Town Convention," *Crawford County [Illinois] Argus*, 9 March 1871, page 3, column 3, imaged, *Robinson History Archives Online* (https://robinson.historyarchives.online/home : accessed 28 January 2024).

294. "The Conference," *Cairo [Illinois] Daily Bulletin*, 28 September 1871, page 3, column 2; imaged, *GenealogyBank* (https://www.genealogybank.com : accessed 17 February 2019).

295. "The Conference," *Cairo [Illinois] Daily Bulletin*, 3 October 1871, page 5, column 4; imaged, *GenealogyBank* (https://www.genealogybank.com : accessed 17 February 2019).

296. *Crawford County Argus* (Robinson, Illinois), 14 September 1871, page 3, column 2; imaged, *Robinson History Archives Online* (https://robinson.historyarchives.online/home : accessed 28 January 2024).

297. *Crawford County Argus* (Robinson, Illinois), 12 October 1871, page 3, column 2; imaged, *Robinson History Archives Online* (https://robinson.historyarchives.online/home : accessed 28 January 2024).

298. *Combined History of Edwards, Lawrence and Wabash Counties*, 266.

299. *History of White County Illinois: Together with Sketches of its Cities, Villages, and Townships, Educational, Religious, Civil, Military and Political History; Portraits of Prominent Persons, and Biographies of Representative Citizens* (Chicago: Inter-State Publishing Company, 1883), 517.

300. *History of White County Illinois*, 554.

301. *100 Years of Methodism, 1850-1950 in Carmi, Illinois* (n.p. : Carmi, Illinois, 1950), unpaginated; imaged, *University of Illinois at Urbana-Champaign and the Open Content Alliance* (http://hdl.handle.net/10111/UIUCOCA:100yearsofmethod00firs : accessed 1 August 2022).

302. "Rev. Wallar's Kindheartedness," *Robinson [Illinois] Argus*, 26 December 1900, page 1, column 6, imaged, *Robinson History Archives Online* (https://www.robinson.historyarchives.online;home : accessed 28 January 2024).

303. *World Population Review* (https://worldpopulationreview.com/us-cities/cairo-il-population : accessed 12 December 2023); and William Henry Perrin, *History of Alexander, Union and Pulaski Counties, Illinois* (Chicago: O.L. Baskin & Company, 1883), 163-164.

304. The church building appears on maps published in both 1867 and 1888, so presumably was at the same location in the early 1870s. *Cairo, Illinois* (Chicago Lithographing Co., 1867); imaged, *Library of Congress Geography and Map Division* (https://lccn.loc.gov/73693346 : accessed 23 April 2022); and *Perspective Map of the City of Cairo, Ill.* (Milwaukee: Henry Wellge & Co., 1888); imaged, *Library of Congress Geography and Map Division* (http://hdl.loc.gov/loc/gmd/g4104c.pm001420 : accessed 23 April 2022).

305. *Cairo [Illinois] Daily Bulletin*, 16 October 1873, page 4, column2; imaged, *GenealogyBank* (http://www.genealogybank.com : accessed 20 February 2019.

306. "The Straight Path," *Cairo [Illinois] Daily Bulletin*, 26 October 1873, page 4, column 4; imaged, *GenealogyBank* (http://www.genealogybank.com : accessed 17 February 2019.

307. "Rev. Dr. Wallar," *Mount Carmel [Illinois] Register*, 27 December 1900, page 1, column 2; imaged, *Newspapers.com* (https://www.newspapers.com/image/440258595/ : accessed 10 March 2019).

308. "Royal Arch Masons," *Crawford County [Illinois]Argus*, 15 March 1870, page 3, column 2; imaged, *Robinson History Archives Online* (https://robinson.historyarchives.online/home : accessed 28 January 2024).

309. "Ascension Day," *[Illinois] Bulletin*, 17 May 1874, page 4, column 2; imaged, *GenealogyBank* (https://www.genealogybank.com : accessed 17 February 2019).

310. S. Brent Morris, *The Complete Idiot's Guide to Freemasonry* (New York: Alpha Books, 2013).

311. L.H. Plogsted, *Knights Templar*. (Cottier & Denton, Buffalo, monographic, 1875). *Notated Music; Library of Congress* (https:www.loc.gov/item/sm1875.07951/ : accessed 26 May 2022).

312. "They Are Coming," *Cairo [Illinois] Bulletin*, 17 May 1874, page 5, column 4; imaged, *GenealogyBank* (https://www.genealogybank.com : accessed 17 February 2019).

313. Patricia Kmiec, "Parading the Children: The Leisure Activities of Ontario's Protestant Sunday Schools, 1840-1870," *Historical Papers 2012: Canadian Society of Church History*, 71; imaged, (https://historicalpapers.journals.yorku.ca/index.php/historicalpapers/article/download/39111/35474 : accessed 24 April 2022).

314. "The Object of the Methodist Excursion," *Cairo [Illinois] Bulletin*, 27 June 1875, page 3, column 5; imaged, *Newspapers.com* (https://www.newspapers.com/image/70850174/ : accessed 17 September 2014).

315. "Come and Gone," *Cairo [Illinois] Bulletin,* 23 May 1874, page 4, columns 3-4; imaged, *GenealogyBank* (https://www.genealogybank.com : accessed 24 April 2022).

316. 1870 U.S. census, Crawford County, Illinois, population schedule, Martin Township, page 77B, dwelling 123, family 127, Fay K. Wallar; digital images, *Ancestry.com* (http://www.ancestry.com : accessed 22 December 2023); citing National Archives microfilm publication M593, roll 214

317. "U.S., School catalogs, 1765-1935," database, *Ancestry.com* (http://www.ancestry.com: accessed 27 December 2023), *Indiana, Union Christian College, 1871, 1872, 1873, 1874, and 1876*, Charles Millard Wallar and Harry Herbert Wallar.

318. "Roll of Honor," *Cairo [Illinois] Bulletin*, 24 May 1874, page 4, column 3; imaged, *GenealogyBank* (https://www.genealogybank.com : accessed 24 April 2022).

319. Perrin, *History of Alexander, Union and Pulaski Counties, Illinois*, 194.

320. "Better," *Cairo [Illinois] Bulletin*, 20 June 1874, page 4, column 2; imaged, *Newspapers.com* (https://www.newspapers.com/image/70838374/ : accessed 24 April 2022).

321. "Mr. Wallar," *Cairo [Illinois] Bulletin*, 27 June 1874, page 4, column 2; imaged, *Newspapers.com* (https://www.newspapers.com/image/46332339/ : accessed 24 April 2022).

322. "Personal Notes," *Cairo [Illinois] Bulletin*, 1 July 1874, page 4, column 3; imaged, *Newspapers.com* (https://www.newspapers.com/image/70838989/ : accessed 27 September 2014).

323. "River, Weather, Steamboats," *New Orleans [Louisiana] Times-Picayune*, 26 November 1874, page 8, column 4; imaged, *Newspapers.com* (https://www.newspapers.com/image/27013268/ : accessed 12 May 2022).

324. "The Knights Templar," *New Orleans [Louisiana] Republican*, 15 November 1874, page 1, column 4; imaged, *Newspapers.com* (https://www.newspapers.com/image/326034952/ : accessed 12 May 2022).

325. Keith Norington, "The Elegant Str. *Thompson Dean*," *The Waterways Journal Weekly*, 4 June 2021, (https://www.waterwaysjournal.net/2021/06/04/the-elegant-str-thompson-dean/ : accessed 14 May 2022).

326. Leonard V. Huber, "The Mississippi Leviathans," *Louisiana History: The Journal of the Louisiana Historical Association*, vol. 22, no. 3, 1981, p. 239-251; imaged, *JSTOR*. (http://www.jstor.org/stable/4232094 : accessed 15 May 2022).

327. "The Knights Templar," *Cairo Bulletin*, 22 November 1874, page 3, columns 4-5; imaged, *Newspapers.com* (https://www.newspapers.com/image/70850939 : accessed 22 April 2022).

328. "The Dawn of Peace," *New Orleans [Louisiana] Times-Picayune*, 28 November 1874, page 8, column 2; imaged, *Newspapers.com* (https://www.newspapers.com/image/27013284/ : accessed 12 May 2022); and "Knights Templar," *New Orleans [Louisiana] Bulletin*, 1 December 1874, page 1, column 1; imaged, *Newspapers.com* (https://www.newspapers.com/image/367227566/ : accessed 12 May 2022).

329. Huber, "The Mississippi Leviathans," 246.

330. "The Dawn of Peace," *New Orleans Times-Picayune*, 28 November 1874.

331. "Knights Templars," Kansas City [Missouri] Daily Journal of Commerce, 9 December 1874, page 3, column 3; imaged, Newspapers.com (https://www.newspapers.com/image/666702646/ : accessed 30 May 2022).

332. "Knights Templar," *New Orleans [Louisiana] Bulletin*, 1 December 1874.

333. "The Levee," *New Orleans [Louisiana] Times-Picayune*, 1 December 1874, page 8, column 1; imaged, *Newspapers.com* (https://www.newspapers.com/image/27013308/ : accessed 12 May 2022).

334. "The Levee," *New Orleans Times-Picayune*, 1 December 1874.

335. "Knights Templar," *New Orleans [Louisiana] Times-Picayune*, 2 December 1874, page 1, columns 5-6, continued on page 8, columns 1-2; imaged, *Newspapers.com* (https://www.newspapers.com/image/27013309/ : accessed 12 May 2022).

336. "Knights Templar," *New Orleans Times-Picayune*, 2 December 1874.

337. "Knights Templar Notes," *New Orleans [Louisiana] Republican*, 2 December 1874, page 1, column 3; imaged, *Newspapers.com* (https://www.newspapers.com/image/326038561/ : accessed 12 May 2022).

338. *New Orleans [Louisiana] Times-Picayune*, 2 December 1874, page 1, column 6; imaged, *Newspapers.com* (https://www.newspapers.com/image/27013309/ : accessed 12 May 2022).

339. "Knights Templar Notes," *New Orleans [Louisiana] Republican*, 5 December 1874, page 1, column 2; imaged, *Newspapers.com* (https://www.newspapers.com/image/326039108/ : accessed 28 May 2022).

340. "Steamboats," *New Orleans [Louisiana] Bulletin*, 4 December 1874, page 7, column 4; imaged, *Newspapers.com* (https://www.newspapers.com/image/367228092/ : accessed 30 May 2022).

341. "The River," *New Orleans [Louisiana] Times-Picayune*, 5 December 1874, page 6, column 5; imaged, *Newspapers.com* (https://www.newspapers.com/image/27013340/ : accessed 30 May 2022).

342. "River Intelligence," *Memphis [Tennessee] Daily Appeal*, 9 December 1874, page 3, column 4; imaged, *Newspapers.com* (https://www.newspapers.com/image/39791697/ : accessed 30 May 2022).

343. "River Telegrams," *Memphis [Tennessee] Public Ledger*, 10 December 1874, page 2, column 4; imaged, *Newspapers.com* (https://www.newspapers.com/image/587060358/ : accessed 30 May 2022).

344. "Mr. Wallar's Lecture," *Cairo [Illinois] Bulletin*, 23 February 1875, page 3, column 2; imaged, *Newspapers.com* (https://www.newspapers.com/image/70840156/ : accessed 12 May 2022).

345. "Lecture," *Cairo [Illinois] Bulletin*, 14 March 1875, page 3, column 2; imaged, *Newspapers.com* (https://www.newspapers.com/image/70841862/ : accessed 12 May 2022).

346. "Temperance Organization," *Cairo [Illinois] Bulletin*, 15 April 1875, page 3, column 2; imaged, *Newspapers.com* (https://newspapers.com : accessed 12 May 2022).

347. "To Leave," *Cairo [Illinois] Bulletin*, 16 September 1875, page 3, column 3; imaged, *Newspapers.com* (https://www.newspapers.com/image/70856395/ : accessed 27 September 2014).

348. "A Great Storm," *Decatur [Illinois] Daily Republican*, 5 June 1877, page 2, column 3; imaged, *Newspapers.com* (https://www.newspapers.com/image/32381004/ : accessed 12 February 2024).

349. Haley Church, "200 Years of Methodism: Trinity United Methodist Plans Celebratory Events," *Hometown Register*, 8 April 2017, archived HTML edition (https://www.hometownregister.com/community.200-years-of-methodism-trinity-united-methodist-plans-celebratory-events/article_90b4faca-1c8b-11e7-b31b-e738201cde5e.html : accessed 8 December 2024).

350. Haley Church, "A New Era: The Register Office is Moving to New Ninth Street Location," *Hometown Register*, 27 May 2017, archived HTML edition (https://www.hometownregister.com/news/a-new-era-the-register-office-is-moving-to-new-ninth-street-location/article_771914d6-42e5-11e7-9f46-f770eefebac3.html : accessed 8 December 2024).

351. *Minutes of the Southern Illinois Conference of the Methodist Episcopal Church, Held at Olney, Illinois, September 13-18, 1876* (St. Louis: Chancy R. Barns, 1876), unpaginated pages and pages 17, 33; imaged, *Divinity Archive* (https://divinityarchive.com/handle/11258/4394 : accessed 10 April 2022).

352. "Marriages," *Mount Carmel [Illinois] Register*, 17 May 1877, page 4, column 7; imaged, *Newspapers.com* (https://www.newspapers.com/image/757467563/ : accessed 5 February 2024).

353. "Cyclone," *Mount Carmel [Illinois] Register*, 7 June 1877, page 1; imaged, *Newspapers.com* (https://www.newspapers.com/image/757467607/ : accessed 12 February 2024).

354. "The Mt. Carmel Horror," *Evansville [Illinois] Journal*, 8 June 1877, page 7, column 3; imaged, *Newspapers.com* (https://www.newspapers.com/image/771751576/ : accessed 2 June 2022).

355. "Casualties," *Chicago [Illinois] Tribune*, 7 June 1877, page 2, column 3, *Newspapers.com* (https://www.newspapers.com/image/349751378/ : accessed 2 June 2022).

356. The former Methodist Episcopal Church in Mount Carmel, Illinois photograph, 2022; privately held by Nancy E. Wiseman. The building, on East Fourth Street between Market and Mulberry Streets is currently used as an antique shop. The arched window openings can still be seen on the sides of the building.

357. "The Mount Carmel Tornado," *Sullivan [Indiana] Democrat,* 13 June 1877, page 2, column 4; imaged, *NewspaperArchive* (https://www.newspaperarchive.com : accessed 12 February 2024).

358. "The Courthouse," *Harper's Weekly*, 21:1070 (June 30, 1877), 508; imaged, *Internet Archive* (https://archive.org/details/sim_harpers-weekly_1877-06-30_21-1070/page/508/mode/2up : accessed 22 February 2024).

359. "Mt. Carmel Cyclone," *New Orleans [Louisiana] Daily Picayune,* 10 June 1877, page 3, column 1; imaged, *Newspapers.com* (https://www.newspapers.com/image/27308770/ : accessed 12 February 2024).

360. "Taking Out the Dead," *Harper's Weekly*, 21:1070 (June 30, 1877), 508; imaged, *Internet Archive* (https://archive.org/details/sim_harpers-weekly_1877-06-30_21-1070/page/508/mode/2up : accessed 22 February 2024).

361. William C. Wallar grave marker in Rose Hill Cemetery, Mount Carmel, Illinois photograph, 2022; privately held by Nancy E. Wiseman. Inscription reads, "WILLIAM C., Son of Rev. J.L. & F.E. WALLAR DIED June 4, 1877 AGED 17 yrs 9 m's, 9 ds." Note: It's unclear whether William's middle initial is C or G. He was not enumerated with a middle initial in either the 1860 or 1870 U.S. censuses.

362. "Hundreds for Humanity," *Evansville [Indiana] Courier and Press*, 8 June 1877, page 4, column 2; imaged, *Newspapers.com* (https://www.newspapers.com/image/768042061/ : accessed 5 February 2024).

363. "Local Breveties," *Cairo [Illinois] Bulletin*, 9 June 1877, page 3, column 3; imaged, *Newspapers.com* (https://www.newspapers.com/image/70857523/: accessed 2 June 2022).

364. "Local Breveties," *Cairo [Illinois] Bulletin*, 8 June 1877, page 3, column 3; imaged, *Newspapers.com* (https://www.newspapers.com/image/70857395/ : accessed 2 June 2022).

365. "Local Breveties," *Cairo [Illinois] Bulletin*, 12 June 1877, page 3, column 3; imaged, *Newspapers.com* (https://www.newspapers.com/image/70857714/ : accessed 2 June 2022).

366. "Hundreds for Humanity," *Evansville Courier and Press*, 8 June 1877.

367. "The Mount Carmel Disaster-A View of the Ruins on Fourth Street," *Frank Leslie's Illustrated Newspaper*, 44: 1135 (June 30, 1877), 293; imaged, *Internet Archive* (https://archive.org/details/sim_leslies-weekly_1877-06-30_44_1135/page/292/mode/2up?view=theater : accessed 14 March 2024).

368. S.A. Changnon, Jr. and G. E. Stout, "Tornadoes in Illinois," *Illinois State Water Survey Circular 63*, (Urbana, Illinois, 1957): 5, Illinois State Water Survey (https://www.isws.illinois.edu/pubdoc/C/ISWSC-63.pdf : accessed 24 February 2024).

369. "Hundreds for Humanity," *Evansville Courier and Press*, 8 June 1877.

370. *Mount Carmel [Illinois] Register*, 10 June 1877, page 2, column 1, *Newspapers.com* (https://www.newspapers.com/image/757467626/ : accessed 14 March 2024).

371. "To Our Country Friends," *Mount Carmel [Illinois] Register*, 14 June 1877, page 4, column 3, *Newspapers.com* (https://www.newspapers.com/image/757467649/ : accessed 14 March 2024).

372. "To Our Country Friends," *Mount Carmel Register*, 14 June 1877.

373. "Repairing the Damage," *Mount Carmel [Illinois] Register*, 21 June 1877, page 4, column 3; imaged, *Newspapers.com* (https://www.newspapers.com/image/757467685/ : accessed 8 December 2024).

374. "Marriages," *Mount Carmel [Illinois] Register*, 31 January 1878, page 4, column 5; imaged, *Newspapers.com* (https://www.newspapers.com/image/757468864/ : accessed 5 February 2024).

375. *The History of Henry and St. Clair Counties, Missouri*, 600.

376. Miami Medical College of Cincinnati, *Alumni Catalogue of Miami Medical College in Cincinnati: Including Members of the Faculty, 1852-1900.* (Cincinnati, 1901), 123; imaged, *Cincinnati & Hamilton County Public Library Digital Library, Yearbooks & School Publications* (https://digital.cincinnatilibrary.org/digital/collection/p16998coll3/id/101392 : accessed 8 August 2024).

377. "Registered Locals, *Mount Carmel [Illinois] Register*, 25 April 1878, page 4, column 1, *Newspapers.com* (https://www.newspapers.com/image/757469414/ : accessed 24 January 2025).

378. *Find a Grave*, database with images (http://www.findagrave.com : accessed 29 March 2020), memorial 123729079, Katie Wallar; Sumner Cemetery, Sumner, Lawrence County, Illinois; grave marker photographed by Find a Grave user B. Pipher.

379. "Illinois, County Marriages, 1810-1940," imaged, *FamilySearch* (https://www.familysearch.org/ark:/61903/1:1:QK92-TDNH : accessed 15 February 2025), marriage of Fay K. Waller to Martha M. Leeper, 1 October 1879.

380. *Minutes of the Southern Illinois Conference of the Methodist Episcopal Church, Held at Mt. Vernon, Illinois, September 20-24, 1877* (St. Lewis: Chancy R. Barns, 1877), unpaginated pages and pages 73, 82, 116; imaged, *Divinity Archive* (https://divinityarchive.com/handle/11258/4395 : accessed 10 April 2022).

381. "Rev. James L. Wallar, D.D.," *Minutes of the Fiftieth Session of the Southern Illinois Conference of the Methodist Episcopal Church Held at Alton, Ills., Sept. 18-23, 1901*, (Saint Louis, Missouri: Perrin & Smith Printing Company, 1901), 39-40, *Illinois Library Digital Collections* (https://libsysdigi.library.uiuc.edu/OCA/Books2009-08/minutesofsession/mi nutesofsession505219011903meth/minutesofsession505219011903meth.pdf) .

382. *Minutes of the Thirty-Third Session of the Southern Illinois Conference of the Methodist Episcopal Church, Held at Fairfield, Illinois, September 24-29, 1884* (Olney, Illinois: News Steam Printing Co., 1884), unpaginated section; imaged, *Divinity Archive* (https://divinityarchive.com/handle/11258/4397 : accessed 12 April 2022.

383. *Minutes and Journal of the Twenty-Ninth Session of the Southern Illinois Conference of the Methodist Episcopal Church, Held at Fairfield, Illinois, September 1-6, 1880* (St. Louis: C. R. Barns, 1880), unpaginated pages and pages 14-16, 19, 21, 35, 69; imaged, *Divinity Archive* (https://divinityarchive.com/handle/11258/4396 : accessed 12 April 2022).

384. Reed to Wiseman, e-mail, 23 April 2022.

385. William Henry Perrin, editor, History of Effingham County, Illinois. (Chicago: O.L. Baskin & Co., 1883), 161.

386. William Henry Perrin, editor, *History of Crawford and Clark Counties, Illinois.* (Chicago: O.L. Baskin & Co., 1883), 181.

387. "Home & Neighborhood," *Robinson Argus* (Robinson, Illinois), 14 November 1883, page 1, column 2; imaged, *Robinson History Archives Online* (https://www.robinson.historyarchives.online : accessed 28 January 2024).

388. *Manual of the General Conference of the Methodist Episcopal Church, at its Session Held in Philadelphia, PA., May 1, 1884* (New York: Phillips & Hunt, 1884), pages 18, 28; imaged, *Divinity Archive* (https://divinityarchive.com/handle/11258/5093 : accessed 12 April 2022).

389. "Doings of the Churches", *Effingham [Illinois] Democrat,* 16 May 1884, page 3, column 4; imaged, *Newspapers.com* (https://www.newspapers.com/image/875085021/ : accessed 18 August 2024).

390. "They Ratify", *Effingham [Illinois] Democrat*, 8 August 1884, page 3, column 5; imaged, *Newspapers.com* (https://www.newspapers.com/image/874306857/ : accessed 18 August 2024).

391. "City Chat", *Effingham [Illinois] Democrat*, 7 November 1884, page 3, column 2; imaged, *Newspapers.com* (https://www.newspapers.com/image/874306932/ : accessed 18 August 2024).

392. "Our History," Garrett Evangelical Theological Seminary, February 16, 2022. (https://www.garrett.edu/about/our-history/ : accessed 16 April 2022).

393. *Minutes of the Thirty-Third Session of the Southern Illinois Conference of the Methodist Episcopal Church, Held at Fairfield, Illinois, September 24-29, 1884,* unpaginated section and pages 31-32, 56.

394. *Altamont [Illinois] News*, page 1, column 3; imaged, *Newspapers.com* (https://www.newspapers.com/image/864573210/ : accessed 18 August 2024).

395. *Proceedings, Sermon, Essays, and Addresses of the Centennial Methodist Conference Held in Mt. Vernon Place Methodist Episcopal Church, Baltimore, MD., December 9-17, 1884. With a Historical Statement* (Cincinnati: Cranston and Stowe, 1885), xiv, 11, 70-72; imaged, *Divinity Archive* (https://divinityarchive.com/handle/11258/4832 : accessed 12 April 2022).

396. "Programme," *Centralia [Illinois] Daily Sentinel*, 28 March 1885, page 1, column 4; imaged, *Newspaper Archive* (https://www.newspaperarchive.com : accessed 18 March 2024).

397. "City Chat," *Effingham [Illinois] Democrat*, 2 January 1885, page 9, column 2; imaged, *Newspapers.com* (https://www.newspapers.com/image/874307008/ : accessed 18 August 2024).

398. "U.S., World War I Draft Registration Cards, 1917-1918," database with images, *Ancestry.com* (https://www.ancestry.com : accessed 22 January 2024), entry for Harry Herbert Wallar.

399. "Memorial Services," *Altamont [Illinois] News*, 13 August 1885, page 1, column 5; imaged, *Newspapers.com* (https://www.newspapers.com/image/864576380/ : accessed 18 August 2024).

400. *Newton [Illinois] Press*, 13 January 1886, page 2, column 3; imaged, *Newspapers.com* (https://www.newspapers.com/image/874231576/ : accessed 19 August 2024).

401. *Effingham [Illinois] Democrat*, 22 January 1886, page 3, column 3; imaged, *Newspapers.com* (https://www.newspapers.com/image/874291297/ : accessed 19 August 2024.

402. *Effingham [Illinois] Democrat*, 12 February 1886, page 6, column 1; imaged, *Newspapers.com* (https://www.newspapers.com/image/874291378/ : accessed 19 August 2024).

403. *Effingham [Illinois] Democrat*, 5 February 1886, page 3, column 3; imaged, *Newspapers.com* https://www.newspapers.com/image/874291346/ : accessed 22 April 2024).

404. "Bellmont," *Mount Carmel [Illinois] Republican*, 30 April 1886, page 1, column 4; imaged, *Newspapers.com* (https://www.newspapers.com/image/754645423/ : accessed 19 August 2024).

405. "Personal," *Mount Carmel [Illinois] Republican*, 2 April 1886, page 4, column 3; imaged, *Newspapers.com* (https://www.newspapers.com/image/754645303/ : accessed 19 August 2024).

406. "Personal," *Mount Carmel [Illinois] Republican*, 19 November 1886, page 4, column 4; imaged, *Newspapers.com* (https://www.newspapers.com/image/754646878/ : accessed 20 August 2024).

407. *Effingham [Illinois] Democrat*, 11 June 1886, page 3, column 3; imaged, *Newspapers.com* (https://www.newspapers.com/image/874291802/ : accessed 22 April 2024).

408. *Effingham [Illinois] Democrat*, 30 July 1886, page 3, column 2; imaged, *Newspapers.com* (https://www.newspapers.com/image/874291974/ : accessed 22 April 2024).

409. "Prohibition convention," *Altamont [Illinois] News*, 19 August 1886, page 4, column 2; imaged, Newspapers.com (https://www.newspapers.com/image/864581144/ : accessed 20 August 2024).

410. "Has Not Repented", *Albion Journal*, 8 July 1886.

411. "Has Not Repented", *Albion Journal*, 8 July 1886.

412. "Personals," *Effingham [Illinois] Democrat*, 8 October 1886, page 3, column 3; imaged; *Newspapers.com* (https://www.newspapers.com/image/874292227 : accessed 20 August 2024).

413. George E. Ross, *Centralia, Illinois: A Pictorial History.* (St. Louis: G. Bradley Publishing, Inc., 1992), 22, 66. The northeast corner of Fifth and Poplar Streets is currently (2023) a parking lot for a tanning salon.

414. Cornerstone on the First United Methodist Church, 103 South Elm Street, Centralia, Illinois photograph, 2022; privately held by Nancy E. Wiseman, Carmel, Indiana.

415. *Centralia [Illinois] Daily Sentinel*, 14 March 1887, page 2, column 3; imaged, *NewspaperArchive* (https://www.newspaperarchive.com : accessed 14 March 2024).

416. "City News," *Centralia [Illinois] Daily Sentinel*, 16 March 1887, page 1, column 3; imaged, *NewspaperArchive* (https://www.newspaperarchive.com : accessed 14 March 2024);

417. "City News," *Centralia [Illinois] Daily Sentinel*, 21 March 1887, page 1, column 2; imaged, *NewspaperArchive* (https://www.newspaperarchive.com : accessed 14 March 2024).

418. *Effingham [Illinois] Democrat*, 1 April 1887, page 3, column 3; imaged, *Newspapers.com* (https://www.newspapers.com/image/874292820/ : accessed 2 May 2024).

419. *Centralia [Illinois] Daily Sentinel*, 5 May 1887, page 4, column 4.

420. "The Sweet Singers," *Centralia [Illinois] Daily Sentinel*, 7 May 1887, page 4, column 2; imaged, *NewspaperArchive* (https://www.newspaperarchive.com : accessed 14 March 2024).

421. "The Camp Fire," *Centralia [Illinois] Daily Sentinel*, 12 May 1887, page 6, column 3; imaged, *NewspaperArchive* (https://www.newspaperarchive.com : accessed 14 March 2024).

422. "Commencement Week," *Centralia [Illinois] Democrat*, 13 May 1887, page 5, column 3; imaged, *NewspaperArchive* (https://www.newspaperarchive.com : accessed 14 March 2024).

423. "State and Neighborhood," *Albion [Illinois] Journal*, 30 June 1887, page 2, column 3; imaged, *Illinois Digital Newspaper Collections* (https://idnc.library.illinois.edu/ : accessed 6 Jul 2022).

424. "Personal," *Mount Carmel [Illinois] Republican*, 24 June 1887, page 4, column 6; imaged, *Newspapers.com* (https://www.newspapers.com/image/754648579/ : accessed 21 August 2024).

425. "Beyond the Vale," *Centralia [Illinois] Daily Sentinel*, 27 June 1887, page 1, column 3; imaged, *NewspaperArchive* (https://www.newspaperarchive.com : accessed 12 March 2024).

426. "Within the Tomb," *Centralia [Illinois] Sentinel*, 30 June 1887, page 1, column 2; imaged, *NewspaperArchive* (https://www.newspaperarchive.com : accessed 12 March 2024).

427. "Her Sufferings Ended," *Centralia [Illinois] Democrat*, 1 July 1887, page 4, column 3; imaged, *NewspaperArchive* (https://www.newspaperarchive.com : accessed 18 March 2024).

428. "City News," *Centralia [Illinois] Daily Sentinel*, 6 July 1887, page 1, column 1; imaged, *NewspaperArchive* (https://www.newspaperarchive.com : accessed 18 March 2024).

429. "Died," *Centralia [Illinois] Daily Sentinel*, 16 April 1888, page 1, column 7; imaged, *NewspaperArchive* (https://www.newspaperarchive.com : accessed 18 March 2024).

430. "Local and Personal," *Centralia [Illinois] Daily Sentinel*, 2 February 1888, page 1, column 1; imaged, *Newspaper Archive* (https://newspaperarchive.com : accessed 31 August 2024).

431. "Local and Personal," *Centralia [Illinois] Daily Sentinel*, 3 February 1888, page 1, column 2; imaged, *Newspaper Archive* (https://newspaperarchive.com: accessed 31 August 2024).

432. "Local and Personal," *Centralia [Illinois] Daily Sentinel*, 6 February 1888, page 1, column 1; imaged, *Newspaper Archive* (https://newspaperarchive.com: accessed 31 August 2024).

433. "Local and Personal," *Centralia [Illinois] Daily Sentinel*, 8 February 1888, page 1, column 1; imaged, *Newspaper Archive* (https://newspaperarchive.com: accessed 31 August 2024).

434. "Church Notes," *Centralia [Illinois] Daily Sentinel*, 10 March 1888, page 4, column 5; imaged, *Newspaper Archive* (https://newspaperarchive.com: accessed 31 August 2024).

435. "Local and Personal," *Centralia [Illinois] Daily Sentinel*, 23 February 1888, page 1, column 4; imaged, *Newspaper Archive* (https://newspaperarchive.com: accessed 31 August 2024).

436. "Local and Personal," *Centralia [Illinois] Daily Sentinel*, 17 April 1888, page 1, column 5; imaged, *Newspaper Archive* (https://newspaperarchive.com: accessed 31 August 2024).

437. "Local and Personal," *Centralia [Illinois] Daily Sentinel*, 12 March 1888, page 1, column 4; imaged, *Newspaper Archive* (https://newspaperarchive.com: accessed 31 August 2024).

438. "Local and Personal," *Centralia [Illinois] Daily Sentinel*, 2 April 1888, page 1, column 4; imaged, *Newspaper Archive* (https://newspaperarchive.com: accessed 31 August 2024).

439. "Died," *Centralia Daily Sentinel,* 16 April 1888.

440. "Local and Personal," *Centralia Daily Sentinel*, 17 April 1888.

441. *Journal of the General Conference of the Methodist Episcopal Church, Held in New York, May 1-31, 1888* (New York: Phillips & Hunt, 1888), pages 11, 80, 377, 380; imaged, *Divinity Archive* (https://divinityarchive.com/handle/11258/2756 : accessed 12 April 2022).

442. *Music Division, The New York Public Library.* "Metropolitan Opera House," 1884. The New York Public Library Digital Collections. (https://digitalcollections.nypl.org/items/ac1c2070-ab79-0134-8d0c-0050568 6a51c : accessed 12 April 2024).

443. "The War of the Operas: New Money vs. Old in *The Gilded Age,*" *History Extra* (https://www.historyextra.com/period/victorian/war-of-the-operas-gilded-age / : accessed 18 April 2024).

444. "Ready for its Sessions," *New York Times,* 1 May 1888, page 8, column 3, *Times Machine* (Timesmachine.nytimes.com/timesmachine/1888/05/01/106320538.html : accessed 18 April 2024)

445. "Local and Personal," *Centralia [Illinois] Daily Sentinel*, 29 May 1888, page 1, column 5; imaged, *Newspaper Archive* (https://newspaperarchive.com: accessed 31 August 2024).

446. "A Social Surprise," *Centralia [Illinois] Daily Sentinel*, 5 July 1888, page 1 column 5; imaged, *Newspaper Archive* (https://newspaperarchive.com: accessed 31 August 2024).

447. "A Midnight Blaze," *Centralia [Illinois] Sentinel*, 26 September 1901, page 2, column 4; imaged, *Newspaper Archive* (https://newspaperarchive.com : accessed 2 September 2024). NOTE: On September 22, 1901, Jeanette Wallar's home burned. After the fire, the property was purchased by the Merchants State Bank on October 5, 1901, the ruins razed, and a bank was built. The address is now 200 East Broadway, Centralia: "Local and Personal," *Centralia [Illinois] Daily Sentinel*, 7 October 1901, page 2, column 4; imaged, *NewspaperArchive* (https://newspaperarchive.com : accessed 2 September 2024).

448. "Local and Personal," *Centralia [Illinois] Daily Sentinel*, 15 August 1889, page 1, column 1; imaged, *Newspaper Archive* (https://newspaperarchive.com: accessed 2 September 2024).

449. *Transactions of the Grand Chapter Royal Arch Masons of the State of Michigan; Fifty-Fourth Annual Convocation* (Coldwater, Michigan: Grand Chapter Royal Arch Masons, 1902), page 16; imaged, *Google Books.* (https://www.google.com/books/edition/Transactions_of_the_Annual_Con vocation/80niAAAAMAAJ : accessed 12 June 2019).

450. "Local and Personal," *Centralia [Illinois] Daily Sentinel*, 10 August 1889, page 4, column 1; imaged, *Newspaper Archive* (https://newspaperarchive.com : accessed 18 April 2024); and "Local and Personal," *Centralia [Illinois] Daily Sentinel*, 22 October 1889, page 2, column 2; imaged, *Newspaper Archive* (https://newspaperarchive.com : accessed 18 April 2024).

451. "Local and Personal," *Centralia [Illinois] Sentinel*, 24 October 1889, page 4, column 5; imaged, *Newspaper Archive* (https://newspaperarchive.com : accessed 18 April 2024).

452. *Minutes of the Thirty-Eighth Session of the Southern Illinois Conference of the Methodist Episcopal Church held at Carbondale, Ills., October 9-14, 1889* (Slawson Printing Company, St. Louis, 1889), page 20; image 276 of 1106, *Hathi Trust Digital Library* (https://babel.hathitrust.org/cgi/pt?id=nyp.33433082256243&seq=266&q1= thirty-eighth : accessed 18 April 2024).

453. "Local and Personal," *Centralia [Illinois] Sentinel*, 22 November 1889, page 2, column 1; imaged, *Newspaper Archive* (https://newspaperarchive.com : accessed 18 April 2024).

454. *McLeansboro, Illinois Illustrated*: Special Supplement to the *McLeansboro Times* (United States: Hamilton County Historical Society, 1900), page 39; imaged, *Google Books* (https://www.google.com/books/edition/McLeansboro_Illinois_Illustrated/h jA6J1QAGAIC : accessed 31 January 2024).

455. *Minutes of the Fortieth Session of the Southern Illinois Conference of the Methodist Episcopal Church held at Mt. Vernon, Ill., September 23-28, 1891.* (Bloomington, Illinois, Pantagraph Printing and Stationery Company, 1891), page 20; image 422 of 1106. *Hathi Trust Digital Library* (https://babel.hathitrust.org/cgi/pt : accessed 18 April 2024).

456. "Local and Personal," *Centralia [Illinois] Daily Sentinel*, 12 December 1889, page 2, column 1; imaged, *Newspaper Archive* (https://newspaperarchive.com : accessed 18 April 2024).

457. Grand Commandery of the Knights Templar of the State of Indiana, *Commandery Officer's Handbook*, 14. *Indiana Knights Templar* (https://www.indianaknightstemplar.org/Articles/2017/Commandery_Officers_Handbook-2017.pdf : accessed 19 April 2024).

458. "Local and Personal," *Centralia [Illinois] Daily Sentinel*, 8 August 1890, page 2, column 2; imaged, *Newspaper Archive* (https://newspaperarchive.com : accessed 18 April 2024).

459. "Local and Personal," *Centralia [Illinois] Daily Sentinel*, 21 August 1890, page 2, column 1; imaged, *Newspaper Archive* (https://newspaperarchive.com : accessed 18 April 2024).

460. "Mistaken in the Amount," *Centralia [Illinois] Sentinel*, 2 October 1890, page 1, column 2; imaged, *Newspaper Archive* (https://www.newspaperarchive.com : accessed 24 May 2017).

461. *Robinson [Illinois] Argus*, 25 February 1891, page 5, column 2, imaged, *Robinson History Archives Online* (https://robinson.historyarchives.online/home : accessed 28 January 2024).

462. "Equal Suffrage Association," *Centralia [Illinois] Daily Sentinel*, 13 March 1891, page 2, column 4; imaged, *Newspaper Archive* (https://newspaperarchive.com : accessed 20 April 2024)

463. "Local and Personal," *Centralia [Illinois] Daily Sentinel*, 14 April 1891, page 2, column 2; imaged, *Newspaper Archive* (https://newspaperarchive.com : accessed 20 April 2024).

464. *Minutes of the Forty-First Session of the Southern Illinois Conference of the Methodist Episcopal Church, Held at Belleville, Illinois, September 28-October 3, 1892* (Bunker Hill, Illinois: J.B. House, Publisher, 1892), unpaginated section; imaged, *Divinity Archive* (https://divinityarchive.com/handle/11258/4398 : accessed 12 April 2022).

465. "July 4, 1893," *Chicagology* (https://chicagology.com/columbiaexpo/fair024/ : accessed 31 January 2024).

466. "Local and Personal," *Centralia [Illinois] Daily Sentinel*, 7 July 1893, page 2, column 2; imaged, *Newspaper Archive* (https://newspaperarchive.com : accessed 21 April 2024).

467. *Minutes of the Forty-Second Session of the Southern Illinois Conference of the Methodist Episcopal Church, Held at Flora, Illinois, September 26-October 1, 1892* (Enfield, Illinois: J.B. House, Publisher, 1893), unpaginated section and page 19; imaged, *Divinity Archive* (https://divinityarchive.com/handle/11258/4399 : accessed 10 April 2022).

468. "Northwestern Memorial Hospital Timeline," *Northwestern Medicine* (https://www.nm.org/about-us/history/northwestern-memorial-hospital-time line : accessed 16 April 2022).

469. *Minutes of the Forty-Third Session of the Southern Illinois Conference of the Methodist Episcopal Church, Held at McLeansboro, Ill., September 26-October 1, 1894* (Mt. Vernon, Illinois: J.W. Van Cleve, Publisher, 1894), unpaginated section and pages 18, 22; imaged, *Divinity Archive* (https://divinityarchive.com/handle/11258/4400 : accessed 12 April 2022).

470. "Local and Personal," *Centralia [Illinois] Sentinel*, 29 November 1894, page 4, column 2; imaged, *Newspaper Archive* (https://newspaperarchive.com : accessed 21 April 2024).

471. "Local and Personal," *Centralia [Illinois] Sentinel*, 7 March 1895, page 2, column 4; imaged, *Newspaper Archive* (https://newspaperarchive.com : accessed 20 April 2024).

472. "Safe Investment," *Centralia [Illinois] Daily Sentinel*, 31 December 1896, page 1, column 4; imaged, *Newspaper Archive* (https://newspaperarchive.com : accessed 22 April 2024).

473. "Home News," *Centralia [Illinois] Sentinel*, 11 August 1887, page 3, column 1; imaged, *Newspaper Archive* (https://newspaperarchive.com : accessed 1 September 2024).

474. "Local and Personal," *Centralia [Illinois] Sentinel*, 18 July 1895, page 4, column 2; imaged, *Newspaper Archive* (https://newspaperarchive.com : accessed 21 April 2024).

475. Edwards County, Illinois, "Death Record Book 1, December 1877-July 1908," page 104; imaged, *FamilySearch* (https://www.familysearch.org/ark:/61903/3:1:3QS7-9924-R8B : accessed 11 November 2015), Family History Library film #007625300, image 152 of 162, Mary M. Wallar.

476. "Local and Personal," *Centralia [Illinois] Daily Sentinel*, 21 June 1895, page 2, column 3; imaged, *Newspaper Archive* (https://newspaperarchive.com : accessed 21 April 2024).

477. "People We Know," *Mount Carmel [Illinois] Register*, 4 July 1895, page 4, column 2; imaged, *Newspapers.com* (https://www.newspapers.com/image/440297955/ : accessed 8 March 2024).

478. *Minutes of the Forty-Fourth Session of the Southern Illinois Conference of the Methodist Episcopal Church, Held at Metropolis, Illinois, September 18-23, 1895* (Mt. Vernon, Illinois: J.W. Van Cleve, Publisher, 1895), page 22; imaged, *Divinity Archive* (https://divinityarchive.com/handle/11258/4401 : accessed 10 April 2022).

479. *Minutes of the Forty-Fifth Session of the Southern Illinois Conference of the Methodist Episcopal Church, Held at Jerseyville, Illinois, September 16-21, 1896* (Mt. Vernon, Illinois: J.W. Van Cleve, Publisher, 1896), page 19; imaged, *Divinity Archive* (https://divinityarchive.com/handle/11258/4402 : accessed 10 April 2022).

480. *Minutes of the Forty-Eighth Session of the Southern Illinois Conference of the Methodist Episcopal Church, Held at Mt. Carmel, Ill., September 27-October 2, 1899* (Cincinnati: Western Methodist Book Concern Press, 1899), page 22; imaged, *Divinity Archive* (https://divinityarchive.com/handle/11258/4403 : accessed 12 April 2022).

481. "Local and Personal," *Centralia [Illinois] Daily Sentinel*, 28 October 1895, page 2, column 2; imaged, *Newspaper Archive* (https://newspaperarchive.com : accessed 22 April 2024).

482. *Centralia [Illinois] Sentinel*, 28 October 1897, page 4, column 3; imaged, *Newspaper Archive* (https://newspaperarchive.com : accessed 23 April 2024).

483. "Lincoln's Birthday Entertainment," *Centralia [Illinois] Sentinel*, 18 February 1897, page 6, column 8; imaged, *Newspaper Archive* (https://newspaperarchive.com : accessed 23 April 2024).

484. *Minutes of the Fifty-First Session of the Southern Illinois Conference of the Methodist Episcopal Church, Held at Fairfield, Ill., September 24-September 29, 1902* (East Saint Louis: Scott Printing Company, 1902), page 139; imaged, *Google Books* (https://www.google.com/books/edition/Minutes_of_the_Session_of_the_Southern_I/I4szAQAAMAAJ : accessed 21 July 2024).

485. "The Bryan Regiment," *Centralia [Illinois] Sentinel*, 21 July 1898, page 4; imaged, *Newspaper Archive* (https://newspaperarchive.com : accessed 24 May 2017).

486. "People We Know," *Mount Carmel [Illinois] Register*, 22 February 1900, page 5, column 3; imaged, *Newspapers.com* : accessed 1 September 2024.

487. "Local and Personal," *Centralia [Illinois] Daily Sentinel*, 24 July 1900, page 2, column 3; imaged, *Newspaper Archive* (https://www.newspaperarchive.com : accessed 1 September 2024).

488. "Local and Personal," *Centralia [Illinois] Daily Sentinel*, 28 July 1900, page 2, column 5; imaged, *Newspaper Archive* (https://www.newspaperarchive.com : accessed 1 September 2024).

489. "Local and Personal," *Centralia [Illinois] Daily Sentinel*, 8 October 1900, page 2, column 3; imaged, *Newspaper Archive* (https://www.newspaperarchive.com : accessed 1 September 2024); and "Local and Personal," *Centralia [Illinois] Daily Sentinel*, 15 October 1900, page 2, column 4; imaged, *Newspaper Archive* (https://www.newspaperarchive.com : accessed 1 September 2024).

490. Grave marker of J.L. and Frances E. Wallar, Elmwood Cemetery, Centralia, Illinois photograph, 2022; privately held by Nancy E. Wiseman, Carmel, Indiana.

491. "Dr. Wallar Drops Dead," *Centralia [Illinois] Daily Sentinel*, 15 December 1900, page 4, column 4; imaged, *Newspaper Archive* (https://www.newspaperarchive.com : accessed 1 September 2024).

492. "Rev. Dr. Wallar," *Mount Carmel [Illinois] Register*, 27 December, 1900, page 1, column 2; imaged, *Newspapers.com* (https://www.newspapers.com/image/440258595 : accessed 2 September 2024).

493. *Minutes and Journal of the Southern Illinois Annual Conference of the Methodist Episcopal Church Held at Alton, Ills., Sept. 18-23,* pages 28, 39-40.

494. "Local and Personal," *Centralia [Illinois] Daily Sentinel*, 19 December 1900, page 2, column 3; imaged, *Newspaper Archive* (newspaperarchive.com : accessed 2 September 2024).

495. "Illinois State News," *Mascoutah [Illinois] Herald*, 27 December 1900, page 2, column 4; imaged, *Newspapers.com* https://www.newspapers.com/image/702572726/ : accessed 2 September 2024).

496. "Funeral of Dr. Wallar," *Centralia [Illinois] Sentinel*, 20 December 1900, page 2, columns 3-4; imaged, *Newspaper Archive* (https://www.newspaperarchive.com : accessed 12 March 2024).

497. Marion County, Illinois, "Executors' Will Record Book F, 1905-1910," pages 190-195. *FamilySearch* (http://www.familysearch.org; accessed 1 November 2022); Family History Library film #1011191, images 501-507 of 560, Jeannette E. Wallar.

498. City of Centralia, Elmwood Cemetery Records, (https://centraliail.govoffice3.com/index.asp : accessed 14 June 2021).

499. Death notice card for Rev. James Lee Wallar, D.D., 1900. A photocopy of the death notice is held by Nancy E. Wiseman, Carmel, Indiana. The note "Great Grandad Wallar" was written by one of my grandfather's (Clarence Scott Bashears) sisters. Three items appear on this photocopied paper: this death notice card, a copy of "The Aged Christian" - a poem written by J.L. Wallar, and an obituary for Martha J. (Medcalf) Brashears Boyd, my grandfather's paternal grandmother.

500. Grave marker of J.L. and Frances E. Wallar, Elmwood Cemetery, Centralia, Illinois photograph, 2022; privately held by Nancy E. Wiseman, Carmel, Indiana.

501. "Rev. James L. Wallar, D.D.," *Minutes of the Fiftieth Session of the Southern Illinois Conference of the Methodist Episcopal Church Held at Alton, Ills., Sept. 18-23, 1901* (Saint Louis, Missouri: Perrin & Smith Printing Company, 1901), 39-40, *Illinois Library Digital Collections* (https://libsysdigi.library.uiuc.edu/OCA/Books2009-08/minutesofsession/mi nutesofsession505219011903meth/minutesofsession505219011903meth.pdf) . Note: The image I had of Reverend James Wallar from this journal was of poor quality and halftone. It was enhanced using AI-based tools by Karl Zemlin of Zemlin Photo.

502. *The Aged Christian*, poem written by Rev. James Lee Wallar, D.D. A photocopy of the poem is held by Nancy E. Wiseman, Carmel, Indiana. The note "Written By Great Grandad Wallar" was written by one of my grandfather's (Clarence Scott Bashears) sisters. Three items appear on this photocopied paper: this copy of "The Aged Christian," a death notice card, and an obituary for Martha J. (Medcalf) Brashears Boyd, my grandfather's paternal grandmother.

503. "Ohio, County Marriages, 1789-2016," imaged, *FamilySearch* (https://www.familysearch.org/ark:/61903/1:1:2QQR-87G : accessed 15 January 2019), James L. Waller and Frances Gammon, 5 December 1847; and 1830 U.S. census, Harrison County, Ohio, town of Cadiz, page 162, Verden Waller; imaged, "1830 United States Federal Census," *Ancestry.com* (https://www.ancestry.com/search/collections/8058/ : accessed 27 August 2021).

504. "Ohio, County Marriages, 1789-2016," *FamilySearch,* James L. Waller and Frances Gammon.

505. "Beyond the Vale," *Centralia [Illinois] Daily Sentinel*, 27 June 1887, page 1, column 3; imaged, *Newspaper Archive* (https://www.newspaperarchive.com : accessed 12 March 2024).

506. "Ohio, County Marriages, 1789-2016," *FamilySearch,* James L. Waller and Frances Gammon.

507. "Beyond the Vale," *Centralia [Illinois] Daily Sentinel*, 27 June 1887.

508. "Beyond the Vale," *Centralia [Illinois] Daily Sentinel*, 27 June 1887

509. *Combined History of Edwards, Lawrence and Wabash Counties, Illinois* (Philadelphia, Pennsylvania: J.L. McDonough & Co., 1883), 309; imaged, *Internet Archive* (https://archive.org/details/combinedhistoryo00phil/page/n379/mode/2up : accessed 6 September 2024).

510. "Marriages," *Mount Carmel [Illinois] Register*, 17 May 1877, page 4, column 7; imaged, *Newspapers.com* (https://www.newspapers.com/image/757467563/ : accessed 5 February 2024).

511. *Find a Grave*, database with images (https://www.findagrave.com/memorial/123729079/katie-wallar : accessed 29 March 2020), memorial #123729079, "Katie Wallar," Sumner Cemetery, Sumner, Lawrence County, Illinois; grave marker photographed by Find a Grave user B. Pipher.

512. "Illinois, County Marriages, 1810-1940," imaged, *FamilySearch* (https://www.familysearch.org/ark:/61903/1:1:QK92-TDNH : accessed 15 February 2025), Fay K. Waller and Martha M. Leeper.

513. "Dr. F.K. Waller Dies; was Civil War Veteran," *Saint Louis [Missouri] Globe-Democrat*, 25 November 1915, page 7, column 6; imaged, *Newspapers.com* (https://www.newspapers.com/image/572142887 : accessed 15 February 2025).

514. "Double Funeral at the Old Folks' Home," *Mattoon [Illinois] Daily Journal-Gazette*, 24 November 1915, page 1, column 4; imaged, *Newspapers.com* (https://www.newspapers.com/image/73203273/ : accessed 20 December 2023). Note: The obituary mistakenly names Fay K. Wallar as Dr. S.K. Waller.

515. "Missouri, Death Certificates, 1910-1973," database with images, *Missouri Digital Heritage* (https://sos.mo.gov/images/archives/deathcerts/1955/1955_00003212.PDF : accessed 28 February 2019), Glen Leeper Wallar.

516. "Illinois, County Marriages, 1810-1940," *FamilySearch* (https://www.familysearch.org/ark:/61903/1:1:Q288-79KB : accessed 28 February 2019), Glen L. Wallar and Grace Tanquary.

517. "Illinois, County Marriages, 1810-1940," *FamilySearch* (https://www.familysearch.org/ark:/61903/1:1:Q28G-Z13 : accessed 28 February 2019), Glen L. Wallar and May Allen.

518. "Missouri, Death Certificates, 1910-1973," *Missouri Digital Heritage,* Glen Leeper Wallar.

519. *Find a Grave*, database with images (https://www.findagrave.com/memorial/262185727/glen-leeper-wallar : accessed 28 February 2019), memorial #262185727, "Glen Leeper Wallar," Resthaven Memorial Cemetery, Louisville, Jefferson County, Kentucky, memorial created by Find a Grave user PMS Sillix.

520. "U.S. World War II Draft Registration Cards, 1942," database with images, *Ancestry.com* (https://www.ancestry.com/search/collections/1002/records/7328556 : accessed 27 April 2020), Orla L. Wallar, citing United States, Selective Service System. Selective Service Registration Cards, World War II: Fourth Registration, Record Group Number 147, Series Number M1986.

521. City of Saint Louis, Missouri, "Marriage Record Book 81, 1914," *FamilySearch* (https://www.familysearch.org : accessed 28 February 2019), license #188254, Orla L. Wallar and Anna L. Krueger.

522. *Find a Grave*, database with images (https://www.findagrave.com/memorial/99929818/orla-l-wallar : accessed 28 February 2019), memorial #99929818, "Orla L. Wallar," Mount Hope Cemetery Mausoleum, Lemay, Saint Louis County, Missouri; memorial created by Find a Grave user Carol Beck.

523. "U.S. World War II Draft Registration Cards, 1942," database with images, *Ancestry.com* (https://www.ancestry.com/search/collections/1002/records/10331401 : accessed 27 April 2020), Herbert Earl Wallar, citing United States, Selective Service System. Selective Service Registration Cards, World War II: Fourth Registration, Record Group Number 147, Box 52.

524. "St. Louis Boy Marries Belmont Girl This Morning," *Mount Carmel [Illinois] Register,* 18 October 1906, page 3, column 3; imaged, *Newspapers.com* (https://www.newspapers.com : accessed 28 December 2023).

525. "Montana, U.S., County Marriages, 1865-1987," database, *Ancestry.com* (https://www.ancestry.com/search/collections/61375/records/148932 : accessed 27 April 2020) Herbert Earl Wallar and Mary Alice Parks, citing Montana County Marriage Records, 1865-1967, Montana State Historical Society, Helena, Montana.

526. "Willamette Valley, Oregon, U.S., Death Records, 1838-2006," imaged; *Ancestry.com* (https://www.ancestry.com/search/collections/2468/records/15265 : accessed 27 April 2020), H. Earl Wallar, citing Capital Monumental Works, Salem Oregon, 1948-1961, Volume II, Willamette Valley Genealogical Society.

527. *Find a Grave*, database with images
(https://www.findagrave.com/memorial/53452118/h-earl-wallar : accessed 28
February 2019), memorial #53452118, "H. Earl Wallar," Apostolic Cemetery,
Silverton, Marion County, Oregon; memorial created by Find a Grave user D.D.
Thompson

528. "U.S. World War II Draft Registration
Cards, 1942," database with images, *Ancestry.com*
(https://www.ancestry.com/search/collections/1002/records/16121438 :
accessed 27 April 2020), Paul Sabine Wallar, citing United States, Selective
Service System. Selective Service Registration Cards, World War II: Fourth
Registration, Record Group Number 147, Box 1139.

529. "Missouri, County Marriage, Naturalization, and Court Records, 1800-1991,"
FamilySearch (https://www.familysearch.org/ark:/61903/1:1:6689-C76G :
accessed 16 February 2025), Paul Sabine Wallar and Clara Elsie Junclaus.

530. "Deaths," *Saint Louis [Missouri] Post-Dispatch*, 9 April 1959, page 29, column
4; imaged, *Newspapers.com* (https://www.newspapers.com/image/140607526/
: accessed 15 February 2025).

531. "U.S., Headstone Applications for Military Veterans, 1861-1985," imaged;
Ancestry.com (https://www.ancestry.com : accessed 27 April 2020), Paul
S. Wallar, citing Applications for Headstones for U.S. Military Veterans,
1935-1941; NAID: 596118, Record Group Number 92; Records of hte Office
of the Quartermaster General.

532. *Find a Grave*, database with images
(https://www.findagrave.com/memorial/70183729/cornelia-fay-waller-lella:
accessed 28 February 2019), memorial #70183729, "Cornelia Fay Waller Lella,"
Our Lady of Seven Dolors Catholic Cemetery, Welsh, Jefferson Davis Parish,
Louisiana; memorial created by Find a Grave user MHARDY.

533. "Jasper County, Missouri Marriage records,
volume 34, 1911-1912," imaged; *FamilySearch*
(https://www.familysearch.org/ark:/61903/3:1:3QS7-9989-M71H : accessed
29 December 2023), digital film #930900, image 299 of 545, Chester B. Hyde
and Cornelia S. Wallar.

534. "New Jersey Bride Index letters E-Z, R-Z,
Reel 33, 1930-1935," index; imaged, *FamilySearch*
(https://www.familysearch.org/ark:/61903/3:1:3Q9M-FSRH-DJN : accessed
29 December 2023), digital film #104478958, image 410 of 591, Cornelia Hyde.

535. *Find a Grave*, memorial #70183729, Cornelia Fay Waller Lella.

536. "Ohio Deaths, 1908-1953," imaged; *FamilySearch* (https://www.familysearch.org/ark:/61903/3:1:33SQ-GPJ1-SP2K : accessed 29 December 2023), 1920 deaths, certificates 1-2920; digital film #004021995, image 1275 of 3297, Etta Reeder.

537. "Crawford County Marriage Record Book B, 1858-1874," imaged, *FamilySearch* (https://www.familysearch.org/ark:/61903/3:1:3QS7-L9V5-LTC6 : accessed 29 December 2023), page 254, digital film #7616150, image 86 of 627, John D. Reeder and Lauretta Waller.

538. "Ohio Deaths, 1908-1953," *FamilySearch,* Etta Reeder.

539. *Find a Grave*, database with images (https://www.findagrave.com/memorial/45999623/lauretta-may-reeder: accessed 29 December 2023), memorial #45999623, "Lauretta May "Etta" Wallar Reeder," Crown Hill Cemetery, Indianapolis, Marion County, Indiana; memorial created by Find a Grave user John C. Anderson.

540. "Illinois Deaths and Stillbirths, 1916-1947," imaged, *FamilySearch* (https://www.familysearch.org : accessed 28 January 2024), William Clyde Reeder.

541. "Illinois, County Marriages, 1810-1940," imaged; *FamilySearch* (https://www.familysearch.org/ark:/61903/3:1:939J-TGXK-H : accessed 14 January 2024), W.C. Reeder and Nettie Davis.

542. "Illinois, County Marriages, 1810-1940," imaged; *FamilySearch* (https://www.familysearch.org/ark:/61903/1:1:X2L2-P56 : accessed 14 January 2024), William Clyde Reeder and Mabel Edna Watkins.

543. "Illinois Deaths and Stillbirths, 1916-1947," *FamilySearch,* William Clyde Reeder.

544. *Find a Grave*, database with images (https://www.findagrave.com/memorial/81222127/william-clyde-reeder: accessed 17 January 2024), memorial #81222127, "Rev William Clyde Reeder," Spring Hill Cemetery, Danville, Vermilion County, Illinois; memorial created by Find a Grave user Lesa Epperson.

545. U.S., World War I Draft Registration Cards, 1917-1918," database with images, *Ancestry.com* (https://www.ancestry.com : accessed 15 January 2024), Arthur Lee Reeder.

546. Illinois, County Marriages, 1810-1940, imaged; FamilySearch (https://www.familysearch.org/ark:/61903/3:1:33SQ-GBLC-1QM : accessed January 15, 2024), Arthur L. Reeder and Adda Sampson.

547. Illinois, County Marriages, 1810-1940, imaged; FamilySearch (https://www.familysearch.org/ark:/61903/3:1:939Z-YXSK-RR : accessed January 15, 2024), Arthur Reeder and Mrs. Stella Mulquin.

548. "Arthur L. Reeder," *San Fernando [California] Valley Times*, 21 June 1945, page 8, column 2; imaged, *Newspapers.com* (https://www.newspapers.com/image/580272977 : accessed 15 January 2024).

549. *Find a Grave*, database with images (https://www.findagrave.com/memorial/47546163/arthur-lee-reeder: accessed 17 January 2024), memorial #47546163, "Arthur Lee Reeder," Grand View Memorial Park, Glendale, Los Angeles County, California; memorial created by Find a Grave user GVMP Vols.

550. Illinois Deaths and Stillbirths, 1916-1947," imaged, *FamilySearch* (https://www.familysearch.org/ark:/61903/1:1:NQ2M-CMG : accessed 28 January 2024), Casey Reeder.

551. Illinois, County Marriages, 1810-1940," imaged, *FamilySearch* (https://www.familysearch.org/ark:/61903/3:1:939J-VTC6-C : 16 January 2024), C.K. Reeder and Ester Crews.

552. Illinois Deaths and Stillbirths, 1916-1947," *FamilySearch*, Casey Reeder.

553. *Find a Grave*, database with images (https://www.findagrave.com/memorial/47546163/cary-kent-reeder: accessed 17 January 2024), memorial #47546163, "Cary Kent Reeder," Mount Hope Cemetery, Belleville, Saint Clair County, Illinois; memorial created by Find a Grave user Robin.

554. 1900 U.S. census, Clay County, Illinois, population schedule, Larkinsburg Township, enumeration district [ED] 0007, sheet 13B, May Reeder; imaged, "United States Census, 1900," *Ancestry.com* (https://www.ancestry.com/search.collections/7602/records/10051417 : accessed 16 January 2024).

555. "Illinois, County Marriages, 1810-1940," imaged, *FamilySearch* (https://www.familysearch.org/ark:/61903/3:1:939Z-YX2C-P : accessed 15 January 2024), John A.L. Edwards and May Reeder.

556. "Illinois, County Marriages, 1810-1940," imaged, *FamilySearch* (https://www.familysearch.org/ark:/61903/3:1:939J-VTHC-Y : accessed 15 January 2024), Everett Osman and May Edwards.

557. "Retired Pastor is Dead After Short Illness," *Indianapolis [Indiana] Times*, 30 August 1933, page 3, column 1; imaged, *Newspapers.com* (https://www.newspapers.com/image/873259967 : accessed 31 March 2025).

558. "Illinois Births and Christenings, 1824-1940," imaged; *FamilySearch* (https://familysearch.org : accessed 17 January 2024), Reeder; and "U.S., World War Draft Registration Cards, 1942," database with images, *Ancestry.com* (https://www.ancestry.com/search/collections/1002/records/9942831 : accessed 16 January 2024), Merril Clark Reeder.

559. "Merrill Reeder, Section Foreman, Beecher City, Dies," *Effingham [Illinois] Daily News*, 14 April 1953, page 1, column 2; imaged, *Newspapers.com* (https://www.newspapers.com/image/898314730 : accessed 31 March 2024).

560. "Missouri, U.S. Marriage Records," imaged, *Ancestry.com* (https://www.ancestry.com/search/collections/1171/records/310399679 : accessed 31 March 2025), Merrill Reeder and Lillie Pauley.

561. "Merrill Reeder, Section Foreman, Beecher City, Dies," *Effingham [Illinois] Daily News*, 14 April 1953.

562. "U.S., World War I Draft Registration Cards, 1917-1918," database with images, *Ancestry.com* (https://www.ancestry.com/search/collections/6482/records/2102180 : accessed 17 January 2024), Wilbur Verden Reeder.

563. Cuyahoga County, Ohio, "Marriage Record Volume 144," imaged, *FamilySearch* (http://www.familysearch.org/ark:/61903/3:1:9392-BLQ2-J : accessed 17 January 2024), digital film #1889014, image 220 of 603, Wilbur V. Reeder and Jane Ruth Burbank.

564. "Wilbur Reeder Succumbs," *San Diego [California] Union*, 25 January 1957, page 43, column 1; imaged, *GenealogyBank* (https://www.genealogybank.com : accessed 17 January 2024.)

565. *Find a Grave*, database with images (https://www.findagrave.com/memorial/190393958/wilbur-verden-reeder: accessed 17 January 2024), memorial #190393958, "Wilbur Verden Reeder," Greenwood Memorial Park, San Diego, San Diego County, California; memorial created by Find a Grave user Linda.

566. "Lula Reeder, Ex-Fontana," *San Bernardino County [California] Sun*, 3 February 1973, page 22, columns 2-3; imaged, *Newspapers.com* (https://www.newspapers.com : accessed 18 January 2024).

567. Clay County, Illinois, "Marriage Record Volume 2, 1895-1915," *FamilySearch* (https://www.familysearch.org : accessed 18 January 2024), page 137, digital film #1008793, Ike Adams and Lula Reeder.

568. Effingham County, Illinois "Register of Marriages Book 3," *FamilySearch* (https://www.familysearch.org : accessed 18 January 2024), digital film #1010049, page 129; Earl Brown and Lula Adams.

569. "Indiana Marriages, 1811-2019," imaged, *FamilySearch* (https://www.familysearch.org/ark:/61903/1:1:844Q-733Z : accessed 3 May 2024), John Hitt and Lula Reeder Brown.

570. "Lula Reeder, Ex-Fontana," *San Bernardino County [California] Sun*, 3 February 1973.

571. "Illinois Deaths and Stillbirths, 1916-1947," imaged, *FamilySearch* (https://www.familysearch.org/ark:/61903/1:1:NQ53-NJW : accessed 28 January 2024), Warren Fergis Reeder.

572. "Illinois County Marriages, 1810-1940," imaged, *FamilySearch* (https://www.familysearch.org/ark:/61903/3:1:9392-96SL-KL : accessed 28 January 2024), Warren Reeder and Julia Thorp.

573. "Edgewood," *Effingham [Illinois] Daily Record*, 14 December 1922, page 2, column 5; imaged, *Newspapers.com* (https://www.newspapers.com/image/875071910/ : accessed 18 January 2024).

574. "California Death Index, 1940-1997," imaged, *FamilySearch* (https://familysearch.org/ark:/61903/1:1:VP25-6XM : accessed 18 January 2024), Bessie J. Battrelle.

575. City of Saint Louis, Missouri "Marriage Records, Volume 79, 1913," *FamilySearch* (https://www.familysearch.org : accessed 18 January 2024), digital film #469564, page 346, Claude Everett Battrelle and Bessie Jean Reeder.

576. "California Death Index, 1940-1997," *FamilySearch*, Bessie J. Battrelle.

577. "Bessie Battrelle, Ex-Fontana," *San Bernardino County [California] Sun*, 12 December 1973, page 17, columns 2-3; imaged, *Newspapers.com* (https://www.newspapers.com/image/61892766 : accessed 18 January 2024).

578. U.S., World War II Draft Registration Cards, 1942," database with images, *Ancestry.com* (https://www.ancestry.com/search/collections/1002/records/9942845 : accessed 19 January 2024), Roy Raymond Reeder.

579. "Central Indiana Deaths," *Decatur [Illinois] Herald*, 9 November 1972, page 43, column 1; imaged, *Newspapers.com* (https://www.newspapers.com/image/85210395/ : accessed 19 January 2024).

580. "Central Indiana Deaths," *Decatur [Illinois] Herald*, 9 November 1972.

581. *Find a Grave*, database with images (https://www.findagrave.com/memorial/74393509/roy-raymond-reeder: accessed 17 January 2024), memorial #74393509, "Roy Raymond Reeder," Red Bank Cemetery, Lakewood, Shelby County, Illinois; memorial created by Find a Grave user (Helen) Jean Kennedy.

582. *The History of Henry and Saint Clair Counties, Missouri* (St. Joseph, Missouri: National Historical Company, 1883),600.

583. "Obituary," *Chicago [Illinois] Inter Ocean*, 4 February 1908, page 2, column 4; imaged, *Newspapers.com* (https://www.newspapers.com/image/3462846/ : accessed 19 January 2024).

584. 1880 U.S. census, Wayne County, Illinois, mortality schedule, village of Fairfield, enumeration district [ED] 144, page 2, family 455, James L. Waller; imaged, "United States Census, 1880," *Ancestry.com* (https://www.ancestry.com/search/collections/8756/records/1971457 : accessed 19 January 2024).

585. "U.S., World War II Draft Registration Cards, 1942," database with images, *Ancestry.com* (https://www.ancestry.com/search/collections/1002/records/10192630 : accessed 19 January 2024), Charlie Burgess Wallar.

586. Wayne County, Illinois "Marriage Record Book D," imaged, *FamilySearch* (https://www.familysearch.org : accessed 3 May 2024), page 301, Charley B. Waller and Grace Harpole.

587. Delaware County, Indiana "Marriage Record book 22, January 1914- March 1915," imaged, *FamilySearch* (https://www.familysearch.org : accessed 28 January 2024) digital film #00476460, page 389, Earl R. Vincent and Grace B. Wallar.

588. "Mrs. Laura C. Wallar," *Evansville [Indiana] Courier*, 21 October 1947, page 5, columns 4-5; imaged, *Newspapers.com* *https://www.newspapers.com/image/760235899 : accessed 19 January 2024).

589. "U.S., World War II Draft Registration Cards, 1942," database with images, *Ancestry.com* (https://www.ancestry.com/search/collections/1002/records/10192631 : accessed 19 January 2024), Edmond Neal Wallar.

590. "Mrs. Laura C. Wallar," *Evansville [Indiana] Courier*, 21 October 1947.

591. "Illinois Marriages, 1815-1935," imaged, *FamilySearch* (https://www.familysearch.org/ark:/61903/1:1:X2G2-1QH : accessed 22 January 2024), Harry H. Waller and Mary M. Belew.

592. Edwards County, Illinois "Death Record Book 1, December 1877-July 1908," imaged, *FamilySearch* (https://www.familysearch.org : accessed 11 November 2015), digital film #007625300, page 104, Mary M. Wallar.

593. *Albion [Illinois] Journal*, 20 June 1895, page 4, column 1; imaged, *Illinois Digital Newspaper Collections* (https://idnc.library.illinois.edu/ : accessed 23 August 2021).

594. "Illinois, County Marriages, 1810-1940," imaged, *FamilySearch* (https://www.familysearch.org : accessed 22 January 2024), Harry H. Waller and Cora F. (Firmin) Coats.

595. 1900 U.S. census, Lawrence County, Arkansas, Dent Township, Imboden, enumeration district [ED] 48, sheet 4, dwelling 85, family 89, Harry H. Wallar; imaged, "United States Census, 1900," *Ancestry.com* (https://www.ancestry.com/search/collections/7602/records/14850202 : accessed 27 January 2024); and 1900 U.S. census, Crawford County, Illinois, city of Robinson, enumeration district [ED] 36, sheet 6, dwelling 74, family 77, H.H. Waller; imaged, "United States Census, 1900," *Ancestry.com* (https://www.ancestry.com/search/collections/7602/records/11874469 : accessed 27 January 2024).

596. "U.S., World War I Draft Registration Cards, 1917-1918," database with images, *Ancestry.com* (https://www.ancestry.com/search/collections/6482/records/23117924 : accessed 22 January 2024), Harry Herbert Wallar.

597. Fulton County, Illinois, death certificate of Henry *[sic]* H. Waller, died 21 June 1915, County Clerk's Office, Lewistown, Illinois.

598. *Find a Grave*, database with images (https://www.findagrave.com/memorial/169298044/h-h-wallar : accessed 28 January 2024), memorial #169298044, "H.H. Wallar," Oak Hill Cemetery, Lewistown, Fulton County, Illinois; memorial created by Find a Grave user nanwise.

599. Edwards County, Illinois "Birth Record Book 1," imaged, **FamilySearch** (https://www.familysearch.org : accessed 19 January 2024), digital film #1401778, page 90, Anna Francis Wallar. Note: On Anna Francis Wallar's birth record, it is noted that Anna was the second child born to the mother.

600. Edwards County, Illinois "Birth Record Book 1," **FamilySearch,** Anna Francis Wallar.

601. "Crawford County, Illinois, "Marriage Record Book C," imaged, *FamilySearch* (https://www.familysearch.org : accessed 19 January 2024, digital film #007616150, page 113, William C. Brashears and Fannie Waller.

602. "Announcements," *[Springfield] Illinois State Journal*, 18 April 1974, page 39, column 2; imaged, *GenealogyBank* (https://www.genealogybank.com : accessed 20 January 2024).

603. *Find a Grave*, database with images
(https://www.findagrave.com/memorial/214132054/frances-lee-bashears :
accessed 28 January 2024), memorial #214132054, "Frances Lee "Fannie" Wallar
Bashears," Robinson New Cemetery, Robinson, Crawford County, Illinois;
memorial created by Find a Grave user Heather Crenwelge.

604. U.S., World War I Draft Registration Cards,
1917-1918," database with images, Ancestry.com
(https://www.ancestry.com/search/collections/6482/records/23117924 :
accessed 22 January 2024), Harry Herbert Wallar.

605. "Illinois, County Marriages 1810-1940," imaged, *FamilySearch*
(https://www.familysearch.org/ark:/61903/1:1:Q2DM-DMQX : accessed 22
January 2024), Harry H. Waller and Josie E. Cann.

606. "Wants a Divorce, " *Belleville [Illinois] Daily Advocate*, 12
October 1912, page 4, column 4; imaged, *Newspapers.com*
(https://www.newspapers.com/images/767226913/ : accessed 9 March 2025).

607. "Default Day Kept the Divorce Mill Grinding," *Belleville [Illinois]
News-Democrat,* 7 March 1913, page 1, column 4; imaged, *Newspapers.com*
(https://www.newspapers.com/image/768942900/ : accessed 9 March 2025).

608. "St. Louis, Missouri, United States records, " imaged, *FamilySearch*
(https://www.familysearch.org/ark:/61903/3:1:3QS7-L98M-YW27 : accessed
8 March 2025), FHL film #007513844, image 105 of 694), Harry H. Waller and
Della McRoy.

609. 1920 U.S. census, Saint Clair County, Illinois, East Saint Louis, part of Precinct
2, ward 4, sheet 11B, enumeration district [ED] 147. Myrtle McBride boarding
with William Rife family and Harry Wallar living with cousin Khery *[sic]*
(Cary) Reeder and family; imaged, "United States Census, 1920," *Ancestry.com*
(https://www.ancestry.com/search/collections/6061/records/96405357 :
accessed 12 March 2025).

610. "Marriage Licenses," *Waterloo [Illinois] Republican*, 28 May 1930, page 2,
column 2; imaged, *Newspapers.com* (https://www.newspapers.com : accessed 9
March 2025).

611. "In Divorce Court," *Omaha [Nebraska] Evening World-Herald*, page 14,
column 4; imaged, *GenealogyBank* (https://www.genealogybank.com : accessed
8 March 2025).

612. "Indiana, U.S., Death Certificates, 1899-2017," database with images, *Ancestry.com* (https://www.ancestry.com :accessed 22 January 2024), Harry Herbert Wallar.

613. C.L. McCredie Dies at age 85," *Belleville [Illinois] News-Democrat*, 10 May 1972, page 2, column 2; imaged, *Newspapers.com* (www.newspapers.com : accessed 22 January 2024).

614. 1900 U.S. census, Hancock County, Illinois, Warsaw city, enumeration district [ED] 36, sheet 6, dwelling 144, family 152, Clarence McCready; imaged, "United States Census, 1900," *Ancestry.com* (https://www.ancestry.com/search/collections/7602/records/12137753 : accessed 27 January 2024).

615. "Illinois, County Marriages, 1810-1940," imaged, *FamilySearch* (https://www.familysearch.org : accessed 22 January 2024), Clarence McCredie and Rita E. Rhodes.

616. "Illinois, County Marriages, 1810-1940," imaged, *FamilySearch* (https://www.familysearch.org : accessed 22 January 2024), Clarence L. McCredie and Mamie Adams.

617. C.L. McCredie Dies at age 85," *Belleville [Illinois] News-Democrat*, 10 May 1972.

618. "Local and Personal," *Centralia [Illinois] Sentinel*, 15 August 1889, page 1, column 1; imaged, *Newspaper Archive* (https://www.newspaperarchive.com : accessed 7 March 2025).

619. 1900 U.S. census, Fayette County, Pennsylvania, Jefferson Township, enumeration district [ED] 34, sheet 6, dwelling 89, family 94, Florence W. Wilkin; imaged, "United States Census, 1900," *Ancestry.com* (https://www.ancestry.com/search/collections/7602, records/52147140 : accessed 27 January 2024).

620. "Indiana Marriages, 1811-2019," imaged, *FamilySearch* (https://www.familysearch.org : accessed 22 January 2024), Earnest W. Bashears and Florence Wallar.

621. Crawford County, Illinois, death certificate no. 1968D-056 (27 March 1968), Florence Jeanette Bashears; County Clerk's office, Robinson, Illinois.

622. "Illinois Deaths and Stillbirths, 1916-1947," imaged, *FamilySearch* (https://www.familysearch.org :accessed 28 January 2024), Ella B. O'Neal.

623. "Mortuary," *Beardstown [Illinois] Illinoian Star*, 26 June 1920, page 2, column 1; imaged, *Newspaper Archive* (https://www.newspaperarchive.com : accessed 7 March 2025).

624. "Illinois Deaths and Stillbirths, 1916-1947," *FamilySearch*, Ella B. O'Neal.

625. U.S., World War II Draft Cards Young Men, 1940-1947," imaged, *Ancestry.com* (https://www.ancestry.com/search/collections/2238/records/300847734 : accessed 21 January 2024), Clinton Harold Waller.

626. "Iowa," County Marriages, 1838-1934," imaged, *FamilySearch* (https://www.familysearch.org : accessed 21 January 2024), Clinton H. Waller and Nellie M. West.

627. *Find a Grave*, database with images (https://www.findagrave.com/memorial/229361960/clinton-h-waller : accessed 21 January 2024), memorial #229361960 "Clinton H. Waller Sr." Oak Hill Cemetery, Lewistown, Fulton County, Illinois; memorial created by Find a Grave user TReed.

628. "Iowa, U.S., Marriage Records, 1880-1947," imaged, *Ancestry.com* (https://www.ancestry.com/search/collections/8823/records/4231601 : accessed 21 January 2024); Gerald T. Graves and Esther R. Rowley.

629. "Esther R. Graves," *Galesburg [Illinois] Register-Mail*, 5 November 2000, page 11, column 2, *GenealogyBank* (www.genealogybank.com : accessed 20 January 2024).

630. "Iowa, U.S., Marriage Records, 1880-1947," *Ancestry.com,* Esther R. Rowley.

631. "Iowa, U.S., Marriage Records, 1880-1947," *Ancestry.com,* Esther R. Rowley.

632. "Esther R. Graves," *Galesburg [Illinois] Register-Mail*, 5 November 2000.

633. *Find a Grave*, database with images (https://www.findagrave.com/memorial/12690408/william-g-wallar : accessed 29 January 2024), memorial #12690408 "William G. Wallar" Rose Hill Cemetery, Mount Carmel, Wabash County, Illinois; memorial created by Find a Grave user Alberta Daniels Withrow. Note: Birthdate calculated from grave marker.

634. 1870 U.S. census, Crawford County, Illinois, population schedule, Robinson Township, page 174 (stamped), dwelling 288, family 282, William Waller; imaged, "United States Census, 1870," *Ancestry.com* (https://www.ancestry.com/search/collections/7163/records/15766874 : accessed 12 March 2025).

635. "Cyclone," *Mount Carmel [Illinois] Register*, 7 June 1877, page 1, column 4; imaged, Newspapers.com (https://www.newspapers.com/image/757467607 : accessed 29 January 2024).

636. *Find a Grave*, memorial #12690408, William G. Wallar.

637. 1870 U.S. census, Crawford County, Illinois, population schedule, Robinson Township, page 174 (stamped), dwelling 288, family 282, Lillie M. Waller; imaged, "United States Census, 1870," *Ancestry.com* (https://www.ancestry.com/search/collections/7163/records/15766874 : accessed 12 March 2025).

638. "Local News Recorded a Half Century Ago," *Robinson [Illinois] Argus*, 16 February 1921, page 5, column 2, imaged, *Robinson History Archives Online* (https://robinson.historyarchives.online/home : accessed 28 January 2024).

639. *Find a Grave*, database with images (https://www.findagrave.com/memorial/96336656/lillie-may-wallar : accessed 29 January 2024), memorial #96336656 "Lillie May Wallar" Old Robinson Cemetery, Robinson, Crawford County, Illinois; memorial created by Find a Grave user Boyd Correll.

SELECT BIBLIOGRAPHY

Andre, Richard, Stan Cohen, and Bill Wintz. *Bullets & Steel: The Fight for the Great Kanawha Valley 1861-1865.* Charleston, West Virginia: Pictorial Histories Publishing Company, 1995.

Bard, David. *Civil War: The New River Valley 1861-1865, 3 One-Day Driving Tours.* Charleston, West Virginia: Quarrier Press, 2004.

Cox, Jacob D. *Military Reminiscences of the Civil War, volume 1: April 1861-November 1863.* New York: C. Scribner's Sons, 1900.

Hayes, Rutherford B., and Charles Richard Williams. *Diary and Letters of Rutherford Birchard Hayes, volume 2, 1861-1865.* Columbus: Ohio State Archaeological and Historical Society, 1922.

Hewett, Janet B. *Supplement to the Official Records of the Union and Confederate Armies.* Wilmington, North Carolina: Broadfoot Publishing Company, 1995.

Humphreys, Milton W. *Military Operations Fayette County, West Virginia 1861-1863.* Fayetteville, West Virginia: Charles W. Goddard, 1926.

Hurd III, Arnold H. *Tears on the Bluestone: A Civil War Portrait of Mercer County, Virginia, Now West Virginia.* Self-published, 2007.

Lang, Theodore F. *Loyal West Virginia from 1861-1865.* Baltimore: Deutsch Publishing Company, 1895.

Lowry, Terry. *The Battle of Charleston and the 1862 Kanawha Valley Campaign.* Charleston, West Virginia: 35th Star Publishing, 2016.

Lowry, Terry. *Last Sleep: The Battle of Droop Mountain November 6, 1863.* Charleston, West Virginia: Pictorial Histories Publishing Company, 1996.

McKinney, Tim. *The Civil War in Fayette County, West Virginia.* Charleston, West Virginia: Quarrier Press, 1988.

Palmer, Jewett. *A Historical Sketch of Company "B", Eighteenth Regiment, Ohio Volunteer Infantry, Three Months' Service.* Publisher not given, 1911.

Snell, Mark A. *West Virginia and the Civil War.* Charleston, South Carolina: The History Press, 2011.

Starr, Stephen Z. *The Union Cavalry in the Civil War.* Baton Rouge: Louisiana State University Press, 1979.

Sutton, J.J. *History of the Second Regiment West Virginia Cavalry Volunteers, During the War of the Rebellion.* Portsmouth, Ohio, 1892.

Wiley, Bell I. *The Life of Billy Yank: the Common Soldier of the Union.* Baton Rouge: Louisiana State University Press, 1952, 1993 printing.

Williams, T. Harry. *Hayes of the Twenty-Third.* Lincoln: University of Nebraska Press, 1965.

United States. War Department. *The War of the Rebellion: A Compilation of the Official Records of the Union and Confederate Armies.* U.S. Government Printing Office, 1885.

ACKNOWLEDGEMENTS

There are many people who have helped me on this long journey of researching and writing about James L. Wallar. I'd like to thank my husband Karl Zemlin for tolerating my genealogy addiction, for accompanying me on road trips, and for his photography skills. Thanks, too, to our daughters Ellen Zemlin and Caroline Zemlin who have listened to me talk about their great-great-great-great grandfather for many years, and to my friends and coworkers who, I'm sure, heard more than they cared to, but smiled and nodded anyway. My son-in-law Max Thornton helped me with editing, for which I am grateful. And lastly, thanks to Lappity-Toppity, my trusty laptop, which has traveled near and far on this journey with me.

LOCATION INDEX

Indiana

    Decker's Station   126

    Evansville   133

    Vincennes   126, 133

Iowa

    Davenport   8

Louisiana

    New Orleans   122-124

Maryland

    Baltimore   137

    Oakland   27

New York

    New York City   152-154

Ohio

    Chester   92

    Cincinnati   91, 133

    Circleville   6, 7

    Gallipolis   69, 72, 88

    Harrison   91

    Harrison County   7

    Marietta   8, 18, 21, 27, 152

    Meigs County   8, 9, 15

    Middleport   92

    Muskingum County   7

    Pomeroy   12, 13, 16, 68, 72, 92

    Portland   92

    Racine   6, 8, 9, 11, 12, 29, 69, 70, 72, 74, 91, 111

    Salineville   92

    Tuscarawas County   7

CIVIL WAR INDEX

NAME INDEX

ABOUT THE AUTHOR

Nancy E. Wiseman has been researching her family history for nearly 50 years. Born a Hoosier and a resident of Indiana for the last 30 years, she is an Illinoisan at heart and a proud University of Illinois graduate. Nancy lives with her husband Karl Zemlin and cat Beatrice in central Indiana, where she works part-time at the local public library. She enjoys spending time with family, volunteering with her Daughters of the American Revolution chapter, lunching with friends, and reading historical fiction.

www.ingramcontent.com/pod-product-compliance
Lightning Source LLC
Chambersburg PA
CBHW041930260326
41914CB00009B/1250